Promising Nothing

PROMISING NOTHING
Christology Suspended from the Cross

Pickwick Publications
An Imprint of Wipf and Stock Publishers
199 W. 8th Ave., Suite 3
Eugene, OR 97401

www.wipfandstock.com

PAPERBACK ISBN: 978-1-7252-8217-9
HARDCOVER ISBN: 978-1-7252-8218-6
EBOOK ISBN: 978-1-7252-8219-3

Cataloguing-in-Publication data:

Names: Anthony, Neal J., author.

Title: Promising nothing : christology suspended from the cross / Neal J. Anthony.

Description: Eugene, OR : Pickwick Publications, 2021 | Includes bibliographical references and index.

Identifiers: ISBN 978-1-7252-8217-9 (paperback) | ISBN 978-1-7252-8218-6 (hardcover) | ISBN 978-1-7252-8219-3 (ebook)

Subjects: LCSH: Luther, Martin, 1483–1546—Influence. | Schweitzer, Albert, 1875–1965—Influence. | Jesus Christ—Person and offices. | Theology, Doctrinal.

Classification: BT77 .A55 2021 (paperback) | BT77 .A55 (ebook)

02/21/21

Promising Nothing

Christology Suspended from the Cross

NEAL J. ANTHONY

PICKWICK *Publications* · Eugene, Oregon

For Vítor Westhelle (1952–2018)
Adviser to many,
Friend,
Body of Promise

"No words, instead a labor of mourning and love connects Friday and Sunday and fills the spaces of death with fragrance. The wind, the breath, the Spirit did not utter words on that day but spread a scent countering the miserable odor of death. There was work to be done even, and above all, in the midst of the apocalypse, a work of another economy, a mad economy . . . that spends for a gift that cannot be returned: spices for a dead and decaying body."
—**Vítor Westhelle,** *The Scandalous God*

May the labor of all those you have mentored be the fragrance which fills the spaces between the world's Fridays and its Promised Sunday. It was through your labor of love that you taught us how to "practice resurrection" together. You have equipped, empowered, and commissioned us for that labor. That labor is the prayer of the whole self, one initiated and sustained by Promise.

"If it weren't for the promise, I wouldn't pray."
—Martin Luther

"If you would like to catch the dew of divinity,
Unwaveringly adhere to its humanity."
—Angelus Silesius, *The Cherubinic Wanderer*

"'My God, my God, why has thou forsaken me?'
There we have the real proof that Christianity is something divine."
—Simone Weil, *Gravity and Grace*

"God speaks to each of us as he makes us,
then walks with us silently out of the night.
These are the words we dimly hear:
You, sent out beyond your recall, go to the limits of your longing.
Embody me."
—Rainer Maria Rilke

"Let us hold fast to the confession of our hope without wavering,
for he who has promised is faithful."
—Hebrews 10:23

Contents

List of Illustrations

A (Longer Than Usual) Preface

Valentine Hausmann. A kindred spirit of sorts. Save the name.

It is a safe bet that even among church historians and theologians who often have a knack for retaining obscure tidbits of knowledge, this name registers no immediate significance. Indeed, it was only within a book whose main subject is someone else that I discovered his name.[1] In that book—divided into such chapters as "Comfort for the Sick and Dying," "Consolation for the Bereaved," "Cheer for the Anxious and Despondent," "Encouragement to the Persecuted and Imprisoned," and "Counsel in Questions of Marriage and Sex"—many of Martin Luther's writings, mainly private correspondences, have been edited and arranged according to various loci of pastoral counsel. Valentine Hausmann's name appears within the chapter titled, "The Perplexed and Doubting."

Hausmann, we are told in the annotation above the letter, was both the burgomaster of Freiburg, Saxony, and the younger sibling of a clergyman by the name of Nicholas Hausmann, who was apparently a friend of Luther. The editor also tells us that he was "assailed for some time by doubts, unbelief, and consequent terror."[2] It is to this situation of spiritual turmoil that Luther penned these words to Hausmann (dated with a degree of uncertainty as February 19, 1532), and I quote him at length:

> . . . this is my faithful counsel: Accept this scourge as laid upon you
> by God for your own good, even as Saint Paul had to bear a thorn
> in the flesh, and thank God that he deems you worthy of such
> unbelief and terror, for they will drive you all the more to pray and
> seek help and say, as it is written in the Gospel, "Lord, help though

1. Luther, *Letters of Spiritual Counsel.*
2. Luther, *Letters of Spiritual Counsel*, 119.

mine unbelief." How many there are who have less faith than you have! Yet they are not aware of it and remain in their unbelief. The fact that God makes you sensible of this is a good sign that he wishes to help you out of your condition. The more you are aware of it, the nearer you are to improvement. Cling calmly to God, and he will cause everything to turn out well.[3]

For those who have an aptitude for absorbing and applying instructions, I suppose we can summarily boil down from Luther's pastoral counsel a rule to be applied for the sake of spiritual well-being when "doubt" and "unbelief" wash over us: employ a habit of viewing "unbelief"—and the experience which issues from it—as God driving you back to God. Sound spiritual advice grounded in solid (Lutheran) theology! Can, perhaps, Valentine Hausmann be considered "exhibit A" with regard to an aptitude for applying spiritual counsel? But then that would sever my kindred connection to Valentine Hausmann.

That is, my kindred connection with Valentine Hausmann has nothing to do with an aptitude of any stripe, be it spiritual or even theological in nature. Rather, just the opposite is the case. Besides, *that* Valentine Hausmann's name, as with anybody's name, would appear in a chapter bearing the title "The Perplexed and Doubting" is nothing extraordinary. It is safe to assume, no doubt, that all are beset by spiritual struggles at some point. Instead, it's the *frequency* of his name's appearance that caught my attention. And what I failed to mention is that the words which come immediately before the block quote above are, "As I have before written to you . . ."[4] Already, this is Luther's second letter of counsel to Hausmann. Another, much longer letter of pastoral counsel awaits. It is this frequency that has created a sense of solidarity surrounding a certain aptitude, or shall I say, its lack.

On the very next page of this edited selection of Luther's pastoral counsel, we are again confronted with yet another letter—a third letter, three times as long, and dated June 24, 1532—written by Luther to Hausmann. The editor's annotation above the letter simply states, "Valentine Hausmann continued to worry about his unbelief . . . and Luther gave him further instructions as to what he ought to do under the circumstances."[5] Though I won't reproduce Luther's third letter *in toto*, his opening line to Hausmann runs as such:

My dear Valentine: I have learned of the trouble you are having on account of your terror. You should not worry too much about

3. Luther, *Letters of Spiritual Counsel*, 119.
4. A footnote explains that this prior letter is not extant.
5. Luther, *Letters of Spiritual Counsel*, 120.

it, for God deals with us in a wondrous way; it may appear to us that he means evil and harm, and yet what he does is for our benefit, even if we do not understand.[6]

Ultimately, Luther's pastoral counsel to Hausmann entails three points: First, though what God does is for our benefit, it is beyond our understanding and often appears as "evil and harm." Ask for patience to bear it! Second, call upon God in prayer when unbelief's terror arrives. Finally, and especially when praying well is difficult, have someone read clearly from the Scriptures, in particular from the Psalms or the New Testament. Listen attentively. Luther adds, "Without the Word of God, the enemy is too strong for us."[7]

Whether this third letter of pastoral counsel was able to draw Hausmann out of his unbelief and subsequent terror, I suppose we'll never know. (My guess is that his malaise was chronic and irreversible. But that guess is only grounded in personal experience extrapolated.) Notwithstanding, there are at least a few points I want to tease out of Luther's correspondence with Hausmann. First, keeping in mind that aptitude is grounded in how quickly we are able to absorb and apply instructions, it is clear that Hausmann's inability, per Luther's pastoral counsel—repeated three times!—to apprehend just how God (in God's "wondrous way"!) works to his benefit and does not appear to disqualify him from any aptitude for apprehending God. Quite the contrary, as Luther points out, "The more you are aware of [your unbelief], the nearer you are to improvement." Second, and closely related, even though "faith" itself is the issue, namely its absence, Luther still counsels him as a "Christian." At no point does Luther call his "Christianness" into question. Simply, a cocksure, uncontested "faith" does not appear to be a prerequisite for one to be considered a Christian. Finally, and closely related, "unbelief," struggle—what will later be developed in this project under the rubric *Anfechtung*—appears to be inherent, indeed, integral to "faith" itself. What else are we to make of the counsel that one's consciousness of one's own "unbelief" is to be recognized simultaneously as God driving one to "belief"?

So what makes Hausmann a "kindred spirit"? Simply, having served as an ordained Lutheran pastor for the past twenty years, having received a PhD in theology from a reputable graduate school ("with distinction," no less!), and even having one book on Christology published, "confessing Jesus Christ as true God and true man" has never come easy. Perhaps in fits and starts, glimpses and glances. More punctiliar than extended into space, if we

6. Luther, *Letters of Spiritual Counsel*, 120.
7. Luther, *Letters of Spiritual Counsel*, 121.

want to put it geometric terms. In particular, confessing his "divinity"—and all the benefits and attributes that theologians have historically ascribed to his "divinity"—has often seemed nothing more than a perpetual struggle, a fool's (for Christ!) errand, in the terms of the Preacher, a "chasing after wind" (Eccl 1:14). Perhaps "confessing Christ as true God and true man" amounts to nothing more than a prayerful struggle, a struggling prayer—a "doubling-down" on Promise!—against experience and reason that the crucified Jesus is the revelation of God's life-giving agency.

In short, I am Valentine Hausmann.

It's a safe bet that perhaps the only difference between us is that I have more letters after my name, letters that should signal either innate or developed (or both) aptitude with regard to apprehending the subject-matter for which I am trained to confidently say something knowledgeable. They do not. As well, if being a credentialed theologian presupposes a certain level of facility for unreservedly experiencing the God-man's benefits, it is obvious that I am no "natural." I read about them. I hear others talking about them. I proclaim them as an ordained minister of "Word and sacrament." I revel in ministering to folks who seemingly experience, confess, and celebrate them without qualification. But such a cocksure confession and unreserved experience for myself is a whole other matter.

Though much has been written on "sick souls,"[8] "wintry spiritualities,"[9] and "walking in the dark" *sans* a "full solar spirituality"[10]—and I commend all of the wonderful works which develop these realities to the reader—this book, though it may appeal to these "spiritual types" (and for those who need labels, one could no doubt label me as being one of these "types"), is something more akin to doing theology, borrowing Joseph's Sittler's terminology, from Mt. Nebo. Specifically, this book is an exercise, a project, in doing Christology *from* Mt. Nebo. Let me develop this point.

Drawing from the biblical narrative in Deuteronomy 34 in which, from the top of Mt. Nebo, the Lord shows Moses all the land he has both sworn to his forebears—Abraham, Isaac, and Jacob—and promised to his descendants, yet with the caveat that "I have let you see it with your eyes, but you shall not cross over there" (Deut 34:4), Sittler, in a Sunday sermon delivered to a summer camp manned by several hundred students, provided a corrective to a caricature of the Christian faith that was previously being expressed in that camp's Sunday services.[11] That is, as expressed in

8. See James, *Varieties of Religious Experience*.

9. See Marty, *Cry of Absence*.

10. See Taylor, *Learning to Walk in the Dark*.

11. Sittler, "View from Mount Nebo," 33–48.

the prefatory remarks, the atmosphere in which Sittler was to preach was colored by a Christian *ethos* that was "experiential, sentimental. Personal testimonies around an emotion-stirring campfire were a regular evening feature."[12] Though for many students, this expression of Christianity was both normal and accustomed, this experiential, sentimental expression of Christianity was also alienating for others. Ultimately, "the students who rejected [this] custom [of expression] felt that they were somehow outside the orbit of normal Christian experience. And the feeling troubled them."[13] It is noted that this sermon was "addressed to outsiders."[14] Briefly, let me develop the main points of this sermon.

As Sittler observed, though faith is a work of the Holy Spirit, it is often the case that the Holy Spirit's work is reduced—no doubt the result of our oversimplifying tendencies—to a single, simple expression best captured in the lines of the well-known hymn, *Blessed Assurance*: "Blessed assurance, Jesus is mine. O what a foretaste of glory divine." What is suggested in these famous lines, observes Sittler, is the reality that nothing is authentically Christian "until and unless it has become a blessed assurance in some specifiable, warm, pervasive, and crucial experience."[15] Though this assumption points to the truth that for humans there is a continuity between our inner state and our outward expressions, that there is a "momentum between confession and total being," the error of this assumption is that the Christian faith can be reduced to this manner of confirmation. The error of this assumption is that "It tempts us to hang the reality of God, the compass of his demands, the scope of biblical and theological meaning, upon a febrile nail: the warmth and immediacy of a feeling of blessed assurance" resulting in a "subjectivizing of the Christian faith."[16] It was as the dean of students in a theological seminary of his church that Sittler observed this reality to be a significant issue for students, especially when tied to reflection upon the vocation for which they were being equipped.

If seminarians—schooled in the study and techniques of preaching—did not have the inner emotional confirmation of the gospel they were called to preach (and frequently they did not), how could their calling to the vocation of Christian ministry be verified? How can one be called to Christian ministry in the absence of "blessed assurance"? Sittler, obviously a theologian of the Christian church, empathized with this predicament.

12. Sittler, "View from Mount Nebo," 33.
13. Sittler, "View from Mount Nebo," 33–4.
14. Sittler, "View from Mount Nebo," 34.
15. Sittler, "View from Mount Nebo," 36.
16. Sittler, "View from Mount Nebo," 36.

Knowing, as well, the experience of feeling an absence of "blessed assurance," Sittler asserted in his sermon, "I, too, make uncertified postulation of the Christian faith, uncertified, that is, by auxiliary feelings that are supposed somehow to make it 'more true.'"[17]

Conjuring a time when, as a pastor, he committed himself to preaching the entirety of Philippians, he had no choice but to reveal this "uncertified postulation." Having to preach from texts such as "To live is Christ, and to die is gain" (Phil 1:21), and having recognized the absence of an emotional state that could underwrite such a declaration, Sittler came to the conclusion that "My duty was to say that grace has this magnificent possibility, it *can* do that to a person, and for Paul, it did."[18] Regardless, it is not the duty of preachers to reduce the message of the gospel to an emotional state they may or may not possess. The truth of one's proclamation is not legitimized, validated, by one's emotional state.

Although, ultimately, Sittler sketches in his sermon the Christian faith both from the perspective of "*within*," or that perspective according to which such elements of the great objective story of Christianity as "nativity," "incarnation," and "death" become inner, experienced realities within Christians, and "*without*," or that perspective according to which attachment to the great objective story of Christianity is expressed through quiet, reflective, critical detachment, the primary thrust of his sermon, as the title suggests, is the elaboration, the benefit, of a third perspective. For the sake of this project, its context and method, it is this "view," "the view from Mt. Nebo"—"the perspective of many today who do not know if they ought to call themselves Christians at all"[19]—that will now be developed.

Looking out from Mt. Nebo—an extensive view, as Scripture details, of "Gilead as far as Dan, all Naphtali, the land of Ephraim and Manasseh, all the land of Judah as far as the Western Sea, the Negeb, and the Plain . . . as far as Zoar" (Deut 34:1–3)—Moses possessed "sight without actuality . . . knowledge without possession."[20] It is a view which, as Sittler asserted, parallels the experience of so many students in his purview:

> Moses on Mt. Nebo is a man in the situation of many of us who feel we must confess and serve a faith whose gifts to us are not given with all the opulence we might desire, and in whose lives

---

17. Sittler, "View from Mount Nebo," 37.
18. Sittler, "View from Mount Nebo," 38.
19. Sittler, "View from Mount Nebo," 43.
20. Sittler, "View from Mount Nebo," 45.

the very gifts of grace do not control us who are the declarers of these same gifts.[21]

Though educated in all disciplines of a seminary education, though gifted with critical and voracious minds for theological training, the "conventional standard psychological equipment of blessed assurance has not been given them."[22] So willing to participate in the emotional confirmation of the Holy Spirit's renewing and transformative presence, theirs is also a "hurt" participation, that is, the fruits of the Spirit's "blessed assurance" are barred to them. "Nevertheless," Sittler asserts, "they want to affirm those very gifts as being a possibility of God for the world."[23] He adds, "this means that we must sometimes envision with the mind what the heart cannot yet confirm, must see and affirm with clear intellectual sight what we have not been given the grace to celebrate in actual life."[24] Perhaps it is the hungry who know best the value, the meaning, the significance of food; food the satiated view from complacency.

Ultimately, Sittler asserts that there are two "mothers" of "precision" when it comes to theological knowledge, one never lifted to the exclusion of the other. Certainly, there is the theological precision of the "insider," of "having"; the precision born of faith's warm experience and the mind's self-convincing that it has apprehended the matter at hand. But there is also the other "precision," for this is the "precision begotten of deprivation, the tormented precision of vision without gift." The ones who possess this other "precision" are those, as Sittler describes,

> who have described the reality of certain graces because they lived their lives, not within the vitality and fragrance of these graces, but because they stood outside longingly looking in and described with tormented precision what they saw. They are the people of Mt. Nebo who see what their feet cannot touch, and out of negation forge those clear descriptions which then become the dear possession of the children of the land. These are the people who in sheer thought forge ideas in longing that others affirm in quiet and unquestioning possession.[25]

21. Sittler, "View from Mount Nebo," 44.

22. Sittler, "View from Mount Nebo," 45.

23. Sittler, "View from Mount Nebo," 46.

24. Sittler, "View from Mount Nebo," 46.

25. Sittler, "View from Mount Nebo," 47.

As Sittler adds, "Without the lean people of Mt. Nebo, the people on Mt. Zion are always tempted to become fat."[26]

So, begging your pardon over this longer-than-usual preface, it is from the perspective of Mt. Nebo that I offer this project in Christology. It is a Christology for those for whom the "standard psychological equipment of blessed assurance" has not been given; a Christology of longing, yearning, "hoping against hope" (Rom 4:18), that what is astir in the man Jesus is the divinity whose attributes of which the theologians speak; the divinity of which so many generations of theologians have written so convincingly and confidently; the divinity who creates, sustains, and redeems all there is. Yet is this also not a divinity who, as the Prophet declares, not only "hides himself" (Isa 45:15), but whose "thoughts are not [our] thoughts, whose ways are not [our] ways" (Isa 55:8)? It is confessed that it is the Spirit of that same divinity who creates faith, as well. At the very least, one would think that such confession would inscribe theology's expressions with a baseline of thoroughgoing humility.

It is a Christology from Mt. Nebo. It is a Christology for Valentine Hausmann and folks emotionally honest enough to confess solidarity with him. It is a "modest" (or, in Sittler's terms, "lean") Christology which not only "knows moments of serious doubt,"[27] but most likely—with doubt and unbelief as its baseline pulse—knows only of a "belief" which is constantly concealed under the opposite of what passes for the "belief" and "blessed assurance" so many have come to associate with it. Certainly this does not make for a want of "theological precision." Instead, it points to a "precision" (and its accompanying methodology) that reveals itself as being more credible to human experience; namely, the "precision" born of a privation whose experience includes an abject, deafening silence—*Anfechtung*—with regard to any such "blessed assurance." Such a "precision" drives hope. Specifically, it is a "theological precision"—a Christology—forged between Promise and experience, a Christology suspended from the cross.

What follows is a "theological precision" that Valentine Hausmann, and folks like him, would understand. That is, a Christology—one that "hopes and against hope" (Rom 4:18)—*from* the Cross, from that ultimate "outsider" location in relation to the experience of "blessed assurance." Or, according to Luther's theology of the cross, is the experience that funds this Christology really nothing other than the privileged location of theology? A *theologia crucis*—a christological existence!—exploring the farthest edges of its privileged perspective?

26. Sittler, "View from Mount Nebo," 47.
27. See Hall, "Theology of the Cross," 52–58.

Certainly this project is academic in nature. Most of it builds from, is an appropriation of, the theology of Martin Luther; in particular, his delineation of the mutual exchange of essential properties of the two natures in the person of Jesus Christ. As such, it can be read as a contribution in Christology. Or constructive theology. Or Lutheran theology. Or pastoral theology. Some will argue that within these pages Luther's Christology is pushed too far. Some will argue that the Christology presented within this project is merely a reduction to anthropology. (Or, instead, is it an existence determined completely by its object, or Jesus Christ?) Some will assert "pantheism." (Though justification of such an accusation in the face of a theology grounded so completely in the *ex nihilo* creating agency of the Word, a Word who causes us to identify preservation with the gift of God's incessant creating [see chapter 2, below], would be interesting.) Some will ask, "Where is 'hell'?" (Look hard enough and you will find it mirrored back at you!) Perhaps some will ask, "Where is talk of the Trinity?" (Do we not confess that the *"opera trinitatis ad extra indivisa sunt"*?) Some will resonate with such a Christology—commensurate with Luther's *theologia crucis*—delineated completely *sub contraria specie*. Some will resonate with an existence—a christological existence—developed completely from the perspective of its object, or the crucified Christ. The christological existence developed in this project is not a forfeiting of Luther's theocentric theology, but one which is understood by its author to be a thoroughgoing expression of God's *ex nihilo*, life-giving presence through the Word.

Indeed, taking a cue from Heiko Oberman's observations regarding the inception of John Calvin's doctrine of predestination, it may be said that the Christology developed within the pages that follow is an existentializing, a returning to the initial context of creation, of classical Lutheranism's christological genera, especially as those genera correspond to Luther's articulation of the *communicatio idiomatum* (communication of attributes within the person of Jesus Christ). A bit of explanation is warranted here.

Far from providing the grounds for dogmatically derived arrogance or dogmatic divisiveness, or even an ecclesiastical litmus test by which the doomed and divinely desired are determined, the doctrine of predestination, Heiko Oberman observed, was born out of the firsthand experience of exile.[28] Oberman added,

> The Calvinist doctrine of predestination is the mighty bulwark
> of the Christian faithful against the fear that they will be unable
> to hold out against the pressure of persecution. Election is the
> Gospel's encouragement to those who have faith, not a message

28. Oberman, "Cutting Edge," 111.

of doom for those who lack it. In particular, it responds to the anguish that Calvin already felt in the early wave of persecution, which spread through Paris on the eve of his escape to Switzerland fearing that torture would force him to betray the other members of his underground cell. Rather than providing grounds for arrogance, predestination offers all true Christians the hope that even under extreme duress they will persevere to the end.[29]

To be sure, Oberman added, it was not until later, when the persecution diminished and the refugees had become "settlers and citizens,"[30] that the scriptural insights which led them through this experience were crystallized into "a systematic theology that lost touch with its initial purpose and hardened its doctrinal crust."[31] Essentially, then, the Christology developed within these pages is an attempt to reconnect the categories of classical Lutheran Christology with their initial context and purpose, one begotten of Luther's *theologia crucis*, one grounded in Promise and inscribed with prayer and prayer's struggle.

Learning from firsthand experience that theological expression risks sounding dogmatic and wooden lest it is written fundamentally from the perspective of existential engagement with the subject matter, I have written this book primarily for myself. Call it a form of "wounded speech,"[32] if you will. A form of address that emanates from an experienced deficit, a wound, a struggle that is unrelenting. Albeit, it is confessed (with more struggle!), it is a deficit, a wound, a struggle, that is life-giving, or better, by which I am given life. It is a Christology which corresponds to my theological existence, one between Promise and the gnawing experience of its absence; one of doubling-down on Promise in the face of experience. It is an existence cultivated through the hundreds of occasions of being situated as a pastor between open grave and the committal rite of "Burial of the Dead." It is an existence of walking with and ministering to, the terminally ill equipped only with the Promise of New Creation. For reason and experience, the "only" is often experienced as the accusation, "Where is your God" (Ps 42:3)? At times that "only" is a "broad place" of deliverance (Pss 18:19 and 118:5). It is my observation, my experience, that the most confident, cocksure expressions of "faith" are often nothing more than masks concealing desperate demands for the "proof" of Promise's efficacy. The Spirit's

29. Oberman, "Cutting Edge," 114–15.
30. Oberman, "Cutting Edge," 115.
31. Oberman, "Cutting Edge," 115.
32. Chrétien, "Wounded Word," 175.

"certainty," instead, remains concealed in the experience of the sinner's horror of complete passivity before the Triune God. Are we not but clay in the
potter's hands (Jer 18:6)?

Perhaps the unceasing struggle, the suspendedness of the struggle, this
work conveys in some way will resonate with your theological existence. If,
as Scripture asserts, "we walk by faith, not by sight" (2 Cor 5:7), then such a
reality informs, and is inscribed into, every jot and tittle of the Christology
found in these pages. Perhaps the christological "crumbs" this work drops
may be a sort of "daily bread" for your theological journey. If not, that, too,
is well and good.

Acknowledgments

It is difficult to pinpoint when this project started.

Certainly the seeds were broadcast at Dana College when, during those final minutes of Koine Greek instruction each class period, Delvin Hutton would field questions by neophyte exegete/theologians over topics ranging from periphrastic constructions and objective genitives to *kenosis*, messianic secrets, and Paul's employment of Hebrew Scripture in Galatians. (It must be noted that, for the duration of all eighteen credit hours over four semesters, the course consisted of three people—including the instructor!)

And the soil was fertilized during my years at Luther Seminary when my passion for Martin Luther's *theologia crucis*—galvanized by Gerhard Forde and Steve Paulson—intersected with gnawing questions about Christology. It always seemed strange how the theology of the cross's methodology—*oratio*, *meditatio*, and *tentatio*—could culminate in the expression of christological verities that seemed so far removed from the Jabbok struggle in which they originated. Christology discussions, regardless of the seminary course in which they occurred, always seemed something like being presented with a fragment of flak with no reference to the reality that it was once the product of a blast that shook everyone around it to the core, transforming their existences forever.

And the soil was unquestionably cultivated in Vítor Westhelle's office at the Lutheran School of Theology at Chicago. In that small, cluttered (not messy!) confine overlooking the courtyard, Vítor not only challenged me to focus more deeply on Luther's Christology as an expression of this *theologia crucis*, but to develop its implications. In many ways, this is a natural follow-up to my first project (published by Pickwick as *Cross Narratives*). As well, in so many ways, this project is a response both to my questions and our conversations about the *genus tapeinoticum*. Why is a *genus* so fundamental to Luther's articulation of the *communicatio idiomatum* omitted from the taxonomies of later orthodox Lutheran theologians? Most importantly, through an appropriation of Luther's *communicatio idiomatum,* this project is an attempt to both revitalize the two-natures metaphysic and genera—in particular the *genus majestaticum* and the *genus tapeinoticum*—of classical Lutheran Christology, and recast them as existential categories of Luther's *theologia crucis*, or the Jabbok struggle of which, ultimately, they are a product.

Though it seems strange to say this, with Vítor's death occurring about a third of the way through this project, it is safe to say that he was a silent conversation partner throughout many of these pages. With that said, I alone am responsible for the implications and connections I have drawn from Luther's Christology. There is no question I have made conclusions he would not have made, or have gone in directions he would not have been comfortable going. Unquestionably, the student wonders what the teacher would think about matters. But this student is eternally thankful for the gifts the teacher imparted. It goes without saying that if teachers have fulfilled their vocation properly, then they have produced a cadre of students standing on their own feet, speaking with their own voice to their own concerns. Vítor was not about creating parrots, a cult of personality, or a school dedicated to himself. He was an empowering teacher in every sense.

I give thanks to Kurt Hendel, another teacher and cherished friend at LSTC, for his close reading of the manuscript and his many incisive suggestions. I am grateful for him. He is a person of intellect, kindness, and grace. On many points he challenged me to clarify my work, especially with regard to elaborating precisely the unity of the Word and the Holy Spirit's certainty. I give thanks to Adam White, a colleague here in Lincoln, Nebraska, for his reading of the manuscript, as well. Although there are long sentences in this work, Adam challenged me to shorten many of them, making them more reader-friendly. As well, *that* chapters 3 and 4 are now two chapters instead of one is due to Adam's advice.

There is a list of other colleagues for whom I give thanks; those who, through conversation—normally impromptu—provoked questions and affirmed answers. Scott Frederickson especially comes to mind.

Writing theology from the vocational location of full-time pastor can be very lonely. So I give thanks for voices of affirmation wherever I find them. I give thanks for Tom Iwand. Allegedly he is only a novice theologian. He is also humble. But I also know that his father's Christology lectures were his catechism classes. Lutheran Christology is in his marrow. Tom has no idea of the manner by which his friendship has shaped and fed me. I give thanks for Pastor Jer Gilbreath. His friendship is bread. In common we share, among other things, a vocation, a friendship, a taste for good beer, and a substantive amount of Welsh heritage.

I give thanks to my wife, Kim, for her support, patience, and understanding. On many an evening—office work complete, hospital and home communion visits made, weekly sermon finished, kids' activities having been tended to—I would slip away to the office and write for hours at a time. And I give thanks for my children, Owen and Shannon, for their understanding, as well, with regard to their father's evening absences (in addition to his ridiculous schedule as a pastor).

I want to thank the folks at Wipf and Stock, their professionalism, their graciousness, and their accessibility: especially Blake Adams, Savanah N. Landerholm, George Callihan, Charlie Collier, and Matthew Wimer. And thank you, again, for the opportunity to publish.

I give thanks for all those who have permitted me to shepherd them, and their families through the dying process and the rites of death and resurrection hope.

Ultimately, I want to recognize all those who have been a "body of Promise" throughout my lifetime; namely, both family and those who have served influential pastoral roles for me, for my family, at various stages of life; those whose deaths are a reminder that Promise is bound to finitude. The life-creating Promise is bound to dust, a dust stirring with Promise. The listing of their names is a Prayer created by Promise:

Dr. James and Carmelia "Carmy" (Peters) Anthony

Alvin "Beans" and Beulah (Schlesiger) Peters

Walter and Muzetta Ellen (Davis) Anthony

Clara (Heldt) Schlesiger

Mary Lillian (Bleything) Davis

Rev. Dr. Vitor Westhelle

Dr. Gerhard O. Forde

Rev. Dr. Mark Thomsen

Rev. Edward Keller

Rev. Ed Roleder

Marion Herforth-Liska

Rev. Bob Berthelsen

Rev. Jack Horner

Rev. Dr. Howard B. Franzen

Rev. Dr. Bruce Berggren

Rev. Harlan Brei

Rev. Wilmer Westman

Rev. Karen Kaye

Rev. Dale Topp

Rev. Nels Ritola

Rev. Darwin Garton

Introduction

In the pages that follow is a Christology developed entirely within the trajectory of Martin Luther's theology of the cross. Perhaps already a restatement is warranted: recognizing that there are only "theologians" of the cross,[1] that God can only be apprehended where there are "no signs of transcendence, no religious clues,"[2] and that, ultimately, a "theologian of the cross . . . can only speak *from* the cross in sheer faith without evidence,"[3] what is developed in the following pages is a Christology from the cross, a Christology suspended from the cross; a *christologia crucis*.

If, for Luther, "true theology and recognition of God," as he asserted in his *Heidelberg Disputation* (1518), "are in the crucified Christ,"[4] then for the theologian of the cross, such an epistemic point of departure—God's *sub contrario* revelation in the crucified Christ—bears profound implications for Christology. Such a point of departure, for Luther, comes to expression in a dual concealment with regard to both Christology and theological existence itself. Ultimately, as it will be demonstrated through a development and application of Luther's *communicatio idiomatum* (the communication of natures within the person of Christ), such a point of departure also necessitates the articulation of Christology as christological existence, an existence suspended between Promise and experience; the experience of both its structure and its absence.

---

1. Forde, *On Being a Theologian of the Cross*, 11. See also theses 19–21 of Luther's *Heidelberg Disputation* in Luther, *Works* 31.52–3.

2. Williams, *Christian Spirituality*, 146.

3. Westhelle, *Scandalous God*, 114.

4. Luther, *Works* 31.53.

At the same time, it should be noted, if Heinrich Schmid's seminal presentation of classical Lutheran theology, *The Doctrinal Theology of the Evangelical Lutheran Church*, served as a textbook—covering the gamut of traditional theological *loci*—for generations of Lutheran theologians and pastors, it is also a testament to just how far classical Lutheran theology deviated from the theologian whose name became identified with the tradition within which it was formulated, or Martin Luther. Nowhere, it can be argued, does this deviation from Luther's theology become more salient than with reference to its excision of Luther's epistemic point of departure, the crucified Christ, especially as that excision manifests itself with regard to Schmid's treatment of both Christology—the *communication idiomatum*—and the subject of "Who is a theologian?" Let us pause in order to develop this discrepancy.

Traditionally coined the *communicatio idiomatum*, or the mutual exchange of essential properties of the divine and human natures in the person of Jesus Christ, Schmid—drawing from the dogmatic statements of fourteen prominent Lutheran theologians spanning the sixteenth and seventeenth centuries, and certainly working within the framework of the *Formula of Concord* (1577)—presents the doctrine of the two natures of Jesus Christ in an outline consisting of three genera.[5] The first genus, according to Schmid's presentation, is the "idiomatic" genus in which the attributes of both natures are ascribed to the person of Jesus Christ. Next is the "majestic" genus—the *genus majestaticum*—in which the divine attributes (such as creating/sustaining, omnipotence, omnipresence, infinitude) are attributed to the human nature. The third and final genus, according to Schmid's outline, is the "apotelesmatic" genus in which the operations/influences of the person may be ascribed to either of the two natures in a manner peculiar to the respective nature. And here let us note: it is the second genus, or the *genus majestaticum*, which came to be known as both the distinctive feature of classical Lutheran Christology and the foundation—contra the Reformed position—of the sacramental slogan "*finitum est capax infiniti*" (the finite is capable of the infinite). But it is also precisely here, on the matter of the "majestic" genus, the *genus majestaticum*, that Schmid's delineation of the two natures of Jesus Christ reveals classical Lutheran theology's deviation from its original wellspring.

Further elaborating upon the dynamics of the *genus majestaticum*, Schmid asserts that

---

5. It should be noted that these three genera appear in the in the *Formula of Concord*, though not in the order Schmid presents them. Their order of presentation in the *Formula of Concord* is first, the *genus idiomaticum*; second, the *genus apotelesmaticum*; and third, the *genus majestaticum*. See Luther, *Book of Concord*, 622–25.

by the personal union, not only the person, but, since person
and nature cannot be separated, the divine also has entered into
communion with the human nature; and the participation in
the divine attributes by the human nature occurs at the very moment in which the [Word] unites itself with the human nature.[6]

Up to this point, we might say, "so far so good." But it is Schmid's very next
sentence that explicitly reveals the deviation of classical Lutheran theology—as presented by Schmid—from its founding source. He adds,

But there is no reciprocal effect produced; for, while the human
nature can become partaker of the idiomata of the divine, and
thus acquire an addition to the idiomata essential to itself, the
contrary cannot be maintained, because the divine nature in its
essence is unchangeable and can suffer no increase.[7]

To be sure, though Schmid, according to the dictates of classical Lutheran
Christology, will allow for the human nature to partake of the divine attributes in the person of Jesus Christ, he will not permit, due to its unchange-
ability, the divine nature to partake of the human attributes in the person
of Jesus Christ. From Luther's perspective though, this can be considered
only a partial *communicatio idiomatum*, an incomplete communication of
attributes.

That is, when we follow Luther on the formulation of the *communicatio
idiomatum*—an expression of his theology of the cross, its epistemic point
of departure, or the crucified Christ—we discover that he insists on a full,
direct communication of natures within the personal unity of Jesus Christ,
and not merely an ascription of operations or attributes of the natures to the
person.[8] According to Luther's radical interpretation of the *communicatio*

6. Schmid, *Doctrinal Theology*, 314.

7. Schmid, *Doctrinal Theology*, 314–15. Italics mine.

8. In order to underscore the difference between Luther and classical Lutheran theology on this point, Schmid asserts, elaborating the idiomatic genus, "While, however,
the idiomata of the two natures are attributed to the concrete of both natures . . . it by
no means follows from this that therefore the idiomata of the one nature become those
of the other; for the two natures are not in substance changed by the personal union,
but each of them retains the idiomata essential and natural to itself." He adds, and here
the difference becomes explicit, "Therefore it is *only to the person* that, without further
distinctions, the idiomata of the one or of the other nature can be ascribed; but this can
in no wise happen between the natures themselves . . . " Schmid, *Doctrinal Theology*,
313. As we will see, it is just this direct communication between natures within the person of Jesus Christ that is necessitated by Luther's *theologia crucis*, its epistemic point of
departure. As well, let us notice: classical Lutheran Christology appears to be more bent
on preserving the integrity of the individual natures, especially that of the divine, than
of stressing the priority of the unity of the person of Jesus Christ, the eternal Word of
God, the divine-human One.

idiomatum, if there is a *genus majestaticum* (a direct communication of the divine nature to the human nature within the person of Jesus Christ), then by necessity of the personal unity of Jesus Christ there must be, for Luther, a *genus tapeinoticum* (a communication of the human nature to the divine nature within the person of Jesus Christ; from *tapeinos,* meaning "humble," "lowly," that which is associated with the finite nature of humanity).[9] To be sure, as Vítor Westhelle has observed, these are not two separate genera, but merely "mutual sides of the same communication between natures."[10] Recognizing, as well, that the *genus majestaticum* is not the quintessential expression of Luther's Christology, Paul Althaus observed that

> [Luther] transcends [the *genus majestaticum*] when he makes statements which point in the direction of a genus tapeinoti[cum] [the doctrine that God in Christ shared the weakness, suffering, and humiliation of Jesus]. Luther holds that the deity of Christ, because of the incarnation and of its personal unity with the humanity, enters into the uttermost depths of its suffering. God suffers in Christ.[11]

Developing the implications of this reality, Althaus states that

> [I]t means nothing else than that God is at once completely above and completely below. He is the creator and the Lord and yet at the same time the lowest creature and a servant subject to all men, yes, even to the devil. This man Jesus who bears the wrath of God, the sin of the world, all earthly trouble, yes, hell itself, is at the same time the highest God.[12]

"The mystery of Christ," Althaus adds, "cannot be expressed without these paradoxes."[13]

If, on the one hand, the Lutheran "slogan" *finitum est capax infiniti* underscores the crucial role of the *genus majestaticum* with reference to the Eucharistic debates of the sixteenth century between the Lutheran and Reformed theological traditions, then, on the other hand, in light of Luther's theology of the cross, its epistemic point of departure, the Lutherans may also, equally so, assert *infinitum est capax finiti* or even *infinitus ferat finem.*

9. There are two variations of spelling with regard to this genus: *tapeinoticon* and *tapeinoticum.* Without getting into the "why" of the variations, I have simply chosen the latter form as this was the one introduced to me by Vítor Westhelle.

10. Westhelle, "Foreword," x.

11. Althaus, *Theology of Martin Luther,* 197. The final set of brackets belong to Althaus.

12. Althaus, *Theology of Martin Luther,* 197–98.

13. Althaus, *Theology of Martin Luther,* 198.

If classical Lutheran theology has taught us that the *genus majestaticum* and its corollary expression *finitum est capax infiniti* are fundamental expressions of the Lutheran theological tradition, this project argues that the *genus tapeinoticum* and its corollary expression *infinitum est capax finiti* are equally fundamental to that same theological tradition. The *genus majestaticum* and the *genus tapeinoticum* are "flip sides" of the same christological coin, so to speak, of a Christology whose epistemic point of departure is the crucified Christ. Both the *genus majestaticum* and the *genus tapeinoticum* express the nature of God's relation and radical commitment to creation through the Word of God.

Therefore, with some theological context in hand, the argument of this book is relatively straightforward. If, again, as Luther asserted in his *Heidelberg Disputation*, the *locus classicus* of his theology of the cross, that "true theology and knowledge of God are in the crucified Christ,"[14] then not only does such an epistemic point of departure—the crucified Christ—transform the taxonomy of the two natures of Jesus Christ as it has been traditionally presented within confessional Lutheranism, as has already been developed, but such a point of departure necessitates the fundamental position of the *genus tapeinoticum*—a category of Christology excised by later confessional Lutheran Christology—for Luther's Christology. Specifically, within the trajectory of the Luther's theology of the cross, as Luther's theology of the cross comes to expression in his radical interpretation of the *communicatio idiomatum*, the *genus tapeinoticum* is the christological genus *sine qua non*, so to speak. Expressing the epistemic point of departure of Luther's theology of the cross, or the crucified humanity of Christ, the *genus tapeinoticum* becomes the fundamental "text" of the incarnate, divine-human One for a theologian of the cross. To be sure, not only does an elaboration of Luther's Christology reveal this to be the case, but, as this project aims to make evident, any foray into constructive Christology from the epistemic point of departure of Luther's theology of the cross will necessarily underscore the priority of the *genus tapeinoticum*.

The *genus majestaticum* (again, including such attributes as creating/sustaining, omnipotence, omnipresence, infinitude), that christological genus traditionally employed by classical Lutheran dogmatics as expressing what is peculiar with regard to Lutheran Christology will, subsequently, be situated—commensurate with God's *sub contrario* revelation in the crucified Christ—within the category of Promise, hidden *sub contraria specie* within the body of Promise. The *genus majestaticum* is the Promise of God's presence and life-giving activity communicated to, stirring within, and

14. Luther, *Works* 31.53.

concealed by, the *genus tapeinoticum* in the Word of God, the incarnate, divine-human One, true God and true man. Indeed, faith confesses that the *genus tapeinoticum* and the *genus majestaticum* are an inseparable unity as the Word of God, the incarnate, crucified Word who expresses the Triune God's loving, self-giving commitment to creation. Again, the argument is relatively straightforward. The implications, as they will be developed in the course of this project, are quite the opposite, perhaps even subversive for traditional delineations of Christology. In essence, this project is a thoroughgoing reinterpretation and appropriation of Christology from the perspective of Luther's epistemic point of departure, or the *genus tapeinoticum*.

If, as Robert Kolb observed, Luther locates the divine-human One "precisely where theologians of glory are horrified to find him . . . [ultimately,] as a corpse in a crypt,"[15] then, as this project asks: What does it mean for a Christology constructed from the epistemic point of departure of Luther's theology of the cross to employ as its fundamental "text," and thus starting point, a "corpse in a crypt," or the mangled, isolated corpse of Jesus Christ, exsanguinated of all references to, evidences of, "divine presence"? What does it mean to permit co-priority (with the *genus majestaticum*) to the *genus tapeinoticum*—*in extremis*—for Christology?

Ultimately, working from the epistemic point of departure of the *genus tapeinoticum*, what will be developed in the following pages is a *christologia crucis*, a Christology for which the dynamics of Luther's theology of the cross—involving such dynamics as the hiddenness of God (both within and beyond revelation), the hiddenness of faith itself, and a theological methodology shaped by *oratio* (prayer), *meditatio* (meditation), and, perhaps most importantly, *tentatio/Anfechtung* (spiritual attack)—are inscribed from start to finish. It is a Christology suspended between Promise and experience, one clinging to the *yes* of God revealed in Jesus Christ against the experience of its opposite. It is a Christology of faith's *extra nos* certainty concealed within the struggle, the suspendedness, of reason and experience's judgments and calculations.[16]

If such a theological point of departure, a God hidden in suffering in death, manifests itself in the reality, for Luther, that "Experience alone makes a theologian . . . It is by living—no, rather it is by dying and being damned that a theologian is made, not by understanding, reading, or

---

15. Kolb, "Luther on the Theology of the Cross," 449.

16. "And this the reason why our theology is certain: it snatches us away from ourselves and places us outside ourselves, so that we do not depend on our own strength, conscience, experience, person, or works but depend on that which is outside ourselves, that is, on the promise and truth of God, which cannot deceive." Luther, *Works* 26.387.

speculating,"[17] then the excision of such a point of departure, according to Schmid's presentation, also manifests itself in a corresponding theological existence. For David Hollaz, one of the Lutheran dogmaticians whose theological formulations is adduced by Schmid, the removal of the crucified Christ as epistemic point of departure, and thus the omission of the *genus tapeinoticum* for Christology, resulted in an articulation of theological existence quite opposite of Luther's. In this case, under the rubric "Who is a theologian?" Hollaz was able to describe "The theologian properly and strictly so-called; a regenerated man, firmly believing in the divine Word, that reveals the mysteries of faith, adhering to it with unshaken confidence, apt in teaching others and confuting opponents."[18] In short, reflecting the epistemic point of departure of Luther's theology of the cross, far from one inflected with "unshaken [confessional] confidence," or even the prerequisite detached objectivity of the academy, a *christologia crucis* is the expression of a concealed christological existence, or one which, suspended between Promise and experience, is inscribed with *Anfechtung*.

Thus, risking redundancy: in this project, the reader will encounter a Christology from the cross, a *christologia crucis*, or a Christology which is inscribed from beginning to end with the theology of the cross, both its epistemic point of departure—the *genus tapeinoticum*—and its corresponding theological—christological!—existence. It is a Christology expressive of Promise-grounded certainty and faith's suspended concealment to experience and reason. It is a Christology which begins and ends with the confession and prayer that the experience of divine absence is really the concealment of divine presence; that the "corpse in the crypt," a corpse exsanguinated of all divine reference, self-designation, and clues, is the body of Promise, the *sub contraria specie* revelation of the Word's life-giving activity. It is a Christology which expresses the confession that the creating Word's activity is not divorced from, but inextricably bound to, *body*; that that which is ephemeral and attracts flies is fundamental to the structure of Promise. It is, ultimately, as will be developed, a Christology which recognizes the *genus tapeinoticum* and the *genus majestaticum* to be co-fundamental categories of christological existence, a christological existence in which one confesses against the experience of cruciformity that the life-giving agency of the latter stirs, is present, within the former.

This project, then, will move through a series of stages in order to develop and elaborate such a *christologia crucis*. Let us, briefly, outline these stages.

17. Luther, *Werke* 5.163, 28.
18. Schmid, *Doctrinal Theology*, 19.

Recognizing that, for the theologian of the cross, the *genus tapeinoti-cum*—as we think of the epistemic point of departure for Luther's theology of the cross—is the primary "text" of theology, the locus of God's *sub contrario* revelation, it is the intention of chapter 1—recognizing that the theology of the cross does not possess exclusive rights to an interpretation of the crucified body of Christ—to pull the crucified Christ from the theology of the cross. In the process of releasing the crucified corpse of Jesus Christ from its confessional point of departure according to the theology of the cross, it will be exposed to the decisions and conclusions, the hermeneutics, of reason and experience, ultimately permitting us to gaze upon the crucified Christ as the silent void of death's abyss which once served as Promise's—for Luther—epistemic point of departure for God's *sub contrario* revelation. It is my hope that I have accomplished this move in convincing fashion. If such a move even sounds sympathetic in its rendering, I will have achieved my goal. Facilitating such a move, as will become clear in the last half of the chapter, is the hermeneutics of deconstruction, especially as they come to expression in the work of John Caputo. Isolating the corpse of Christ from Luther's theology of the cross, it will be viewed from an *in media res* perspective amid the flux and flow of competing interpretations, *sans* all divine designation with no hermeneutical recourse beyond the "text," or the isolated corpse of Christ. Again, the intention is this: that such a sustained consideration of the crucified body of Christ—pulled from the interpretive framework of Luther's theology of the cross and isolated and exsanguinated of all designation—permits us to perceive it as the locus of "referential instability." In order to establish such a perspective, chapter 1 will move through several stages. Starting with Julia Kristeva's (assisted by Dostoyevsky's Ippolit and Prince Myshkin) gaze of Hans Holbein's *The Body of the Dead Christ in the Tomb*, chapter 1 will begin from an artistic point of departure, gazing upon the crucified body of Christ with no recourse to divine designation within the borders of the work itself. From there, with the assistance of Richard Beck, we will consider the implications of incarnation itself, especially as it has given rise to—reflected, according to Beck, in the christological controversies of the past—a certain "incarnational ambivalence." Ultimately, Beck will assist us, from the perspective of terror management theory (TMT), in considering how the corpse of Jesus itself is received among many Christians. From there we will move to Elaine Scarry's treatment of human bodies ripped apart in their defense of nation-states and the manner by which wounded bodies take on a referential instability with reference to "sides." Dovetailing with Scarry, we will consider Theresa Sanders' articulation of the "death of designation" with reference to the crucified body of Christ, as well. Ultimately chapter 1 will move to a treatment of, from the perspective of deconstruction, employing John Caputo as our chief guide, the One who, incarnate without remainder, is the primary "text" of theology. At this stage we will consider the incarnate One—the primary "text"—from the perspective of an absence of both an "Authorizing Presence," and a "Divine Referent." It is a combined absence, as we will see, which culminates in an ultimate "undecidability" at play with regard to the decisions of hermeneutics conducted *in media res*. Again, the purpose of this chapter, or—ultimately—pulling the corpse of Christ from the framework of Luther's theology of the cross, is to delineate the crucified Christ within a context of referential instability. Ultimately, our gaze will be filled with a silent, exsanguinated corpse resting in death's repose. God's *sub contrario* promise of life? Perhaps. Or maybe—from the perspective delineated by Caputo and others—it is just one interpretation among an infinite supply of others.

Beginning with the development of "promise"—the "undeconstructible"—under the direction of Jacques Derrida and Caputo, chapter 2 will develop the structure of Promise as it is expressed according to Martin Luther's radical interpretation of the *communicatio idiomatum*. Caputo's— informed by Derrida—delineation of "promise" is provided at the outset for a couple of reasons. First, the conceptualization of "promise" that is expressed within this framework provides an excellent contrasting background against which to develop the structure of Promise through Luther's *communicatio idiomatum*. And, second, it can be argued, it is through this combined, prolific corpus of Derrida and Caputo (and especially Caputo's for an American audience) that "promise" has been given its most sustained contemporary application.[19] But let us note: a prior level of engagement, a certain level of facility, with Derrida and Caputo is not required, as this line of thinking with regard to "promise" will be unpacked and explained for the reader within the text itself (within the context of "undecidability," which will also be unpacked). Ultimately, as will be developed, the structure of Promise—per Luther's *communcatio idiomatum*—is anything but "undeconstructible." Moreover, Luther's radical interpretation of the *communicatio idiomatum* will permit us to delineate the structure of Promise, literally, with creational proportions. Reminding ourselves that, for a theologian of the cross, the revelation of God's *yes* is always concealed under the experience of a *no*, that for a theologian of the cross the calculations of reason and

---

19. Caputo and Derrida's *Deconstruction in a Nutshell* will serve as our guide to developing "promise" in this sub-section. I also refer readers to—among others—Caputo's *The Weakness of God* and *The Insistence of God*. These latter two titles are informed by a conceptualization of "promise"—one whose fundaments are developed in *Deconstruction in a Nutshell*—which funds Caputo's fundamental poetics of the "event."

the judgments of experience remain in this life, and, subsequently, the experience of *Anfechtung*, Promise's structure will be considered from a dual perspective: Is this the *Promise* of nihil, or the promise of *nihil*? Let it also be noted here: "promise" will be capitalized only upon reaching Luther's elaboration of the *communicatio idiomatum*. Until this point, it will appear in quotation marks. This is done to indicate explicitly that the "promise" being discussed is the one articulated by Luther's radical interpretation of the *communicatio idiomatum*, and is thus bound to what "is," what is created, what attracts flies.

Originally intended as a single chapter, chapters 3 and 4—for all intents and purposes—can be considered "3A" and "3B." Chapter 4 is to be read as the development of a christological hermeneutic in light of the framework delineated in chapter 3 through the lens of Albert Schweitzer's seminal work. Specifically, a close reading of key passages from Schweitzer's *The Quest of the Historical Jesus* will be employed to frame the christological heremeneutic developed in chapter 4. Schweitzer's diagnosis of the so-called "historical Jesus" as produced by those engaged in the nineteenth-century "quest of the historical Jesus," in addition to his analysis of the "life of Jesus" as it is specifically presented by the Synoptic Gospels, will serve as a framework for our task of developing the manner by which Scripture conveys both Jesus Christ, and the value of those whose gaze is directed at him. As will be developed, Schweitzer's redirect of the "life of Jesus" from "mirror" to "window" will both shape chapter 3, and provide both a foundation for and contrast to chapter 4. In the process, we will also be able to discern the manner by which Schweitzer navigates the silence of the text, a silence manifest both in the eschatological peculiarity of Jesus, and the seams and gaps of the text which presents him. Ultimately, our analysis of Schweitzer will beg the question: Is Scripture—the text—a "window" (to the "timeless" and "spiritual") or a "mirror" (of matters more "timely")?

With Schweitzer's treatment of the "historical Jesus" in hand, we will then, in chapter 4, turn to Martin Luther's understanding of Scripture. It is here that we will develop his christological hermeneutic, or, let us call it, the kenotic authority of the unveiled text. But chapter 4 will push the hermeneutic even further. Indeed, asserting that the crucified Christ, the *genus tapeinoticum*, is the primary text for a theologian of the cross, chapter 4 will develop and elaborate the implications of Luther's *communicatio idiomatum*, especially with regard to expanding the scope of the text. Chapter 4 will culminate with our gaze directed squarely at the Isenheim Altarpiece, at Grünewald's *Crucifixion*. Gazing at his work, let us ask: How extensive is the crucified "text"? Is there such a reality as a "plural crucified One"? Grünewald, as does Holbein in chapter 1, reminds us of art's capacity for theological profundity *sans* the prolixity which is so common in academic works of theology. Ultimately, chapter 4 will arrive at a full development of a Christology suspended from the cross, a *christologia crucis*.

Chapter 5 will dive into two of Luther's "works," a sermon and a lecture, in order to reveal a dynamic at play in Luther's writings which has been central to the development and application of Luther's *communicatio idiomatum* all through this project: the narrating of Christology. It is the narrating of a Christology inscribed with the theology of the cross, thus reflecting its "undecideness" and "suspendedness" with regard to God's concealed *yes*, God's *sub contrario* revelation, or the judgments of experience and reason which fund *Anfechtung*. If chapter 4 is a delineation of a Christology suspended from the cross through a development and application of Luther's *communicatio idiomatum* (the structure of Promise), then chapter 5 is a delineation of a Christology suspended from the cross gleaned from Luther's own narration (the experience of Promise). Perhaps it may be the case that chapter 5 leaves the reader wanting to dive back into both Luther's *Lectures on Genesis,* or his sermons, spotting the ways by which he narrates the experience Christology for his readers and listeners, preaching and teaching a God whose *yes* is concealed under a *no*; discerning how he narrates an existence between Promise and experience. Recognizing the concealed nature of God's revealed *yes* in Jesus Christ, chapter 5—near its conclusion—will also present the reader with something that can be best described as a "Barthian (intra-textual) footnote." It will consist of a discussion, from Lutheran sources, regarding the "hiddenness of faith," a faith which corresponds to the crucified Christ. Who is the active agent, the subject, of "faith?" How do we speak of such a "faith"?

Between chapters 2 and 3, 4 and 5, and 5 and the conclusion, are situated three "interludes" (the author was unable to conjure a more profound word). These interludes develop and address the engagements of significant theologians with aspects of Luther's theology of the cross and Christology. To be sure, these interludes not only present engagements with Luther's theology of the cross and Christology from perspectives beyond the circle of Lutheranism—two of the three through a Reformed theological lens—but, in their development, in formulating a response to these voices, these interludes have forced the author to further clarify his understanding—and presentation—of Luther's theology of the cross and Christology at various points. The reader may enjoy this project without reading the interludes. If one chooses to read them, it is hoped that a fuller understanding of Luther's theology of the cross and Christology emerge.

Ultimately, the conclusion will, as conclusions often do, tie up the project while, in the process, providing some new perspectives on the material.

Finally, let me give what is perhaps a confession of sorts.

That is, theology has always been an existence. There is nothing contrived here. To be sure, the seeds of the argument developed in this project were planted many years ago during college and seminary as the result of perceived inadequacies and unanswered questions surrounding the matter of ecumenical and confessional Christology—especially on the matter of confessional Christology. Why was the *Anfechtung* of Luther's theology of the cross, the concealed nature of revelation and faith, absent from—never seemed to be translated into—confessional Christology?

Some days, this theological existence is experienced as something of a curse, a "slough of despond," a "negative sign" hanging over life and vocation itself. Most often it is experienced as a blessing the depths of which I can only begin to understand. It is a theological existence that situates me between two poles, perhaps best expressed by Luther, an existence not wanting "to be the nothing out of which the Lord can create,"[20] and confessing that "The love of God does not find, but creates, that which is pleasing to it."[21]

It is the recognition that, in the words of Karl Barth, "Implicitly and explicitly, proper theology will have to be a *Proslogion*, *Suspirium*, or prayer. It will mediate on the fact that God can be its object only because he is the acting and speaking subject upon whom all depends."[22] I await this acting and speaking, in the words of the psalmist, "more than those who watch for the morning, more than those who watch for the morning" (Ps 130:6).

20. Luther, *Works* 25.158.

21. Luther, *Works* 31.58.

22. Barth, *Evangelical Theology*, 165.

1

Interpreting Crucified Corpses

Inhabiting Ippolit's Gaze

As Julia Kristeva observes, Italian iconography has a tradition of embellishing and ennobling the face of Jesus during the Passion, inscribing lingering traces of transcendence, if you will. And certainly this tradition of iconography is noted for the manner by which it surrounds Jesus with individuals who appear to be absorbed simultaneously in the throes of grief and the certainty, perhaps a "glow," of the impending resurrection, "as if to suggest the attitude we should ourselves adopt facing the Passion."[1] As if to say, if reference to transcendence cannot be discerned within the lines of Jesus' body, his *post mortem* expression, it can certainly be detected—with Jesus as the referent—in the countenances of those surrounding him. On the contrary, she points out, Hans Holbein the Younger (1497–1543), captures on canvas a visage bearing no such resemblance.

1. Kristeva, "Holbein's Dead Christ," 112.

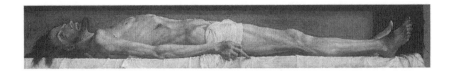

**Hans Holbein the Younger, *The Body of the Dead Christ in the Tomb* (1520–1522)
Kunstmuseum, Basel, Switzerland**

Casting her eyes upon the image of Jesus produced by Holbein entitled *The Body of the Dead Christ in the Tomb* (1521), Julia Kristeva's gaze is filled with the lifeless corpse of Jesus stretched out on a slab, viewed from the side, from an angle slightly below the subject, body scarred, emaciated and exsanguinated of any hint of animation and transcendent reference. Elaborating Kristeva's gaze in detail:

> Holbein's painting represents a corpse stretched out by itself on a slab covered with a cloth that is scarcely draped. Life size, the painted corpse is seen from the side, its head slightly turned toward the viewer, the hair spread out on the sheet. The right arm is in full view, resting alongside the emaciated, tortured body, and the hand protrudes slightly from the slab. The rounded chest suggests a triangle within the very low, elongated rectangle of the recess that constitutes the painting's frame. The chest bears the bloody mark of a spear, and the hand shows the stigmata of the crucifixion, which stiffen the outstretched middle finger. Imprints of nails mark Christ's feet. The martyr's face bears the expression of a hopeless grief; the empty stare, the sharp-lined profile, the dull blue-green complexion are those of a man who is truly dead, of Christ forsaken by the Father ("My God, my God, why have you deserted me?") and without promise of Resurrection.[2]

As well, not only is the body alone, bereft of living company to convey an appropriate *pathos* worthy of the gravity of the scene, but the body is also, per the logistics of its depiction, "cut off from us by its base but without any prospect toward heaven, for the ceiling in the recess comes down low, Holbein's *Dead Christ* is inaccessible, distant, but without a beyond. It is a way of looking at mankind from afar, even in death . . . "[3] And it is not simply the logistics of the painting, the aloneness of the subject, that draws our

2. Kristeva, "Holbein's Dead Christ," 110.
3. Kristeva, "Holbein's Dead Christ," 113.

imagination into the unrepresentable abyss of death and what it means to be dead, but, as well, it is the depiction of Jesus himself, a dismal rendering captured in nondescript and parsimonious strokes, that reveals, perhaps, "the most disturbing sign is the most ordinary one."[4] Regarding this subject, the *Dead Christ*, Kristeva reflects:

> The unadorned representation of human death, the well-nigh anatomical stripping of the corpse convey to viewers an unbearable anguish before the death of God, here blended with our own, since there is not the slightest suggestion of transcendency. What is more, Hans Holbein has given up all architectural or compositional fancy. The tombstone weighs down on the upper portion of the painting, which is merely twelve inches high, and intensifies the feeling of permanent death: *this corpse shall never rise again*.[5]

Indeed, Kristeva hearkens us to Dostoyevsky's *The Idiot*, wherein it is Prince Myshkin who, upon seeing a reproduction of this work at Rogozhin's house, exclaimed, "A man could even lose his faith from that painting!"[6] And it is Ippolit—a young nihilist who is nearing death from tuberculosis—who, later in the novel, is afforded an opportunity to describe this work, and the impression it makes, of Holbein's in greater detail for the reader. I quote him at length:

> The picture portrays Christ just taken down from the cross. It seems to me that painters are usually in the habit of portraying Christ, both on the cross and taken down from the cross, as still having a shade of extraordinary beauty in his face; they seek to preserve this beauty for him even in his most horrible suffering. But in Rogozhin's picture there is not a word about beauty; this is in the fullest sense the corpse of a man who had endured infinite suffering before the cross, wounds, torture, beating by the guards, beating by the people as he carried the cross and fell down under it, and had finally suffered on the cross for six hours (at least according to my calculation). True, it is the face of a man who has *only just* been taken down from the cross, that is, retaining in itself a great deal of life, of warmth; nothing has had time to become rigid yet, so that the dead man's face even shows suffering as if he were feeling it now (the artist has caught that very well); but the face has not been spared in the least; it

4. Kristeva, "Holbein's Dead Christ," 115.
5. Kristeva, "Holbein's Dead Christ," 110. Italics mine.
6. Kristeva, "Holbein's Dead Christ," 107. See also Dostoyevsky, *Idiot*, 218.

is nature alone, and truly as the dead body of any man must be after such torments. I know that in the first centuries the Christian Church already established that Christ suffered not in appearance but in reality, and that on the cross his body, therefore, was fully and completely subject to the laws of nature. In the picture this face is horribly hurt by blows, swollen, with horrible, swollen, and bloody bruises, the eyelids are open, the eyes cross; the large, open whites have a sort of deathly, glassy shine. But, strangely, when you look at the corpse of this tortured man, a particular and curious question arises: if all his disciples, his chief future apostles, if the women who followed him and stood by the cross, if all those who believed in him and worshipped him had seen a corpse like that (and it was bound to be exactly like that), how could they believe, looking at such a corpse, that this sufferer would resurrect? Here the notion involuntarily occurs to you that if death is so terrible and the laws of nature are so powerful, how can they be overcome? How overcome them, if they were not even defeated now, by the one who defeated nature while he lived, whom nature obeyed, who exclaimed: "*Talitha cumi*" and the girl arose, "Lazarus, come forth" and the dead man came out? Nature appears to the viewer of this painting in the shape of some enormous, implacable, and dumb beast, or, to put it more correctly, much more correctly, strange though it is—in the shape of some huge machine of the most modern construction, which has senselessly seized, crushed, and swallowed up, blankly and unfeelingly, a great and priceless being—such a being as by himself was worth the whole of nature and all its laws, the whole earth, which was perhaps created solely for the appearance of this being alone! The painting seems precisely to express this notion of a dark, insolent, and senselessly eternal power, to which everything is subjected, and it is conveyed to you involuntarily. The people who surrounded the dead man, none of whom is in the painting, must have felt horrible anguish and confusion on that evening, which at once smashed all their hopes and almost their beliefs. They must have gone off in terrible fear, though each carried within himself a tremendous thought that could never be torn out of him. And if this same teacher could have seen his own image on the eve of the execution, would he have gone to the cross and died as he did? That question also comes to you involuntarily as you look at the painting.[7]

7. Dostoyevsky, *Idiot*, 407–9; also cited in Kristeva, "Holbein's Dead Christ," 107–9.

Ippolit finally asks, perhaps words aimed at death itself, the unrepresentable abyss worked by that "dumb beast" called "nature," "Can something that has no image come as an image?"[8] As if to say, perhaps, if "that infinite power, that blank, dark, and dumb being" has an ultimate, crystallized form, it is the "strange and impossible form" captured by Holbein.[9]

It is a form which bears the marks of humanity's brutality, the deafeningly silenced, suffocatingly confined isolation of death, and the implacable indifference of a reality—called by many "nature"—that both "gives" and "takes" with equal portions of eternal insouciance. Stated otherwise, Holbein's Jesus ironically becomes a depiction of a divine void, a vacuum with regard to any trace of transcendence. A witness to absence, capital "A." But this may be only the beginning of why Holbein's Jesus may horrify us. As will be developed below, the wages of brutality—its wounds, its deaths, its corpses (its crucified!)—bear in themselves no stabilized significance or crystalized direction of reference. Essentially, if Holbein has provoked an irreducible, existential ambivalence with regard to the crucified Christ, then, as we will see, this very ambivalence extends back to the conceptualization of "incarnation" itself. And, more often than not, it is an ambivalence concealed by contemporary Christian artists. Why?

If religious belief, as both Sigmund Freud and William James concurred within their respective frameworks of functional analysis of religion, serves the function of minimalizing existential discomfort, an emotional coping mechanism expressed through the adoption of supernatural beliefs employed to assuage and even deny existential anxiety in the face of death,[10] then the human body, as Ernest Becker began to observe, and has since been developed through terror management theory (TMT)[11]—especially

8. Dostoyevsky, *Idiot*, 409.

9. Dostoyevsky, *Idiot*, 409.

10. Let us note that, for James, not only is religion not limited to this function, but, contrary to Freud, he observed that there are religious persons—"sick souls"—who both eschew the employment of religious belief in order to assuage or insulate themselves from existential anxiety, and embrace such categories as protest, lament, and complaint. For an overview and application of the functional analysis of religion, see Beck, *Authenticity of Faith*.

11. At a fundamental level, terror management theory (TMT) is focused on two questions: (1) Why are people so intensely concerned with their self-esteem; and (2) why do people cling so tenaciously to their own cultural beliefs and have such a difficult time coexisting with others different than themselves? Ultimately, as TMT has developed, cultural worldviews assist in managing the terror which accompanies awareness of mortality. It does so fundamentally through the mechanism of self-esteem, or the "belief that one is a valuable contributor to a meaningful universe." Effective terror management, then, requires a "meaningful conception of reality" combined with the recognition that one is able to achieve the "standards of value prescribed by worldview."

with reference to Christian religious beliefs—presents its own set of complications with regard to that same anxiety.[12] Nowhere is this dynamic more profoundly revealed than on the matter of the incarnation. Approaching the matter from the perspective of psychology, as Richard Beck observes, and as it has been historically expressed in the Gnostic and Docetic controversies, the idea of God assuming a fully human form has been for many, to say the least, far from an existential comfort. This discomfort with regard to imagining an incarnation, of God becoming fully human, is what Beck calls "incarnational ambivalence"[13] But, let us ask, what is it that drives this ambivalence?

Beck offers that recent work in *TMT* may provide one answer as to what drives this "incarnational ambivalence." As a variety of recent studies have demonstrated, not only are people ambivalent toward their own bodies and bodily functions, but the body itself is a constant reminder of death. From this perspective, Beck asserts, the incarnation of Jesus Christ ceases to be a solace against anxiety in the face of death. Beck elaborates,

> Perhaps a fully human Jesus is theologically and psychologically worrisome because Jesus becomes too vulnerable to the forces of decay, the very forces that cause us such existential dread. Phrased another way, a superhuman Jesus, not affected by bodily functions, pain, or vulnerability, might seem a better prospect, psychologically speaking, to rescue us from our existential anxieties.[14]

If our physical bodies—including everything from our vulnerabilities, our sexual appetites, our fecal production, to the reality that, at long last, we will decompose and attract flies—perpetuate reminders of mortality, then the reality of the Divine Son of God participating fully in human existence is certainly no comfort, no buffer against the existential dread of death.[15] If, for one, the great beauty and comfort of the incarnation of Jesus Christ lies in God's involvement in human existence without remainder, then, for another, this same involvement may be the engine that fires existential anxiety.

Ultimately though, in Beck's view, the manner by which religious beliefs and doctrines and, in this case, the incarnation "are adopted, shifted, deployed, and managed to repress or reduce existential anxiety . . . hints at the intriguing possibility that doctrinal disputes among Christians,

Beck, *Authenticity of Faith*, 87.

12. Beck, *Authenticity of Faith*, 198.

13. Beck, *Authenticity of Faith*, 198.

14. Beck, *Authenticity of Faith*, 199.

15. Beck, *Authenticity of Faith*, 204.

historically and in our present day, might have less to do with theology than with psychology."[16] Could it be—is it not fair to ask?—that instead of prompting dogmatic finger-pointing and words of anathema by that circle of mutual adulation who fancy themselves "orthodox" in all matters theological and confessional, that Gnostic and Docetic positions can be engaged from the perspective of naming the very anxieties and dread regarding putridity and death these positions are elaborated to avoid, from which they insulate their subscribers? Could it be the case that, though Christology, and in this case the doctrine of the two natures of Christ—the full participation of the Word of God in human existence—cannot be reduced to "functional analysis" with regard to articulating its fundamental role for Christian theology, "functional analysis" can be employed to assist in an understanding—dare I say, empathizing!—with regard to why such a doctrine may be abbreviated? But if a function of religious belief is the management of existential anxiety in the face of death, if a purpose of religious belief is palliative care in the face of such matters as randomness and mortality, then this dynamic may be most profoundly expressed in the form of modern Christian visual art.

As Beck points out, art, and, for our purpose, visual art in particular, has traditionally been a medium by which cultures have either confronted their existential predicaments or have been comforted in the face of existential realities such as uncertainty and death. Therefore, visual art can either serve an "escapist" function by which reality is avoided or it can function to address the darkest elements of human existence, and in particular, Christian existence.[17] And certainly in line with the reality that visual art has long served as a fundamental component of Christian church design, worship, personal devotion, and culture at large, there is no question that Christian retail—so-called Christian bookstores and retail outlets—has capitalized on just this matter. For many Christian artists, though, this can only be an occasion for lament. As Beck observes, thinking about much of the visual art that is popular today, much of which that adorns the homes of the devout, worship spaces, and church walls, "[M]any Christian artists see a general decline in Christian aesthetic judgment, as poor or superficial artwork appears to be dominating the Christian visual culture."[18] Elaborating upon what he means by a "decline in Christian aesthetic judgment," Beck cites the observations of Ned Bustard, who asserts,

> Inevitably it seems that most attempts to picture good tend to offer the viewer disingenuous, sugary sweet propaganda. Ignoring

16. Beck, *Authenticity of Faith*, 204–5.
17. Beck, *Authenticity of Faith*, 212–13.
18. Beck, *Authenticity of Faith*, 212.

the implications of [the painful elements of human life], these artists paint the world as a shiny, happy place. The quintessential example of this in our day is found in Thomas Kinkade's general philosophy. Kinkade professes to be a Christian but has said, "I like to portray a world without the Fall."[19]

Beck labels this "disingenuous," "sugary sweet" attempt to capture the world in the medium of visual art devoid of the dark, painful, ugly, or even ambiguous elements of human existence "The Thomas Kinkade effect."[20] Thus, if contemporary Christian visual art has a tendency to be commercial, superficial, and syrupy, perhaps all of this nothing more than a symptom of the function—managing existential anxiety—it is serving and, therefore, how the artist chooses to edit the more troubling aspects of human existence in light of that function.

The "flip-side" of the coin: mirroring the logic discussed above, if that which is considered beautiful and comforting is due to the manner by which it corresponds to human experience—in this case, the Word of God's complete involvement in human existence without remainder; if "true beauty is not achieved by willfully removing the signs of death, suffering, or brokenness,"[21] then the measure of Christian visual art will also be reflected by just how deeply it mirrors and represents human life. Even when that life is depicted at the farthest point on the continuum of what provokes dread. But this "beauty"—especially on the matter of depicting the incarnation— may also provoke our deepest suspicions and greatest fears with regard to the *shear possibility* of discerning traces of transcendence. If Ippolit (and Myshkin) has observed in Holbein's depiction of the dead Christ an image devoid of all traces of transcendence, a divine void, provoking in many what Beck has termed an "incarnational ambivalence," Elaine Scarry traces the dynamics and implications of just such a reality.

Whose Body?

If, as Scarry has observed, the human body during peacetime is irreducibly an expression, however subtly—into to the deepest levels of the unconscious, penetrating the deepest fibers of personhood (its habits, expressions, demeanors, gestures, etc.)—of the nation-state, the polis, the locale in which it has been weened, then warfare—its injuries, its gaping wounds—makes

19. Bustard, "God Is Good," 18; cited in Beck, *Authenticity of Faith*, 214–15.
20. Beck, *Authenticity of Faith*, 220.
21. Beck, *Authenticity of Faith*, 215.

this dynamic profoundly more explicit.[22] The wounds of warfare, Scarry points out, express the "extreme literalness" by which the nation "inscribes itself in the body," by which "the human body opens itself and allows 'the nation' to be registered in the wound."[23] The wounds of warfare also serve to memorialize in human bodies—both alive and buried—the event of warfare, of the body's participation in warfare.[24] But of ultimate significance, Scarry suggests, is the human body's special ability to authenticate beliefs and ideological positions that account for the perpetual presence of warfare. Concretely: what authority, may we ask, does a gaping wound, an eviscerated and mangled corpse, have over, say, the victorious outcome of a tennis match? Scarry offers a helpful framework for thinking about this question.

As Scarry observes, there are three areas of damage with reference to warfare: first, embodied human beings; second, the "material culture" (a self-extension of embodied humans); and third, the "immaterial culture" (expressed in the form of collective national self-definition, especially with regard to a nation's collective self-identity and political beliefs).[25] Thus, according to Scarry, "The object in war . . . is the third; for it is the national self-definitions of the disputing countries that have collided, and the dispute disappears if at least one of them agrees to retract, relinquish, or alter its own form of self-belief, its own form of self-extension."[26] Subsequently, the first and second areas of damage produced by warfare dictate which of the competing sides endures the third area of damage. Although competing sides may suffer damage, only one side is designated "loser," thus incurring the third form of damage. As well, damage sustained in the first and second areas serve as an "abiding record" of the third area.[27] But it is also precisely here that the "abiding record" of warfare's expressions—its wounds, its corpses—becomes problematic, as well.

As Scarry observes, though the first and second forms of damage—and in this case, especially the first—determine which side will incur the third form of damage (and, subsequently, be declared "loser"), the damage inflicted by warfare does not objectify, make explicit, "winners" and "losers," only *that* there was warfare. That is, the physical damage of war—its wounds, its corpses—serves essentially only to memorialize war without

---

22. See Scarry, *Body in Pain*, 108–33.
23. Scarry, *Body in Pain*, 112.
24. Scarry, *Body in Pain*, 113.
25. Scarry, *Body in Pain*, 114.
26. Scarry, *Body in Pain*, 114.
27. Scarry, *Body in Pain*, 114.

specifying winner or loser.[28] Inherent within the gaping wounds of humanity, Scarry observes, is a "fluidity of referential direction,"[29] or a "referential instability"[30] which reflects the reality that wounds and corpses are not only mute to the ideologies that were contested on the field of battle, but are eternally silent with reference to the outcome of those same contests. If the damage of warfare—its body counts and casualty figures—can initially be parsed into a dual framework for the sake of interpreting a "winner" and a "loser," then such damage, with the passage of time, acquiesces into a single numerical figure, perhaps under the rubric of an ideology contested, reflecting merely the fact that a war had been waged by two sides. Concretely, we might say, though the Union and Confederate sides in the American Civil War each may have sustained particular casualty figures, both are ultimately tallied together to reflect the "cost" of a war to "end slavery." But if it is the case, once warfare is finished, that all casualties eventually fall under the umbrella of a single figure, expressing the single phenomenon of a war completed, then Scarry also notices a second habit at play.

According to Scarry, "A second and kindred verbal habit is to keep the injuries of the two sides separate, but to cite those that occurred to one side *either* to make manifest the fact that that side won *or* to make manifest the fact that they lost. That is," she adds, "juxtaposed to the assertion that a country won or lost is the assertion of the number of injuries that occurred, showing that injuries are perceived to be demonstrable 'proof' of either victory or defeat . . . "[31] Ultimately, then, though the declaration that "30,000 Russians died that day in battle, the Russians 'lost'" is meaningful, it can also be said, without canceling out the prior declaration, its logic, that "20,000,000 Russians were killed fighting Germany, the Russians 'won.'" This ability for injury, and ultimately death, to "substantiate disparate phenomena" (as "winning" and "losing") points to the reality of the "referential instability of the body that allows it to confer its reality on whatever outcome occurred."[32]

But—keeping before us Scarry's initial observation that human bodies are irreducibly expressions of the nation-states, the locales of their weening—if the injuries and wounds of war express the "extreme literalness" by which the nation-state "inscribes itself in the body," then they also, in their extreme expression, drain the human body of the cultural and ideological

28. Scarry, *Body in Pain*, 115.

29. Scarry, *Body in Pain*, 115.

30. Scarry, *Body in Pain*, 117.

31. Scarry, *Body in Pain*, 117.

32. Scarry, *Body in Pain*, 117.

identities to which it was aligned and associated and according to which war was waged. To be sure, in death the savaged corpse is not only rendered mute to any sense of self-designated identity, but, perhaps more significantly, it attains a referential freedom indifferent to the original identities and intentions to which the body was once oriented in life. Putting the matter poignantly, Scarry asserts, "Only alive did he sing [his national hymn]: that is, only alive did he determine and control the referential direction of his body, did he determine the ideas and beliefs that would be substantiated by his own embodied person and presence."[33] Placed in perspective: if the wounds of war can initially serve as a testament to the profound manner by which the nation-state "inscribes itself in the body," then by a cruel twist of irony those wounds expressed *in extremis*—a corpse—drain the body of all national inscription and self-designation; of all the conscious designation and meanings by which he aligned himself and for which he fought, which propelled him into battle. But even more fundamentally, the corpse, reveals a referential freedom which raises the question of just who—which side?!—is able to claim the corpse. Once a human body is drained of national and self-designation, once a human body becomes a corpse, it can be co-opted to justify, to substantiate, the very ideas and beliefs of the enemy by whose hands its wounds were inflicted. In short, we may ask, to which side does the corpse belong? Again, to quote Scarry at some length:

> Does this dead [soldier's] body "belong" to his side, the side "for which" he died, or does it "belong" to the side "for which" someone killed him, the side that "took" him? That it belongs to both or neither makes manifest the nonreferential character of the dead body that will become operative in war's aftermath, a nonreferentiality that rather than eliminating all referential activity instead gives it a frightening freedom of referential activity, one whose direction is no longer limited and controlled by the original contexts of personhood and motive, thus increasing the directions in which at the end of the war it can now move.[34]

What military recruiter, we might ask, would tell prospective recruits that sacrificing one's life on behalf of his nation is certainly not the most significant "sacrifice" that can occur with such an event? That indeed the prospective recruit's possible death may well be the sacrifice of his sacrifice on behalf of his nation, or a substantiation of the cause against to which he consciously sacrificed his life!

33. Scarry, *Body in Pain*, 118.
34. Scarry, *Body in Pain*, 119.

Ultimately, though, the conundrum of war is just this: if the gaping wound, the eviscerated and mangled corpse, has a profound ability to substantiate beliefs and ideological positions, thus accounting for the perpetual presence of warfare, as Scarry observes, then those same gaping wounds and forever silenced, eviscerated bodies also render eternally silent the self-designations which once propelled the human body into warfare, creating a referential instability which, at the very least, permits that same body to be employed in the substantiation of the other side's beliefs. Or as Theresa Sanders asserts regarding the dead body, "it makes no claim or promises of its own, can be appropriated by any number of successive, competing, and even contradictory causes. But, by that very fact, it remains subject to none of them."[35] She adds, "One can't really predict what a [dead] body will end up saying."[36] Indeed, as Sanders asserts, "In death the body opens itself up to this or that meaning, or, most horrifying, to no meaning at all. [In death] one risks being insignificant. One risks the death of designation."[37]

And it is this "referential instability" of the silent, savaged, mangled combatant, of the exsanguinated corpse, a deconstruction of the nation- and self-designated identity which once animated and aligned his body— ultimately what Sanders has coined the "death of designation"—that may very well justify fears lurking at the far edge of "incarnational ambivalence," while most certainly reinforcing a deeper "silence" inscribed in texts and, ultimately, mangled (crucified!) corpses.

Descent into Undecidability

As John Caputo observes, though Christianity is certainly considered a religion of the Book, a religious tradition grounded in a sacred text(s), a text(s) allegedly even containing special, divine revelation, "[t]here is no escaping the textuality, the play of traces, no faith that is not a certain *hermeneia*."[38] That is, with the authorizing Origin—the Word—always receding behind the trace—the words—it leaves behind, and, subsequently, with no recourse to "The Meaning"[39] or "The Secret"[40] behind the surface of the text, one may perhaps recognize that the sacrifice concealed in a sacred text—the Bible—is the giving up, the forfeiture, of any claim to direct,

35. Sanders, *Body and Belief*, 4.
36. Sanders, *Body and Belief*, 5.
37. Sanders, *Body and Belief*, 120.
38. Caputo, "Holy Hermeneutics," 196.
39. Caputo, "Hermeneutics and the Secret," 2.
40. Caputo, "Hermeneutics and the Secret," 2.

immediate access to the "living presence" who originally inspired that same text. Never granted absolute access to the Absolute Referent of the text, never granted an orthodox perspective of privilege beyond *in media res*, beyond signs and traces and competing interpretations, the "inescapable play of interpretation,"[41] the interpreter of sacred texts is confronted with, to say the least, a Sisyphean task.

Perhaps the interpreter of the text is confronted with multiple, justifiable choices with regard to interpretation. Perhaps the interpreter of the text is compelled to make a hermeneutical decision beyond the scope of what is deemed logical, deducible, or calculable within the range of what is considered "rational," reaching an impasse with regard to a text's meaning. Perhaps the interpreter of the text is given insufficient evidence upon which to make a hermeneutical decision. Regardless, in all cases, the interpreter is confronted with silence, the silence of the Word who has—in the interpreter's estimation—retreated behind the words of the text.

It is precisely here that the interpreter of the sacred text has arrived at undecidability.[42] "For whenever a decision is really a decision, whenever it is more than a programmable, deducible, calculable, computable result of a logarithm, that is because it has passed through 'the ordeal of undecidability.'"[43] In short, according to Caputo, a true hermeneutical decision—a situation of undecidability—is sustained by its own impossibility, sanctioned by the very absence of—and an absence of recourse to—the Referent in whose name the text was originally sanctioned as sacred. But it is precisely here that we need to be reminded: sacred texts are not merely confined to scrolls and books.

As undecidability draws us into the deep structure of reality itself, so also bodies—especially crucified bodies—can be considered within the domain of "text." To be sure, for the purpose of this project, Christianity is ultimately a religion not merely of a *book*, but of a *body*, a crucified body; and of "reading," of "interpreting" a crucified body. *This*—ultimately the incarnate, crucified One—is the text of Christianity for theologians. But before we advance to our discussion to crucified bodies, let us briefly treat the matter of living, breathing, speaking bodies. Especially with regard to the living, breathing, speaking body of Jesus Christ.

No doubt bearing in mind the divine incognito witnessed by the Gospel narratives (one need only adduce the earliest Gospel's—the Gospel of

41. Caputo, "Hermeneutics and the Secret," 3.

42. For a treatment of the theme undecidability, see my entry, "Undecidability" in *Encylopedia of Martin Luther and the Reformation*, 784.

43. Derrida and Caputo, *Deconstruction in a Nutshell*, 137.

Mark—presentation of Jesus Christ, for example, with reference to the disciples' inability to understand the nature of Jesus' identity, see Mark 8:31–33, 9:30–37, 10:35–40; and certainly, to this same phenomenon expressed with reference to the disciples, crowd, and political leaders through the course of the trial and crucifixion of Jesus, see Mark 14:53—15:20), Caputo makes explicit reference to the "Road to Emmaus" narrative (Luke 24:13–35) in order to raise a "red flag" with regard to possible vantage-points of privilege on the matter of discerning Jesus' identity. That is, the phenomenon of the ever-retreating presence of the authorizing Origin is not merely confined to chronological latecomers, arriving by chance too late on the historical timeline. In this case, the Word is not even to be corralled via contemporaneity of lifespan, as if there was a privileged perspective accessed by chronological contemporaneity which qualifies one for special, privileged access to glean the god-like in what is given. To quote Caputo—echoing Kierkegaard—on this point,

> Even if we walked along the dusty road to Emmaus, we would be as slow of wit, slow of heart, slow of step as Cleophas. Even if we belonged to the first generation, walking the dusty roads of Galilee with Jesus, Johannes Climacus argued, we would still have needed the "condition," faith, to recognize him, so that even when Jesus was *present* the God with or within him was not "unconditionally *given*." The idea that we would catch a glimpse of the *tout autre* in the gleam of his penetrating eyes is paganism, Climacus said.[44]

In short, even standing in the presence of a living, first-century Jesus is not a point of privileged access with regard to an interpretation of his identity, with regard to arresting the play of possible interpretations, thus bailing us from the responsibility of risking one interpretation among others. In reality, perhaps, fated with the gift of contemporaneity before the divine incognito of this first-century Galilean, we simply find ourselves to be nothing more than comfortable co-conspirators with regard to the other contemporaries who fill the scene, who fit the bill of dull disciples, bloodthirsty crowds, and duty-driven executioners. But let us press deeper on the matter of the incarnation of Jesus Christ, the matter of an incarnate God, especially with regard to the implications of such a submission to the human condition.

Whether we agree on *how* the incarnation of Jesus Christ is delineated—will you, by the time theological debate is finished, accuse the other of Arianism? And the other detect a whiff of Docetism in you? Will you, from your perspective of Lutheran (Roman Catholic, Reformed, Orthodox,

---

44. Caputo, "Holy Hermeneutics," 206.

et al.) confessionalism, label the other a "heretic"? And will others sense that Jesus has no stomach for the confessional boundaries from within which you write?—regardless, what can be mutually appreciated is the wider atmosphere, the wider context to which an incarnate God submits. (If it is, in fact, a complete incarnation!) As Caputo points out in so many ways, as an incarnate God *de facto* submits to the human condition, this God submits his verbal communication to human language, *a* human language—just imagine the unending task of observing and interpreting his body language!—and thus to words, especially words that will require translation from one language to another, not to mention the endless play of possible interpretations with regard to his own "incar-native" language. It is an endless fray of words, lines of ink, transmitted to mediating texts, their traces endlessly copied, endlessly retranslated and eternally bereft of their Inspiring Origin, what we have been calling the Word. But more than this, by assuming and submitting to human language an incarnate God "descends into the play of traces, and risks being misunderstood, misremembered, misquoted, misused by people with intentions quite the opposite of his, risks having his (or her) sayings corrupted by corrupt manuscripts or by copyists in Irish monasteries having a bad day."[45]

And just as self-professing carnate, contextual Christians cannot flee from the *in media res* fray and flux of life to a privileged perspective by which the whole landscape may be coolly, calmly surveyed, so also—lest it be merely a feigned, duplicitous form of *kenosis*, something like an incarnational card-reveal yet while keeping one card "up the sleeve"—an incarnate God, one who seeks complete solidarity with humanity without remainder, must, as Caputo points out, be willing to abide by the terms of this incarnational agreement, "to cope with the difficulties this imposes, without attempting to bail out of this textual fix by means of some extratextual, holy hermeneutical hook . . . "[46] Again, for religions grounded in a Book, a Text, in this case Christianity, Caputo avers that "the words of God are the words of the Scriptures, which are the traces of the god who has descended into the play, who has assumed the form of the play, not as a jest but in earnest."[47] An incarnate God—for it to be an incarnation on the terms of humanity without remainder and *sans* divine duplicity—must submit to receding behind the words of the scroll, must forfeit all claims as the Absolute Referent of the traces which mark and dot the text, whether that text is papyrus, paper, or—even—a human body, especially a crucified human body.

45. Caputo, "Holy Hermeneutics," 208.
46. Caputo, "Holy Hermeneutics," 209.
47. Caputo, "Holy Hermeneutics," 209.

Silence: The Beginning of Christology?

If undecidability is essentially the "silence" occasioned by the withdrawal of the Authorizing Presence, the Word, behind the traces and marks of the text it has left in its wake, thereby abandoning all recourse to divinely sanctioning an orthodox, stabilized meaning, then this "silence" must be considered in its ultimate manifestation. If Jesus Christ is the Word of God incarnate without remainder, to the point of silence, sans Authorizing Presence, then Christology is necessarily "radical [C]hristology." That is, as Mark C. Taylor observes,

> Radical [C]hristology is *thoroughly* incarnational—the divine "*is*" the incarnate word. Furthermore, this embodiment of the divine is the death of God. With the appearance of the divine that is not only itself but is at the same time other, the God who alone is God disappears. The death of God is the sacrifice of the transcendent Author/Creator/Master who governs from afar. Incarnation *irrevocably* erases the disembodied logos and inscribes a word that becomes the script enacted in the infinite play of interpretation.[48]

To be sure, this silence must be considered with regard to a text in which the traces and marks are those of bruises, lash marks, contusions, nail-holes, signs of asphyxiation and shock, and certainly streaks of clotted blood; a mangled, crucified text in which all recourse to a Divine Referent has been exsanguinated not merely in theory, as a hermeneutical model or proposal or method, but as a concrete phenomenon of human experience. This text—a crucified body—not only reveals the profound silence to which an incarnate God submits, and is thus exposed, without remainder, but it also reveals the gaping abyss, the silence, over which a "decision" (regarding the identity and significance of this crucified body) is perpetually suspended and renewed.

And perhaps Jesus himself gives us a foretaste of just what it is we must endure—the unremitting silence—as those who are called to confess, to exegete the eternal significance of a crucified body; a hint by the so-called Revealer of Absolute Origin himself that his Authorizer, the Absolute Origin, will not be captured, arrested—so to speak—in order to confirm, to stabilize, the identity of the One who cries out to him/her from such a destabilized context. Indeed—in a manner reminiscent of Holbein's *The Body of the Dead Christ in the Tomb*, a brutalized, crucified Jesus bereft of any external designation, especially that of the Father's—the Authorizer, the

---

48. Taylor, *Erring*, 103.

Absolute Origin, must as well, remain out of frame, concealed beyond the marks and traces of the text, in this case the vast text of creation itself. To be sure, "When it was noon, darkness came over the earth until three in the afternoon. At three o'clock Jesus cried out with a loud voice, 'Eloi, Eloi, lema sabachthani?' which means, 'My God, my God, why have you forsaken me (Mark 15:33–34)?'" A cry, a lament? Yes. For the one who confesses the incarnation of Jesus Christ: a confirmation that Jesus Christ truly is the Word of God incarnate without remainder? Perhaps. Or perhaps this is simply the final cry of exasperation before the final exhalation, and thus the final silencing of a personality. On one hand, this may be an expression of the profundity of Christology. On the other hand, this may be the stark reality, the final word, of anthropology. In either case: silence. Is this the silence where true Christology—expressive of an incarnation without remainder—begins? Bereft of self-designation, bereft of any stabilizing external confirmation? Christology, from this perspective, suffers the silence created in the void left by incarnation's death of designation.

But if the ability to seek a perspective beyond the silence, to still the hermeneutical flux, to seek a perspective beyond the *in media res* of life, to arrest the play and possibility of multiple, competing interpretations, is simply an illusion, then the theologian gives priority to the crucified Christ not because she *knows* once and for all that this where Truth is Finally Revealed, and thus where all theology must begin if one truly wants to practice theology that is "official," "confessional," and "orthodox." No. It is perhaps due to the reality that there is no other point of departure that corresponds to the structure of experience and the world, its profound undecidability, and the competing possibilities which stir within its cracks and fissures, its traces, its wounds. It is perhaps due to the sober recognition that such a point of departure corresponds (if God is to be incarnate without remainder, in solidarity with humanity without deception and duplicity) to the silence—the silence of undecidability, the silence of our sufferings, the silence of our deaths, the silence of our tombs—which is the deepest, most profound expression of the text of humanity into which God has descended, submitted. The theologian experiences, to use Caputo's terms, "a brush with the deep undecidability in things, with the wavering instability in things, with what we have been calling the silence of God that we cannot avoid even as it elicits a choice from us."[49] An incarnate God must submit to this undecidability, an undecidability whose silence is the fundamental datum of theology; the silence of crucified body, a text whose traces are torture marks and wounds. From this perspective, silence is the only point of departure for doing a

49. Caputo, "Undecidability and the Empty Tomb," 237.

theology that corresponds to human experience. Which means, from this perspective: absence, absence of both Divine Referent and Authorizing Origin, may be the litmus test for theology *qua* theology; for theologians who have not confused their context, their method, their self, their tradition, as the Official Point of Access.

If it is from this location—gaze fixed on the mangled, isolated corpse of Jesus, exsanguinated of all references to "divine presence"—that a theologian conducts theology, then the theologian also recognizes the possibility from which he can never extricate himself, which engenders his prayers in the key of lament and inscribes all his theological formulations with provisionality and humility.

The theologian never surpasses the location, or the perspective of Dostoyevsky's Ippolit who stands before Holbein's *Dead Christ* and ruminates upon the possibility that there is another authority—indifferent and impersonal, distant, unchanging—that has actually dictated the significance, the identity, of the one whose ravaged, crucified corpse sits on the cold, enclosed slab. Again, the words of Ippolit:

> Nature appears to the viewer of this painting in the shape of some enormous, implacable, and dumb beast, or, to put it more correctly, much more correctly, strange though it is—in the shape of some huge machine of the most modern construction, which has senselessly seized, crushed, and swallowed up, blankly and unfeelingly, a great and priceless being—such a being as by himself was worth the whole of nature and all its laws, the whole earth, which was perhaps created solely for the appearance of this being alone! The painting seems precisely to express this notion of a dark, insolent, and senselessly eternal power, to which everything is subjected, and it is conveyed to you involuntarily.[50]

Is this *Christus Victor*? Is this the agent of Abelard's "atonement theory," or Anselm's? Is this the incarnate Son of God, second person of the Trinity, two natures, without confusion and without separation? Is this the Word of God through whom all things came into existence, to whose authority all things are subjected? Or is this—and really, I harbor no animus toward the "Jesus Seminar" scholars, as they are conducting historical criticism honestly, according to the fashion in which it was conceived, *sans* ecclesiastical recourse, *sans* a lifeline from going too far into the abyss and swimming within the maelstrom of honest conclusions—merely a rabbi? Or a "sage"?

50. Dostoyevsky, *Idiot*, 408–9.

Or a "miracle worker"? Or an "itinerant preacher"? Or just an "apocalyptic prophet"?

This corpse, viewed so soberly by Ippolit, raises the question of which "side"—thinking of Scarry's observations—it affirms, it justifies, which ideology it vindicates; it raises the distinct possibility that this corpse is a "statistic" reinforcing the policies of the Roman Emperor and, perhaps, the threatened perspective, and thus maneuverings, of the religious authorities—"See what you get when you blaspheme!" Does this corpse "belong" to the "kingdom of God" or to the "kingdom of the world" (and if the latter, which one?)? May not both sides claim it for their own accounting? Does this corpse—bruised, with gaping wounds—raise the possibility that violence, in the end, is the final word on human society that is ultimately nothing more than a microcosm of a world-at-large, one that is irreducibly "red in tooth and claw"? Or is this corpse, exsanguinated of all reference to matters transcendent, simply a witness—in Ippolit's words—to the "dark, insolent, and senselessly eternal power, to which everything is subjected"? Merely a witness to "some huge machine of the most modern construction," which is impersonal, indifferent, eternally in charge? And let us be reminded, such an observation certainly is not new to the history of christological discourse. Albert Schweitzer observes near the end of his famous, long study presenting the results of research into the historical Jesus that

> Soon after [the appearance of John the Baptist] comes Jesus, and in the knowledge that He is the coming Son of Man lays hold of the wheel of the world to set it moving on the last revolution which is to bring all ordinary history to a close. It refuses to turn, and He throws Himself upon it. Then it does turn; and crushes Him. Instead of bringing in the eschatological conditions, He has destroyed them. The wheel rolls onward, and the mangled body of the one immeasurably great Man, who was strong enough to think of Himself as the spiritual ruler of mankind and to bend history to His purpose, is hanging upon it still. That is His victory and His reign.[51]

Is Schweitzer the New Testament scholar concurring with Dostoyevsky's Ippolit?

Such a theological perspective, as is developed in this chapter, will not claim to see traces of divine glitter or an outline of divine aura where others simply see wounds and smell death, but will consider, situate, this exsanguinated, cold, isolated corpse against the "horizon, indeed the specter that perhaps history has no point at all, that undeserved suffering has no

---

51. Schweitzer, *Quest of the Historical Jesus*, 368–69. Herafter cited as *Quest*.

meaning, that the cosmos does not know we are here."[52] Indeed, recognizing that no hermeneutic and its results *must* conform to the *ecclesia*, its official confessional statements, such a theological perspective will not shy away from the conclusions of those who practice the historical critical method in thoroughgoing fashion. That is, as Caputo points out with regard to the crucifixion narrative: "[No] heavens opening up at the crack of 3:00 P.M., no centurion confessing that this was the Son of God in truth. Just abandonment, death, and maybe even no empty tomb at all, just burial in a common grave, maybe even . . . no burial at all, just exposure to the dogs."[53] Again, such a perspective, ultimately, understands that the "silence" of undecidability, of the tomb, is the only authentic expression of a Word of God incarnate without remainder who corresponds to human experience. Subsequently, recognizing the deceit involved, such a theological perspective resists the temptation in "still[ing] the hermeneutical flux, to arrest the play that is set in motion" once the "inescapable undecidability in things"[54] has been conceded. It is dishonesty—or perhaps a theologian who has confused their vocation for magic, or confused their point of departure for The Point of the Departure—who looks upon the exsanguinated corpse of Jesus as though it was clearly transparent to the divine majesty he may (or may not) have claimed to embody when air filled his lungs.

Standing with Ippolit before the exsanguinated corpse of Jesus, observing the abyssal silence of the isolated tomb, drained of all reference to what might possibly be deemed as "divinity," perhaps it is Sanders' observation that best captures the location from which such a gaze emanates, a perspective which will never be superceded in this life; a perspective which will creep into, and corrode, any christological formulation that is ventured, rendering all such formulations tenuous and provisional, tendered with trembling hands. That is, regarding the corpse of Jesus and the silence of the tomb, cut off from all communication—both human and divine, such a reality raises the

> deeply troubling possibility that whatever meaning we think we find in life is simply *one* meaning . . . among thousands of potential meanings . . . It raises the possibility that in the end we have no way of knowing if the cross is really a sign of the impossible, unmasterable kingdom of God or is a justification for murder.[55]

---

52. Caputo, "Undecidability and the Empty Tomb," 243.
53. Caputo, "Undecidability and the Empty Tomb," 244–45.
54. Caputo, "Undecidability and the Empty Tomb," 242.
55. Sanders, "Festivals of Holy Pain," 47.

If the only point of departure for theology that corresponds to the deep structure of human experience is an incarnate God without remainder, then the only "text" commensurate with such a starting point, which captures the concrete phenomenon of such an experience, is the wounded, exsanguinated corpse of Jesus; a corpse drained not simply of life, but adrift in the undecidable, silent play of traces, in the abyssal absence of a divine referent, sacrificed on the altar of self-reference, given up to a "death of designation."

Subsequently, a theologian who operates from such a point of departure, such a datum—the exsanguinated corpse of Jesus—understands that such a hermeneutical point of departure corresponds to the deep structure of existence, an existence whose structure, whose flux and flow, cannot be arrested by confessional or ecclesiastical fiat. It is an exsanguinated corpse whose piercing silence cannot be drowned out by chatter—no matter how profoundly it has masqueraded itself in the jargon of theological and ecclesiastical technicality and authority—even if that chatter is presumed of its elocutionists to be divinely authorized. Such a one utterly despairs of all manufactured pretensions with regard to divine accessibility; of all presumptions of orthodoxy or a confessional community's claim to privileged immunity from the silent play of traces.

Christology's Promising Point of Departure

Before the same crucified text stands the theologian of the cross who—gaze fixed on the traces and marks, the bruises and the gaping wounds of a corpse emptied of all self-designation, exsanguinated of all reference and clues to divine presence or authorization; a crucified body in the abyssal silence of death's repose—confesses, against experience's judgments and reason's calculations, that this is God's *sub contrario* revelation of life. The theologian of the cross confesses that within the vacuum of silenced words bursts the Word's communication; that pulsating within the mangled absence of all divine signifiers is the presence of the Creator's life-giving *modus operandae*. With incessant praying engendered by a Promise, the theologian of the cross "hopes against hope" (Rom 4:18) that the Promise of God's kingdom, of a new creation, a "new Jerusalem," and hence of a new heaven and a new earth (Rev 21:1–5) is revealed precisely here. The theologian of the cross confesses, with a confession that may even be hidden to itself, that this corpse is the life-creating Word, the body of Promise.

If a Christology is to correspond to the a theology of the cross, to be constructed from the location of the cross, certainly within the trajectory of Luther's theology of the cross, then—this project asserts—the abyssal silence of this undecidable play of traces, the abject absence of any divine referent within, or divine authorizer beyond, the crucified text, the mangled body exsanguinated of all divine signifiers, and drained of all self-designation *is* theology's epistemic point of departure, God's *sub contrario* revelation, indeed the mask of Promise.

Whatever else we might say can only be an extension of that fundamental *sine qua non* confession and its corresponding prayer. Without Promise, there is no prayer. Or, as Luther is quoted to have said, "If it weren't for the promise, I wouldn't pray."[56]

Without Promise we would not be standing before this crucified corpse . . . confessing it to be the body of Promise.

At the same time, now casting a retrospective gaze back over this chapter, let us ask: if "A theologian of the cross calls the thing what it actually is,"[57] then with how much soberness is such a naming to be conducted? Have we not, in our sobriety, pushed the hermeneutics of reason and experience to their point of crucifixion? So that we may be ready to conduct Christology in a context of prayer generated by Promise?

56. Luther, *Works* 54.42.
57. Luther, *Works* 31.53.

2

Body Is Promise

Luther's Communicatio Idiomatum

If, as was developed in the Introduction, "true theology and recognition of God," for Martin Luther, "are in the crucified Christ,"[1] then—for a theologian of the cross—Christianity is fundamentally a religion whose primary text is a body, specifically, the body of the crucified Christ. In the terminology of classical Lutheran Christology that text is the *genus tapeinoticum*. At the same time, as its implications were explored in the previous chapter, the body of the crucified Christ is not the exclusive possession, or exclusive hermeneutical province, of Luther's theology of the cross.

Pulling the crucified body of Christ from the framework of Luther's theology of the cross, from its epistemic point of departure as God's *sub contrario* revelation, the previous chapter explored the hermeneutical implications of just this reality: the abyssal silence of a "text," exsanguinated of all self-designated reference, reduced to an interminable "referential instability," a "death of designation"; a mangled, silent body drained of the "promise" which once coursed through its words and gestures, inspiring and galvanizing its existence. All of which provokes a line of questions (implied within the trajectory of this project): should not such a "promise" be more durable, more indestructible than its medium, the one who bears such a "promise"? Should not such a "promise"—of God's kingdom, a new creation, "a new

---

1. Luther, *Works* 31.53.

35

heaven and a new earth"—*not* be bound to the one who bears it? Even if its bearer is destroyed, should not the "promise" borne be indestructible? How might we understand "promise's" durability—if there is such a thing—according to such a reality?

At the outset of this chapter, and continuing within the trajectory of the previous chapter, "promise" will be developed as it is expressive of that dynamic of deconstruction—associated with the philosophy of Jacques Derrida and explicitly delineated with reference to the task of theology by John Caputo—coined "undecidability." How, may we ask, does a text—in this case, the crucified Christ—relate to, convey, "promise"? Or, ironically, we might ask: What is the structure of "promise" according to deconstruction?

By delineating "promise" by means of deconstruction—through Derrida and Caputo—we are simply providing a counter-pole, a contrasting background, against which Luther's "promise," its structure, will be developed. In doing so, the radicality of Luther's conceptualization of "promise" will be more deeply appreciated. As we will see, these two conceptualizations of "promise" could not be more antithetical.

The Promise of Deconstruction

Whether the text before us is sacred Scripture consisting of papyrus or paper, ink, and manual markings, or the *in media res* experience of life itself, deconstruction "is driven by the absolute secret,"[2] a "structural non-knowing."[3] That is, permitted no access to "The Meaning"[4] or "The Secret"[5] behind the surface of the text, deconstruction recognizes, and binds itself to, "The inescapable play of interpretation" within the text itself.[6] Subsequently, with no access to a vantage point outside of the text, it is often the case that the interpreter is forced to make a decision outside the trajectory of what is logical, sequential, deducible, or calculable within the boundaries of the text, thereby reaching an impasse with regard to the determination of a text's meaning. For example, perhaps it is the case that a given text yields multiple, justifiable interpretations; perhaps it is the case that the text contains conflicting elements; perhaps it is the case that the text gives insufficient evidence on a matter; perhaps the text—a crucified body!—yields only silence, abyssal silence. It is here that the interpreter has arrived

2. Caputo, "Hermeneutics and the Secret," 2.
3. Caputo, "Hermeneutics and the Secret," 3.
4. Caputo, "Hermeneutics and the Secret," 2.
5. Caputo, "Hermeneutics and the Secret," 2.
6. Caputo, "Hermeneutics and the Secret," 3.

at undecidability. As Caputo asserts, "For whenever a decision is really a decision, whenever it is more than a programmable, deducible, calculable, computable result of a logarithm, that is because it has passed through 'the ordeal of undecidability.'"[7] Essentially, a *true decision*—a situation of un-decidability—is sustained and perpetuated by the impossibility of its own definitive resolution. Which means: undecidability opens one up to that which lies beyond the calculable, the possible, the foreseeable.

Ultimately, then, undecidability both draws one into the deep struc-ture of experience itself, an experience extending beyond scrolls and sacred books to life itself, which is "a brush with the deep undecidability in things, with the wavering instability in things,"[8] an undecidabilty that extends to "the silence of God that we cannot avoid even as it solicits a choice from us."[9] An incarnate God must submit without remainder to this undecidability; an undecidability occasioned by the text of a silent, crucified body, a text whose traces, jots, and tittles are torture marks and wounds. At the same time, if undecidability draws us into the deep structure of experience, its "waver-ing instability," it also lures us into a distinction; a distinction between the aforementioned text, or structure, and what is harbored, stirring within it. It is precisely here that "promise" emerges.

Instead of being sustained by an extrapolation of what *is*, what is pres-ent, an extrapolation of present possibilities Caputo has coined the "future present,"[10] undecidability is sustained by the messianic, or "absolute future."[11] It is the absolute, or "messianic future"[12]—impossible, unforeseeable, inde-terminate, always to-come—which is both the structure of the "promise," constantly exposing and revealing the contingency, the open-endedness, of what *is*, while also freighting it with an infinite surplus of possibility. For if deconstruction is driven by the keen awareness of the "deeply historical, social, and linguistic 'constructedness' of our beliefs and practices,"[13] then the messianic future intensifies just such an awareness. So asserts Caputo:

> The messianic future is an absolute future, the very structure
> of the to-come that cannot in principle come about, the very
> open-endedness of the present that makes it impossible for the
> present to draw itself into a circle, to close in and gather around

7. Derrida and Caputo, *Deconstruction in a Nutshell*, 137.

8. Caputo, "Undecidability and the Empty Tomb," 237.

9. Caputo, "Undecidability and the Empty Tomb," 237.

10. Caputo, "Hermeneutics and the Secret," 6.

11. Caputo, "Hermeneutics and the Secret," 6.

12. Derrida and Caputo, *Deconstruction in a Nutshell*, 161.

13. Derrida and Caputo, *Deconstruction in a Nutshell*, 52.

itself. The messianic is the structure of the to-come that exposes
the contingency and deconstructibility of the present, exposing
the alterability of what we like to call in English the "powers
that be," the powers that are present, the prestigious power of
the present. The messianic future, the unformable figure of the
Messiah in deconstruction, has to do with something absolutely
unpresentable and unrepresentable that compromises the pres-
tige of the present, the absolutely undeconstructible that breaks
the spell of the present constructions.[14]

He adds, "The essential indeterminacy of the messianic future, of the figure
of the Messiah, is of the essence of its non-essence. The non-presence of
the Messiah is the very stuff of his promise."[15] Perhaps we can say that it is
the structure of "promise," the messianic future—indeterminate, "disturbing whatever is present and phenomenalizable"[16]—which endlessly opens
determinate messianisms (read: historical Christian traditions, confessions,
Jesus Christ himself!) to the "promise" of the undeconstructible they have
always been anticipating in a multitude of contingent, particular forms.

With regard to the interpretation of texts (reminding ourselves of the
scope of "text"), undecidability is not only an expression of the contingency,
the incompleteness of reason's conclusions and, ultimately, interpretations,
always conducted *in media res* within the play of interpretation, but, perhaps more significantly, reveals the nature of interpretation itself, situated
within unremitting textual silence and competing interpretive options, as
an act of faith. From this perspective, then, undecidability is an expression,
indeed the experience, of "promise" exposing reason—its judgments and
conclusions—to its own relativity. "Promise" bares one's decisions to their
contingency and incompleteness. The messianic, indeterminate structure of
"promise" exposes the reality that there is no decision, no interpretation, no
expression of reason, which is not deeply inscribed by an act of faith. Undecidability is reason grappling with the very faith that is inscribed in its own
decisions. Faith, then, identified on the same plane as reason, can be viewed
both as the suppressed justification of human decisions, never surpassing
their incompleteness in their deliberations and conclusions, and, ultimately,
the passionate non-knowing of what is to-come. Again: to recognize the
dynamic of undecidability is to recognize that faith is freed from tacitly justifying what *is* to an unknowing desire for the indeterminate, unconditional
surplus stirring within the contingency, the provisional nature of reality's *is*.

14. Derrida and Caputo, *Deconstruction in a Nutshell*, 162.

15. Derrida and Caputo, *Deconstruction in a Nutshell*, 162.

16. Derrida and Caputo, *Deconstruction in a Nutshell*, 165.

Ultimately, undecidability itself is the experience of the structure of "promise," the messianic future's coming, its perpetual arriving. To move beyond undecidability would be a shift back into the foreseeable, the repetition of present possibilities. Within the fissures and obsolescence of the contingent, the determinate, undecidability is the name given to the provocation of "promise"; the messianic pulse of the deep structure of existence, the unforeseeable, the undeconstructible, always to-come future, stirring within—but never identified, synonymous with—what *is*.

But, having developed "promise" within the trajectory by which this project began, let us now turn to Martin Luther, to the manner by which he understood "promise," its communication and, ultimately, its structure. If, up to this point, "promise"—as elaborated by the dynamic of deconstruction—is the indeterminate, undeconstructible, to-come "messianic future" perpetually stirring within—but never identified within—the contingent, then, for Luther, Promise is given *body*, structured by the determinate, historically contingent, has-come, the incarnate One; in short, the Crucified Christ.

The Structure of Promise: Luther's
Communicatio Idiomatum[17]

Luther's refusal to know of God, to apprehend God, apart from the incarnate, crucified One, Jesus Christ, true God and true man created profound implications for his theology. If it has been observed that Luther's "[C]hristology is above all soteriology,"[18] it can also be asserted that his Christology is the *communicatio idiomatum*.[19] Essentially, according to Kjell Ove Nilsson,

> for Luther everything depends on the matter that Christ—truly the unified God-man—has accomplished the work of redemption *pro nobis*. And because the unity of the action itself is connected with the unity of the person, in which the *communicatio* doctrine is the center, therefore the *communicatio* comprises the core of Luther's theology.[20]

According to Johan Anselm Steiger, Luther's radical interpretation of the Council of Chalcedon's (451) doctrine of the two natures of Christ, the

17. For a thorough overview of Luther's radical interpretation of the *communicatio idiomatum* as a fundamental expression of Luther's *theologia crucis*, see Anthony, *Cross Narratives*, 106–13.

18. Lienhard, *Luther*, 372.

19. Bayer, *Creator est Creatura*, 23.

20. Nilsson, *Simul*, 228.

communicatio idiomatum, "carries this doctrine to its peak and radicalizes it as he makes it the hermeneutical motor of his whole theology, or an axle around which many other theological themes . . . turn."[21] In addition to expressing the peculiar, particular living God attested by Scripture against traditional, metaphysical conceptions of God, Luther's radical interpretation of the *communicatio idiomatum* can be identified as expressing, underscoring four central, closely connected functions. They are: (1) the reality that, since the incarnation, there is no relationship with God that is not a relationship with the *man* Jesus; (2) that creator and redeemer are one, or precisely, that the God of creation is the man who was crucified under Pontius Pilate on Golgotha; (3) that the event of salvation is both divinely authored yet never separated from the man Jesus in whom God is revealed *pro nobis*; and (4) the "soteriological historicization"[22] of Chalcedon's two natures metaphysic for the sake of the *pro nobis* in which all things stated with reference to the human nature of Christ may also be asserted with reference to those who are baptized into Christ. Or as Steiger explains,

> By becoming a human, God takes on not only a human nature but also the whole of humanity and makes his own everything that constitutes this humanity: mortality, neediness, sin and corruption, yes, the whole judgment of God's anger over humans. But, in the opposite direction, everything that really belongs to God alone is made proper to the human: righteousness, eternal life and glory.[23]

But if, as Steiger has asserted, Luther's *communicatio idiomatum* serves as the "hermeneutical motor of his whole theology," as "an axle" around which many theological *loci* turn, then—to remain metaphorically consistent—it can also be asserted that Promise is what necessitates the very vehicle of theology for Luther.

Elaborating upon the centrality of Promise, that indeed the doctrine of justification by faith itself is the expression of the taking of hold of God's Promise,[24] Luther asserts in the course of his lectures on Genesis, specifically his treatment of Genesis 15:6, that

> The chief and most important part of the doctrine [of justification] is the promise; to it faith attaches itself, or, to speak more clearly, faith lays hold of it. Moreover, the confident laying hold

21. Steiger, "*Communicatio Idiomatum*," 125.

22. Steiger, "*Communicatio Idiomatum*," 128–29.

23. Steiger, "*Communicatio Idiomatum*," 138.

24. Luther, *Works* 3.22.

of the promise is called faith; and it justifies, not as our own work but as the work of God. For the promise is a gift, a thought of God by which He offers us something. It is not some work of ours, when we do something from Him, and that solely through His mercy.[25]

Luther adds, "Therefore he who believes God when He promises, he who is convinced that God is truthful and will carry out whatever He has promised, is righteous or is reckoned as righteous."[26] Indeed, faith lays hold of the Promise that, through Christ, "[God's] thoughts concerning us are thoughts of peace, not of affliction or wrath."[27] Promise, for Luther, is the faith-creating means by which God addresses humanity. But, for the sake of this project, it is not simply the centrality of Promise for Luther that is of significance, but, most importantly, its bodiliness. There is no communication of Promise, for Luther, that is not corporeal, inextricably bound to the crucified Christ.

Though it has been rightly observed that the theology of the "young Luther" is a "theology of testament,"[28] it can be argued that Luther's theological program in general, especially when viewed from its core, or Christology, is fundamentally a "theology of testament." More pointedly, Luther's Christology—which "is really the doctrine of the *communicatio idiomatum*"[29]—is a testamental Christology. In other words, if Luther is able to assert that "God does not deal, nor has he ever dealt, with [humanity] otherwise than

25. Luther, *Works* 3.23.

26. Luther, *Works* 3.23.

27. Luther, *Works* 3.22.

28. See Hagen, "Testament of a Worm." Hagen delineates five crucial elements with regard to Luther's "theology of testament." The first element with regard to his theology of testament "is the promise initiated by God from the beginning." Hagen, "Testament of a Worm," 373. God alone initiates without any input from the side of humanity. The second element with regard to his theology of testament is "Luther's theology of the word. The Word is the living eternal promise of the testament of Christ." Or, as Hagen observes, "The Word is the promise, the Word is the testament, the Word is Christ." Hagen, "Testament of a Worm," 375. The third element with regard to his theology of testament is Luther's theology of the cross. The cross, according to Hagen, provides both an "anti-speculative force" and thus, an epistemological center to Luther's theology while also historicizing, "making credible God's eternal promises." Hagen, "Testament of a Worm," 377–8. The fourth element with regard to his theology of testament is grace, or the matter that testament is unilateral gift. The testator wills the inheritance without regard for the merits of the heir. Hagen, "Testament of a Worm," 376. And the fifth element of his theology of testament is "faith or trust in the inheritance." That is, "One receives faith through the Word accomplishing its purpose. Faith is a gift of grace." Hagen, "Testament of a Worm," 376.

29. Bayer, *Creator est Creatura*, 23.

through a word of promise,"[30] then it is the context of that Promise—testament—which both necessitates his Christology and elaborates the substance of the Word, or Promise. As we will see, the *communicatio idiomatum* is the structure of that Promise, its communication, the structure of God's bodily Word.

"A testament," as Luther points out in his treatise *The Babylonian Captivity of the Church* (1520),[31] "as everyone knows, is a promise made by one about to die, in which he designates his bequest and appoints his heirs. A testament, therefore, involves first, the death of the testator, and second, the promise of an inheritance and the naming of an heir." Essentially, Luther continues, "what we call the mass is a promise of the forgiveness of sins made to us by God, and such a promise as has been confirmed by the death of the Son of God."[32] It is "testament" which forms the context of the incarnation, and ultimately, Luther's Christology. So Luther asserts, "Now God made a testament; therefore, it was necessary that he should die. But God could not die unless he became a man. Thus the incarnation and the death of Christ are both comprehended most concisely in this one word, 'testament.'"[33] Which means: Promise, its communication, is the bodily Word of God, or God's complete self-giving through the Son of God by which "life and salvation" (the inheritance) is unilaterally and irrevocably given apart from any human input or merit. Which also means: if the divine Word is not to be sought apart from the *man* Jesus Christ, it is the equivalent, for Luther, of saying that God wishes not to be sought apart from his crucified body of Promise. The body of Jesus Christ—true God and true man—is Promise. There is no communication of Promise—the Word who is Jesus Christ—that is not body.

And nowhere, for Luther, is the structure of that Promise more thoroughly delineated than in his treatise *On the Councils and the Church* (1539).[34] It is here, in the context of retracing the prominent positions which most significantly impacted the proceedings and outcome of the Council of Chalcedon (451), specifically those of Nestorius and Eutyches as they sought to relate the two natures of Jesus Christ, that Luther offers his radical interpretation of the two natures of Jesus Christ.

Stripping the matter to its core logic, failing to privilege the unity of Christ's person, according to Luther, is the chief, common error of Nestorius

30. Luther, *Works* 36.42.
31. Luther, *Works* 36.3–126.
32. Luther, *Works* 36.38.
33. Luther, *Works* 36.38.
34. Luther, *Works* 41.9–178.

and Eutyches. Because they fail to privilege the unity of the Christ's person, neither Nestorius nor Eutyches will allow for a *communicatio idiomatum*, or a full, direct communication of natures within the person of Jesus Christ. As we will see, it is an error with profound implications, especially within the context of a testamental Christology.

Contrary to popular characterization, Nestorius did not posit two Christ's, or two persons, but one Christ, one person. And certainly, as Luther observes, Nestorius adhered to the confession that "Christ was true God born of the Father in eternity, as the Nicene council had defended, and afterward born of a true man of the Virgin Mary."[35] Hence, "staunchly did he regard Christ as true God and man."[36] More precisely, Luther observes, "he also conceded that Christ, God's Son, was born of the Virgin Mary into his humanity, not into his divinity, which we and all Christians also say."[37] The point of contention for Nestorius—according to Luther—was this: "[H]e did not want Mary to be called mother of God because of this since Christ did not derive his divinity, or, to express it plainly, since Christ did not derive his divinity from her as he did his humanity."[38] Critiquing Nestorius on this matter, Luther asserted that although "We too know very well that God did not derive his divinity from Mary . . . [we know that] it does not follow that it is therefore wrong to say that God was born of Mary, that God is Mary's Son, and that Mary is God's mother."[39] Therefore, asserts Luther contrary to traditional caricatures, Nestorius' error was not that "he believed Christ to be a pure man, or that he made two persons of him" but that "after he concedes that God and man are united and fused into one person, he can in no way deny that the *idiomata* of the two natures should also be united and fused. Otherwise, what could God and man united in one person be?"[40]

Instead of relating the two natures of Christ from the priority of the unity of the person of Christ, Nestorius allows the individual integrity of the natures, and specifically, the divinity, to determine his conceptualization of the unity of Christ's person. How can we assert, argues Luther, that God and man are united and fused in the one person of Jesus Christ and *not* declare that "Mary suckled God, rocked God to sleep, prepared broth and soup for God?"[41] Would this not contradict the original premise of unity from

35. Luther, *Works* 41.98.

36. Luther, *Works* 41.98.

37. Luther, *Works* 41.98.

38. Luther, *Works* 41.98.

39. Luther, *Works* 41.99.

40. Luther, *Works* 41.100.

41. Luther, *Works* 41.101.

which our thinking about Jesus Christ started? Thus, as Luther observes, if it seems strange that God assumes human attributes, should it not have been "equally strange that God becomes man . . . [in the first place]?"[42]

Ultimately, the core of the matter for Nestorius was that he would not permit *communicatio idiomatum*. So Luther observes, "This crude, unlearned man did not see that he was asserting the impossible when simultaneously he seriously took Christ to be God and man in one person and yet declined to ascribe the *idiomata* of the natures to the same person of Christ."[43] Pressing this logic against Nestorius, Luther elaborates:

> [I]f I were to say, "There goes God down the street, fetching water and bread so that he might eat and drink with his mother," Nestorius would not grant me this, but says, "To fetch water, buy bread, to have a mother, to eat and drink with her, are *idiomata* or attributes of human not of divine nature." And again, if I say "The carpenter Jesus was crucified by the Jews and the same Jesus is true God," Nestorius would agree that this is true. But if I say, "God was crucified by the Jews," he says, "No! For crucifixion and death are *idiomata* or attributes not of divine but of human nature.[44]

Fundamentally, since for Nestorius the *idiomata naturae humanae,* those attributes peculiar to the nature of humanity ("such as dying, suffering, weeping, speaking, laughing, eating, drinking, sleeping, sorrowing, standing, working, sitting, lying down")[45] are not allowed to directly communicate with the *idiomata Dei,* or those attributes peculiar to the divine nature (immortality, omnipotence, infinity, unbegottenness; the non-applicability of eating, drinking, sleeping, standing, walking, sorrowing, weeping),[46] then Nestorius "means to say with this that Christ is indeed God, but God is not crucified."[47] For, ultimately Nestorius "had in mind . . . that God and death are irreconcilable. It seemed terrible to him to hear that God should die. His meaning was that Christ, in his divinity, was immortal[.]"[48]

Briefly, examining Nestorius' logic with reference to Luther's testamental Christology, a salient deficit arises. Specifically, if for Luther testament forms the context of the incarnation, and subsequently "the incarnation

42. Luther, *Works* 41.100.
43. Luther, *Works* 41.102.
44. Luther, *Works* 41.101.
45. Luther, *Works* 41.100.
46. Luther, *Works* 41.101.
47. Luther, *Works* 41.102.
48. Luther, *Works* 41.102.

and the death of Christ are both comprehended most concisely in this one word, 'testament,'"[49] then for Nestorius "inheritance" ("life and salvation") is removed from the category of irrevocable Promise. The last will and testament of a God who cannot die—who is *not* a divine-*human*—cannot be executed. Therefore "inheritance" cannot be distributed in the form of unilateral Promise. To put it coarsely, the distribution of "life and salvation" would look something more akin to a divine estate sale. One, in economic terms, of inelastic demand.

Ultimately Mary is *Theotokos* and God is crucified. The fundamental error of Nestorius, according to Luther, is that "Nestorius does not want to give the *idiomata* of the humanity to the divinity in Christ, even though he maintains that Christ is God and man . . . "[50] If the Word is one, the *idiomata* of the human nature must be directly communicated to the divine nature. If the Word is one, then the *infinitus ferat finem* (the infinite suffers the finite).[51] God is crucified. God dies. God is buried. If the Word is one, then Nestorius must recognize a *genus tapeinoticum* (the giving of the humble attributes of the human nature to the divine nature). The infinite is revealed only in this particular human, Jesus. Ultimately, if the Word is one, then we have on the slab before us Holbein's Christ.

This same logic was applied to Eutyches. If Nestorius, though recognizing the unity of Christ, did not want to give the human *idiomata* to the divine nature in Christ, then Eutyches, as well, was also unable to think about the relationship of the two natures from the priority of the unity of Christ's person. And so Luther observes regarding Eutyches that he "does not want to give the *idiomata* of divinity to the humanity, though he also maintains that Christ is true God and true man."[52] And so, pressing this logic against Eutyches—in a manner mirroring his handling of Nestorius—Luther asserts:

> [I]f I continue and preach that this same man Christ is creator of heaven and earth, then Eutyches takes offense and is outraged at the words, 'A man created heaven and earth,' and says 'No! Such a divine *idioma* (as creating heaven) does not appertain to man.' But he forgets that he previously conceded that Christ is true God and man in one person and nevertheless refuses to admit the conclusion or 'the premise for a good conclusion.'[53]

49. Luther, *Works* 36.38.
50. Luther, *Works* 41.109.
51. Or: *infinitum capax finiti.*
52. Luther, *Works* 41.109.
53. Luther, *Works* 41.109.

Again, a cursory examination of Euytches' logic with reference to Luther's testamental Christology also reveals a salient deficit. Namely, if the "inheritance" of "life and salvation" requires a *divine*-human to guarantee the substance of the "inheritance," then, for Eutyches such a Promise is underwritten with "insufficient funds." To put it coarsely, "life and salvation" is a check that cannot be underwritten by a mere man. No matter how sincere and pious!

The man Jesus is creator. The man Jesus is omnipotent. Again: if Nestorius was unable to give the human *idiomata* to the divine nature in Christ, Eutyches was unable to give the divine *idiomata* to the human nature in Christ. This time, addressing Eutyches, if the Word is one, then the *finitum capax infiniti* (the finite is capable of the infinite). Jesus of Nazareth created the universe. The man Jesus is God. If the Word is one, then Eutyches must recognize a *genus majestaticum* (the giving of the majestic attributes of God to the human nature).

Returning to Luther's interpretation of Chalcedon, for both men—Nestorius and Eutyches—the fundamental error lay in their inability to permit the priority of the unity of Christ's person to dictate the relationship between the divine and human natures; to redefine *a priori*, abstract conceptualizations of "divine" and "human." "For Luther," as Vítor Westhelle observed, "the problem surrounding [Nestorius' and Eutyches' respective] interpretations of Chalcedon was not the one that pertains to the relationship between the natures and the person, but of the undivided person in whom the natures are perichoretically related."[54] Indeed, "As Luther would say, we could not be more wrong if we start from the purity (aseity) of the divine or of the human nature as such. These can only be obtained from them being in the hypostasis."[55] Both natures can only be spoken of on the basis of the enhypostatic union. To begin the task of theology, and ultimately Christology, with assumptions, preconceptions, of "divinity" and "humanity" apart from the testament of Jesus Christ is to undertake a discipline whose foundation is fractured deeply to the core already from the very beginning. In Luther's words, "whoever confesses the two natures in Christ, God and man, must also ascribe the *idiomata* of both to the person; for to be God and man means nothing if they do not share their *idiomata*."[56]

If we step back and place Luther's interpretation of Chalcedon within the wider context of Lutheranism, in general, especially with regard to the *communicatio idiomatum* as it is delineated by Heinrich Schmid in his

---

54. Luther, *Works* 41.108.

55. Luther, *Works* 41.108.

56. Luther, *Works* 41.118.

classical dogmatics text (see Introduction, above), we discover a profound shift in how the two natures of Christ are related. Although they are listed as the first and third genres respectively, the *idiomatic genus* and the *apotelesmatic* genus establish the fundamental parameters in which the person of Jesus Christ has traditionally been conceptualized, namely through the relationship of the natures to the person.[57] According to the *idiomatic genus,* as Schmid points out, the attributes of both natures are ascribed to the person of Jesus Christ.[58] According to the *apotelesmatic genus* the operations/influences of the person may be ascribed to either of the two natures in a manner peculiar to the respective nature.[59] In the case of both genres, the "person" serves as a buffer which protects the integrity of the *a priori* conceptualized natures.

At the same time, though the traditional Lutheran reading of Chalcedon prioritized the relationship of the two natures to the person, the traditional Lutheran interpretation also leaves us with a partial, incomplete sense of the logic by which Luther originally articulated the *communicatio idiomatum.* That is, if Luther stressed—as we observed through his assessment of Nestorius' and Eutyches' errors—that a true *communicatio idiomatum* involves a giving of the *idiomata* of both natures to each other within the unity of Jesus Christ's person, then traditional Lutheran dogmatics, in this case as elaborated by Schmid, has given Luther's Christology a partial, unfinished rendering.

Though Schmid only elaborates the *genus majestaticum* (in which the divine attributes are ascribed to the human nature)—and certainly the prioritizing of the *genus majestaticum* can be justified against both the sacramental debates of the 1520's and the Reformed position's sacramental rally cry "*finitum non capax infiniti*"—in reality it is only "one side of the *communicatio* coin." One cannot assert a *genus majestaticum* without simultaneously accepting a *genus tapeinoticum.* To do so would be tantamount to saying there is only a "bright side of the moon." It is the expression of a christological naiveté: as if one will not entertain the reality of a "dark side of the moon" because they have not been explicitly informed of it. Thus, with regard to both the *genus majestaticum* and the *genus tapeinoticum,* as Westhelle so succinctly expressed it, "They are, in fact, not two different genres referring to different procedures in *union* of the natures, but only

57. See Westhelle, "Beholding the Core," 106–8, for an elaboration of traditional Lutheran Christology through the lens of hybridity.

58. As Westhelle elaborates it, "Christ is the son of Mary—Christ is the son of God." Westhelle, "Beholding the Core," 106.

59. "[T]he man Jesus died—we are atoned by the son of God." Westhelle, "Beholding the Core," 106.

the mutual sides of the same communication between natures, the double transit from the majestic to the humble and vice versa."[60] One cannot assert that the *finitum capax infiniti* without simultaneously recognizing that the *infinitum capax finiti.*

With reference to this project: if God wishes no longer to be known, sought, apart from the body of God's Promise—Jesus Christ, true God and true man—then, as an analysis of Luther's interpretation of the *communicatio idiomatum* has demonstrated, that same Promise is bound to, and suffers, the finite, evanescent elements by which it is revealed. As the Promise is body, so there is no recourse to a Promise that is "undeconstructible" (Derrida/Caputo), who is not communicated in thoroughgoing frailty and fragility; not bound, identified completely with the meager, determinate structure of what *is*.

But if God is not to be sought apart from the Word of Promise, from the man Jesus, the implications—as they are elaborated by Luther—are striking, especially when we begin to consider that Word, that body, as he both relates to "space" and "takes place." To quote Luther at length:

> And if you could show me one place where God is and not the man, then the person is already divided and I could at once say truthfully, 'Here is God who is not man and has never become man.' But no God like that for me! For it would follow from this that space and place had separated the two natures from one another and thus had divided the person, even though death and all the devils had been unable to separate and tear them apart. This would leave me a poor sort of Christ, if he were present at one single place, as a divine and human person, and if at all other places he had to be nothing more than a mere isolated God and a divine person without humanity. No, comrade, wherever you place God for me, you must also place the humanity for me. They simply will not let themselves be separated and divided from each other.[61]

So now, perhaps, the question begs: what does Luther have in mind when he references "God"? Specifically, how does he understand God's relationship to the world? God's agency? God's creating activity? If the *commuincatio idiomatum* is the structure of Promise, its communication—and, hence, Promise is body—then we are on the verge of discovering the breadth of Promise. But, more fundamentally, we are now prepared to discover the

---

60. Westhelle, "Beholding the Core," 107.

61. Luther, *Works* 37.218–19.

extent of the *genus tapeinoticum*, and, ultimately, the *nihil*, the abyss, which is integral to the structure of Promise, to which Promise is bound.

World Is Promise: The "Third Mode" of Christ's Presence

If Luther was able to assert—countering Ulrich Zwingli's spatially circumscribed depiction—that the "'right hand of God' is not a specific place" but instead "the almighty power of God" which simultaneously "can be nowhere and yet must be everywhere,"[62] then underwriting such an assertion is Luther's core understanding of "God." Not only, as Paul Althaus observed, is God "God" for Luther "because he and only he creates,"[63] but it is the manner of that creating that is crucial for understanding Luther's "God." It is the manner of creating that directly impacts the breadth of Promise and the extent of the *genus tapeinoticum*.

For Luther the fundamental attribute of divinity is immanent, ubiquitous creativity, the "most active working of God"[64] by which God's creating presence is understood to be everywhere "and in all things to the innermost and outermost degree, through and through, as it must be if he is to make and preserve all things everywhere."[65] If Luther understands that creation itself comes into being from nothing (*ex nihilo*) and is itself capable of nothing (*nihil . . . potest*),[66] it is because nothing is either created or sustained apart from God's *ex nihilo* creating activity through the Word.[67] The doctrines of *creatio ex nihilo* and *creatio continua* are identical.[68] As David Löfgren notes, "between God as 'agent' and creation as 'effect' always there is a 'nothing' which excludes every relation of causality in the standard sense."[69] Löfgren adds,

> For Luther the world is not a ship that is constructed in order to sail by itself. The 'nothing' of the world, from which it has

62. Luther, *Works* 37.57.

63. Althaus, *Theology of Martin Luther*, 105.

64. Luther, *Works* 33.233.

65. Luther, *Works* 37.61.

66. Luther, *Works* 4.61.

67. See Althaus, *Theology of Martin Luther*, 105. As well: "If God were to withdraw His hand, this [creation] and everything in it would collapse." Luther, *Works* 22.27. Again: "[I]t is a perpetual and unparalleled rule of the works of God to make all things out of nothing." Luther, *Works* 7.210.

68. Luther, *Works* 4.136.

69. Löfgren, *Die Theologie der Schöpfung*, 23–24.

come, does not lie somewhere in the past, but rather is that from which every new creature, every new human appears at their birth, indeed every moment and every hour are constantly created by God.[70]

Certainly, then, as Johannes Schwanke has observed, the *ex nihilo* formula "is, therefore, not a peripheral concept concerning divine action, but rather the basic matrix of his dealing with humanity and the world."[71]

To be sure, not only does the *nihil* perpetually loom central in Luther's theology as both creation's ever present "whence" and "whither," but the *ex nihilo* formula fundamentally elaborates the Creator-creature/creation relationship, both the complete dependence of the latter upon the former, and the irreversible distinction between the two. Specifically, as we will see, the *nihil*—the abyssal side of God's creating activity—is inscribed into Luther's articulation of Promise, its agency.[72] Ultimately, then, it is this divinity, this creative agency, that is directly communicated to the humanity—ultimately its *nihil*—within the person of Jesus Christ. As well, it is this humanity, its ultimate state of *nihil*, that is communicated to the divinity within the person of Jesus Christ.

The doctrine of *creatio ex nihilo*, we are permitted say from the perspective of Luther's *communicatio idiomatum*, expresses the Promise that within the *nihil* (the vast breadth of the created order) stirs divinity's creating agency, that the creativity of divinity is bound, communicated, to the *nihil*. Simultaneously, *creatio ex nihilo* bears the Promise that the *nihil* (again, the vast breadth of the created order) is the exclusive location and medium of divine creativity, that the *nihil* is bound, communicated, to divinity. Ultimately, this dynamic allows us to arrive at what Luther coined the "third mode" of Christ's presence, a necessary expression of the *communicatio idiomatum*.

If the first mode of Christ's presence is his corporeal, circumscribed presence as the historical man Jesus of Nazareth who walked the earth in the first century, then the second mode is best understood against the background of Luther's sacramental debates with regard to the Real Presence; a "spiritual" mode of presence which allows one to affirm the presence of Christ in the elements of the Lord's Supper without abrogating the integrity of creation. Ultimately, for the Luther, the third mode places Jesus beyond a

70. Löfgren, *Die Theologie der Schöpfung*, 25.

71. Schwanke, "Luther on Creation," 4.

72. Perhaps it is worth nothing for the time being that the doctrine of *creatio ex nihilo* may be of more comfort when the *per-spective* from which it is viewed is *retro-spective*, as opposed to *pro-spective*.

circumscribable, recognizable place, subsequently identifying the person of Jesus Christ with the realm of creation itself.

That is, according to Luther, if "apart from the man there is no God, it must follow that according to the supernatural mode, he is and can be wherever God is, and that everything is full of Christ through and through, even according to his humanity."[73] On the third mode of Christ's presence Luther elaborates,

> You must place this existence of Christ, which constitutes him as one person with God, far, far, beyond things created, as far as God transcends them; and on the other hand, place it as deep in and as near to all created things as God is in them. For he is one indivisible person with God, and wherever God is, he must be also, otherwise our faith is false.[74]

From the perspective of the mechanics of the *communicatio idiomatum*, the third mode of Christ's presence is an expression of the *genus majestaticum* extending the structure of the Promise from the crucified man Jesus to the scope of creation.

It is not simply in redemption, but already in creation—and again let us consider how closely Luther ties *creatio ex nihilo* with *creatio continua*—that God gives completely of Godself. Certainly God's "omnipotence is humble."[75] And if Christ is present everywhere according to his humanity, the *genus tapeinoticum*, its ultimate state of *nihil* (certainly in a manner flirting with pantheism),[76] then the incarnate God is the life-creating Promise stirring, harbored within, all matter; indeed creation—all matter—is the body of Promise, its communication, the testament of the self-giving God. Briefly, let us further elaborate just this point.

If Luther can assert that "The whole creation is a face or mask of God,"[77] that God will only deal with humanity through masks,[78] then the logic behind Luther's "mask" (*larva*) language[79] is the recognition that wherever God is active, that activity is an expression of the incarnate One, true God and true man. Thus, in the words of Löfgren, "It is thus important to be clear on the matter that God, who governs the world through his creatures,

73. Luther, *Works* 37.218.
74. Luther, *Works* 37.223.
75. Bayer, "Creation as History," 259.
76. Westhelle, "Apocalypse," 159. See footnote 81.
77. Luther, *Works* 26.95.
78. Luther, *Works* 1.14.
79. Luther employed such terms as *larva* (mask), *vestitus* (clothing), and *involucrum* (wrapping) to speak of God's presence in creation.

his 'larvae' . . . who consequently is the Lord of history without whom noth- ing occurs—that for Luther this God is none other than the God revealed in Christ who governs his creation and leads it toward its destiny."[80] To be sure, Luther's "mask" language is grounded in the epistemic point of de- parture of his *theologia crucis*—the *genus tapeinoticum*, a divine revelation under the form of its opposite extended from crucified Christ to creation. Luther's "mask" language, then, implies what we have been able to make explicit through his *communicatio idiomatum*. That is, if the third mode of Christ's presence entails the identification of the man Jesus with God's creat- ing agency and is therefore the extension of the humanity of Christ to the scope of creation (as the divinity is communicated to the humanity of Christ within the *communicatio idiomatum*), then not only is creation a testament of Christ, but is, fundamentally, the structure—the body!—of Promise. The third mode of Christ's presence is the *genus tapeinoticum* writ-large. Cre- ation is both body of Promise and the Promise of *nihil*.

The masks of God (*larvae dei*) both express the body of Promise—the *genus tapeinoticum* writ-large according to its manifold particularity—and reveal the creating majesty of God, or the *sub contrario* manner of Prom- ise's *ex nihilo* creating agency.[81] Therefore, the *theologia crucis* is not sim- ply the epistemic principle of Promise (by which its presence and agency

---

80. Löfgren, *Die Theologie der Schöpfung*, 213.

81. Recognizing that, according to Luther, "God deals with people through cover- ings and masks," H. S. Wilson in his "Luther on Preaching as God Speaking" adds, "But God does not become one with these masks, his creations. They are simply his masks. He is hidden behind them. Only a person of faith is given the understanding that God himself is active behind the masks." He adds, " . . . the wisdom to distinguish God from his masks comes from God. A person who is given this kind of wisdom will give attention to God's will and put trust in nothing but God himself, who is operating behind these masks." Ultimately, "God will continue to confront human beings through masks, but wants people to pay attention to the will and Word hidden behind the mask and not the mask itself." Wilson, "Luther on Preaching," 104–5. In response to Wilson, I would simply point out that the only God we know is the *human* God revealed in Jesus Christ. Extending the humanity of Christ, the *genus tapeinoticum*, to the realm of creation through the third mode of Christ's presence, we may confess "mask is God" with the same integrity as confessing that the man Jesus is God. Let us be reminded that Luther refers to the humanity of Jesus Christ with "mask" (*larva*) terminology in his *Lectures on Galatians*. See Luther, *Works* 26.284. The logic of the *communicatio idiomatum*—now writ-large through the third mode—would indicate that the "distinc- tion" does not fracture the prior unity. There is no question that such a dynamic—the third mode of Christ's presence—flirts, when taken out of context with regard to the *communicatio idiomatum*, wildly with pantheism. At the same time, it is the priority of the *communicatio idiomatum* that orders and dictates the relationship between God and creation, and not vice-versa. What also needs to be factored into the conversation is how the third mode of Christ's presence could be construed as pantheism when divinity is understood as incessant, *ex nihilo* creating agency.

is perceived),[82] but provides—considering the *communicatio idiomatum* to be its fundamental christological expression—as well, the structure of Promise, the body of its communication, in all of its modes of expression; a Promise both concealed *sub contraria specie* and bound to fragility, ephemerality, *nihil*. Indeed, if the cross is the material principle of creation, the crucified Christ is the form—the body—of creation. Commensurate with this epistemic point of departure, or the crucified Christ, though "mask" is employed by Luther to speak of Christ's presence throughout creation, let us be reminded that it denies to sight (in a manner corresponding to the first mode of Christ's presence) "evidence of its content, or even existence."[83] To employ "mask" with reference to creation is to confess that the crucified Christ is the creating Promise of all matter.

It must also be observed that, for Luther, the external mediation of Promise, the ministry of Word, and therefore the ministry of the church is, as well, viewed as an expression of the *genus tapeinoticum*, or the humanity of Christ. According to Nilsson,

> [T]he humanity [*Menschlichkeit*] of Christ appears to signify, not only the *historical and biological being of the man Jesus*, which took form in a human body [*einem menschlichen Körper*], but all of what Luther calls *indumenta Dei* [garments of God], the Word, Baptism, and the Lord's Supper, for it is in these human things [*menschlichen Dingen*] that God manifests himself and acts toward us. Wherever such *species Dei* [forms of God] appear, they rightly express the humanity of Christ [*humanitas Christi*].[84]

The ministry of the church, the mediation of the Promise, is qualitatively no different from the wider body of Promise out of which it is called. Perhaps, we could say, a fundamental emphasis of the ministry of the sacraments[85] is to awaken the assembly, ultimately the cosmos, to the structure of its own being, or the Promise who both gives it existence, perpetually animates it, and unilaterally, by grace and love, bestows on it a future *ex nihilo* apart

82. Vercruysse, "Luther's Theology of the Cross," 542.

83. Westhelle, *Scandalous God*, 98.

84. Nilsson, *Simul*, 155. Italics are Nilsson's.

85. A simple, yet fundamental, question needs to be raised here. Could it be, contrary to those who assert "Word and Sacrament," that it is, in reality, simply "Sacrament"? That is, if through Baptism and the Lord's Supper, the Promise is mediated by the physical, external elements of water, bread, and wine, respectively, then preaching is no different. Are not sound waves an expression of the physical universe? In this case, can we not consider the Promise to be mediated by sound waves? Are we aware of Word, a Promise, who is *not* sacramentally mediated, who is not mediated in creation's wrappings?

from its own agency. Stated summarily: the church's mediation of Promise through the ministry of the sacraments (the second mode of Christ's presence) provides the epistemic point of departure by which the world (the third mode of Christ's presence) is perceived according to its structure and destiny as Promise (revealed in the first mode of Christ's presence). This point is certainly echoed by Dietrich Bonhoeffer when he asserts that "The doctrine of ubiquity [third mode of Christ's presence] teaches a Christ outside of revelation." He follows, "[R]evelation becomes the accident of a substance already there."[86] The ministry grounded in the *indumenta Dei*—proclamation, Baptism, Lord's Supper—awakens the world to the recognition that it is the *indumentum* [garment] of Promise, the Promise in whom it is given existence and to whom responsibility is required. Ultimately then, when the world is perceived as body of Promise, as *indumentum* of Promise, it is—specifically—the *genus tapeinoticum* writ-large.

But if the third mode of Christ's presence—"the masked God"—permits us to confess an incarnate God who "holds the promise of all matter,"[87] that creation is the body of Promise, then the very structure of that Promise also conveys an ambivalence, a referential instability, which cannot be transcended for the time being. It is this dynamic we will now explore.

The Promise of Nihil

In the course of elaborating the third mode of Christ's presence we have observed that God's omnipotence is "humble." But only if we settle with understatement. That is, if God will only deal with creation through masks, then God is not only "willing to have those [masks] receive the credit," but is even willing to *appear* unnecessary with regard to the very creation to which God is committed as its creator.[88] Pushing God's "humble" omnipotence even farther, if Luther's "mask" terminology conveys the structure of Promise writ-large, then the very body of Promise—creation—is the chief witness, ultimately, to the ephemerality, the evanescence—ultimately, the *nihil*—which bears that same Promise.

Drawing out the implications of the *communicatio idiomatum*, just as the *genus majestaticum* extends the structure of the Promise from the crucified Christ (first mode of Christ's presence) to the breadth and depth of creation (third mode of Christ's presence), so creation may serve both as a witness to the *ex nihilo* nature of Promise's structure and agency through

---

86. Bonhoeffer, *Christ the Center*, 56.

87. Westhelle, "Apocalypse," 159.

88. Murphy, "Theology of the Cross and God's Work in the World," 225.

which it exists, and—with reference to the *genus tapeinoticum*—as a reflection of the world's unmitigated horrors, its collective, meaningless suffering and death, the experience of divine absence, and ultimately the *nihil* which perpetually bounds the world on all sides. In other words, through the *communcatio idiomatum* the crucified Christ is both communicated to, and mirrored, by creation.

The blessing of the *theologia crucis* is that it prohibits us from seeing through or looking beyond the masks of creation—the text of the third mode of Christ's presence—for the divine. We are bound to *this* text of Promise, *creation as text*. There is no hermeneutical perspective beyond its letters, lines, spaces, and borders. To be sure, at the core of the *theologia crucis* is the confession that "The masked God, the embodied, incarnate God holds [the] promise of all matter. What it reveals is all there is, the mask itself. This divine pantomime, a dancing of masks conveying the word that is never uttered, is all there is."[89] The promise of the *theologia crucis* is that what is *is* Promise's body.

But when the world is no longer believed as *promised*, to be the *body* of Promise, when it ceases to be experienced as the medium of Promise, it mirrors the silent, brutalized, exsanguinated corpse of Jesus Christ, and its corresponding "death of designation." As well, when no longer believed as Promise's body, the world is viewed as confined to the fate of what is. What was once believed as promised, the blessings of life, the gift of community, the life-giving rhythms of nature, is now experienced according to a "horrible naturality."[90] Is this simply another point within the "infinite space" of terrifying "eternal silence?"[91] Is this merely a "cosmic prison" whose "creative spark," especially as it comes to expression through evolution, specifically in the case of humanity, is interminably, irreducibly, reduced to "an inner solitude that is linked to the nature of life itself?"[92] When no longer perceived as the body of Promise, the *genus tapeinoticum* writ-large comes to express the "death of designation." *Nihil* may be infinite grave as justifiably as perpetual womb. Within the void of Promise the structure of Promise may well simply be the quiet guarantee of, and testament to, inevitably ultimate destruction. "In such falling silent and such coldness of the world, God's wrath is experienced[.]"[93] In the silent void of Promise creation shifts from mask of the hidden God whose *ex nihilo* life-giving agency is revealed

89. Westhelle, "Apocalypse," 159.

90. See Bayer, "Creation as History," 258.

91. Pascal, *Pensées*, 73

92. Eiseley, *Invisible Pyramid*, 48.

93. Bayer, "Creation as History," 258.

in the crucified Christ to something far more impersonal, indifferent, inhuman. *Nihil.*

Up to this point we have confined ourselves to a Promise who is revealed *sub contraria specie* (under the form of its opposite) according to all three modes of expression, from cross to creation; a God who is hidden *in* suffering and death, a Promise who is bound to fragility, ephemerality, what is crucified, dies, is destroyed. But the hiddenness of God must be pressed farther. For, as David Tracy has noted,

> [Luther] even dares to speak of a second sense of hiddenness as
> behind or even 'beyond' the word [or, Promise]. At the very least,
> this literally awful, ambivalent sense of God's hiddenness can
> be so overwhelming that God sometimes experienced as purely
> frightening, not tender, sometimes even as an impersonal reali-
> ty—"it"—of sheer power and energy signified by such metaphors,
> such *fragmentary* metaphors as abyss, chasm, chaos, horror.[94]

There is no question that Tracy is correct on the matter of a "second sense of hiddenness" in Luther.[95] It pervades his theology, animating "faith" as a constantly renewed flight from God hidden (in this horrifying, abyssal second sense) to God revealed *sub contraria specie* (hidden in the first sense). Which means: if all of creation can be considered—on account of the third mode of Christ's presence—the body of Promise, then, when the world is no longer believed as Promise, this "second sense of hiddenness," this "literally awful, ambivalent sense of God's hiddenness" expressed by such terms as "abyss," "chasm," "chaos," and "horror," becomes the lurking horror *in*, the looming specter creeping up through the cracks of what *was previously* confessed as "for us."[96] This "second sense of hiddenness" is the horrifying,

---

94. Tracy, "Form and Fragment," 10.

95. For the *locus classicus* of this second sense of hiddenness in Luther, see his *Bondage of the Will* (1525). "God must therefore be left to himself in his own majesty, for in this regard we have nothing to do with him, nor has he willed that we should have anything to do with him. But we have something to do with him insofar as he is clothed and set forth in his Word, through which he offers himself to us and which is the beauty and glory with which the psalmist celebrates him as being clothed. In this regard, we say, the good God does not deplore the death of his people which he works in them, but he deplores the death which he finds in his people and desires to remove it from them. For it is this that God as he is preached is concerned with, namely, that sin and death should be taken away and we should be saved. For 'he sent his word and healed them' [Ps 107:20]. But God hidden in his majesty neither deplores nor takes away death, but works life, death, and all in all. For there he has not bound himself by his word, but has kept himself free over all things." Luther, *Works* 33.139–40.

96. See previous footnote. Luther would disagree with me on this point. This "second sense of hiddenness" is one which Luther posits beyond, outside the Word. I have

impersonal abyss lurking *within* a world no longer perceived through the Word as the Word's creation, or the body of Promise. Creation is either body of Promise, the *Promise* of nihil, or—when no longer perceived through the lens of Promise—an unmitigated, indifferent theater of destruction and horror: the promise of *Nihil*. For a theologian of the cross the experience of this "second sense of hiddenness" drives one back into the arms of the Promise concealed in suffering and death.

According to Eugene Thacker—a contemporary philosopher writing from the burgeoning discipline within philosophy conducted at the intersection of philosophy and horror—contemporary philosophy is confronted with, and struggles to assimilate, a similar horror. Let us briefly pursue this line of thought. It is here we will discover a similar dynamic, a parallel path, one which can certainly inform our thinking with regard to the abyss, the horror within the cracks and fissures of a creation originally understood as "for us."

If, according to Thacker, the world has become "increasingly unthinkable,"[97] it is because humanity has become increasingly aware that we inhabit a fundamentally "non-human" world, or one which will no longer submit to an anthropocentrically derived framework of meaning, especially when the world manifests itself in the form of natural disaster and looming global cataclysm. Such a realization, according to Thacker, has spawned a strain of philosophy he calls "the horror of philosophy" (as opposed to "the philosophy of horror") which perpetually isolates and grapples with "those moments in which philosophy reveals its own limitations and constraints, moments in which thinking enigmatically confronts the horizon of its possibility—the thought of the unthinkable that philosophy cannot pronounce but via non-philosophical language."[98] "Horror," and specifically, the genre of "supernatural horror," has traditionally been both the "privileged site" and the "non-philosophical attempt" to think about the impersonal and indifferent world which will not be domesticated by a framework of meaning.[99]

Throughout history, Thacker observes, when the world has manifested itself in the form of natural/ecological disasters, or has posed the threat of

---

taken the step of assigning this "second sense of hiddenness" as one which—when the body of Promise, the third mode presence is no longer believed, or when faith is afflicted with *Anfechtung* (see chapter 5, below)—looms and lurks within the cracks of creation itself; certainly as the experience of creation no longer perceived as body of Promise; when it becomes indifferent, abyssal.

97. Thacker, *In the Dust of This Planet*, 1. See especially pages 1–9 for an overview of this perspective.

98. Thacker, *In the Dust of This Planet*, 2.

99. Thacker, *In the Dust of This Planet*, 2.

global cataclysm, humanity has been able to counter with a corresponding interpretative framework in order to give meaning to these realities; to a world of such indiscriminate, inhuman expressions. Thacker briefly identifies three such frameworks by which meaning is established, especially with an eye to the envelopment of its non-human elements. For the classical Greeks such an interpretative framework, often circling around questions of fate and destiny, was fundamentally mythological, or personification of the impersonal world through a pantheon of gods driven by all-too-human emotions, or a "world at once familiar and unfamiliar, a world within our control or a world as a plaything of the gods."[100] With regard to Medieval and early modern Christianity, the interpretive framework was fundamentally theological. No less personifying of the impersonal world, this time through the employment of a paternal God, angels, and demons, Medieval and early modern Christianity—most notably through its apocalyptic and Scholastic influences, according to Thacker—cast the non-human world within the context of a "moral-economic framework of sin, debt, and redemption in a life after life."[101] The interpretive framework of modernity is essentially existential. Or, at the crossroads of scientific hegemony, industrial capitalism, and the "death of God" (in the trajectory of Nietzsche's prophesy), the response of modernity is a "questioning of the role of human individuals and human groups in light of modern science, high technology, industrial and post-industrial capitalism, and world wars."[102] This modern existential framework, Thacker adds, "with its ethical imperative of choice, freedom, and will, in the face of both scientific and religious determinisms, ultimately constricts the entire world into a solipsistic, angst-ridden vortex of the individual human subject."[103] Summarily, Thacker observes, all of these interpretive frameworks consist, according to their fundamental assumptions, of "a view of the world as a human-centric world, as a world 'for us' as human beings, living in human cultures, governed by human values."[104] Ultimately, when the world manifests itself in the form of disaster, of looming cataclysm, it is humanity's perpetual proclivity to "recuperate that non-human world into whatever the dominant, human-centric worldview is at the time."[105] Countering this tendency, Thacker proposes a new framework,

100. Thacker, *In the Dust of This Planet*, 3.

101. Thacker, *In the Dust of This Planet*, 4.

102. Thacker, *In the Dust of This Planet*, 3.

103. Thacker, *In the Dust of This Planet*, 3.

104. Thacker, *In the Dust of This Planet*, 4.

105. Thacker, *In the Dust of This Planet*, 4.

new terminology, for thinking through a world which cannot be completely domesticated by, reduced to, anthropocentric frameworks of meaning.

The world which reveals itself to human subjects is a both a territory of familiarity and constant exploration; both zone of life-giving habitat and collective force of hostility. Nevertheless, it is a world which humans "interpret and give meaning to,"[106] a world which Thacker has coined *"the world-for-us."*[107] Its shorthand is "World."[108] But the "world-for-us," as Thacker observes, does not reside completely within the purview of human control, of humanity's "wants and desires," for it "bites back," it "resists . . . our attempts to mold it into the world-for-us."[109] This is the world which preeminently exists as an object in some prior, inaccessible state, now retrieved through the instruments of the various earth sciences and ultimately subsumed into an overarching framework of meaning. This is called the *"world-in-itself."*[110] Its shorthand is "Earth."[111] The logical paradox of the "world-in-itself," as Thacker observes, is that the moment it becomes accessible, the moment we "think it and attempt to act on it, it ceases to be the world-in-itself and becomes the world-for-us."[112] But it is here that the warning sounds: "Anything that reveals itself does not reveal itself in total."[113] The "world-in-itself" is at once both "world-for-us," and—to employ Thacker's third term—*"world-without-us."*[114]

The "world-in-itself" gives itself as the "world-for-us." But the "world-in-itself" will never submit completely to the logical paradox by which its revelation is its dissolution; perpetually, infinitely resisting being funneled into a comprehensive interpretive framework of meaning. "Even though there is something out there that is not the world-for-us, and even though we can name it the world-in-itself, this latter constitutes a horizon for thought, always receding just beyond the bounds of intelligibility";[115] a horizon which draws humans to consider that which is spectral, which can never be directly fathomed, or the world sans humanity, the

106. Thacker, *In the Dust of This Planet*, 4.
107. Thacker, *In the Dust of This Planet*, 4.
108. Thacker, *In the Dust of This Planet*, 6.
109. Thacker, *In the Dust of This Planet*, 4.
110. Thacker, *In the Dust of This Planet*, 5.
111. Thacker, *In the Dust of This Planet*, 6.
112. Thacker, *In the Dust of This Planet*, 5.
113. Thacker, *In the Dust of This Planet*, 7.
114. Thacker, *In the Dust of This Planet*, 5.
115. Thacker, *In the Dust of This Planet*, 5.

"world-without-us." Its shorthand is "Planet."[116] The "world-without-us" looms as a specter which "moves beyond the subjective World, but . . . also recedes behind the objective Earth.[117] The "world-without-us" is the impersonal, indifferent, abyssal "world-in-itself" which will not be collapsed into a "world-for-us"; the "world-without-us" is the "world-in-itself" which has not submitted to the logical paradox of being thought. It is the "Planet" which has both existed long before and will exist long after humanity's interpretive frameworks. Ultimately, as Thacker asserts,

> [T]he world-without-us is not to be found in a "great beyond" that is exterior to the World (the world-for-us) or the Earth (the world-in-itself); rather, it is in the very fissures, lapses, or lacunae in the World and the Earth. The Planet (the world-without-us) is, in the words of the darkness of mysticism, the "dark intelligible abyss" that is paradoxically manifest as the Word and the Earth.[118]

Within the context of our discussion regarding the "second sense of hiddenness," that "literally awful, ambivalent sense of God's hiddenness," Thacker delineates for us the "world-without-us," the indifferent, impersonal Planet which we can only infer indirectly, perhaps as a shadow suspicion, via the "world-in-itself" which will not be brought to heel by the "world-for-us."[119] Parallel with, but certainly not identical to, what has been developed with regard to Luther's "second sense of hiddenness," the "world-without-us" is not "behind" or "beyond" the "world-for-us," but resides precisely within the "world-in-itself," lurking as the possibility of the true substance concealed by the masks which have been constructed as frameworks of meaning via the multitude expressions of the "world-for-us." In the end, these frameworks may be nothing more than therapies to assuage the abyss, the horror, the eternal indifference of the universe. Perhaps we may say that the "world-without-us" is nothing more than the "world-in-itself" loaning its long view perspective through the cracks and fissures of human meaning

116. Thacker, *In the Dust of This Planet*, 6.

117. Thacker, *In the Dust of This Planet*, 7.

118. Thacker, *In the Dust of This Planet*, 7–8.

119. Let it be pointed out quite clearly: Thacker's "world-for-us" is not to be understood as synonymous with the third mode of Christ's presence, or the world perceived as body of Promise. The point of lifting up Thacker is to delineate a conceptual parallel to the "second sense of hiddenness" (which I have further developed, certainly in disagreement with Luther), or the "world-without-us." This "second sense of hiddenness"—whether delineated by Luther or Thacker—is the cul-de-sac of crucifixion for reason and experience. It is not the sole province of theology. It is, though, where theology begins.

erected over it; teasing humanity to think from the spectral vantage point of its own void. Perhaps it is reminding us that, due to cataclysmic realities that are unthinkable in nature, what we currently have named "World" and "Earth" will be eventually "unthought." A Planet. Indifferent. Impersonal.

But if it is Thacker's intention to have us consider, to give us an avenue to contemplate in prolonged fashion, the "world-without-us" apart from the "world-for-us,"[120] then Luther's understanding of that "second sense of [divine] hiddenness" is intended to have the opposite effect. That is, God's "second sense of hiddenness" is intended to drive us back to God's first sense of hiddenness, or the *sub contrario* revelation of the life-giving Word, the body of Promise. Lay claim to God where God has revealed Godself as "for us." Whether God's "second sense of hiddenness" is conceived of as the "world-without-us," or God experienced apart from revelation, and thus world apart from Promise, who has the wherewithal to maintain such an abyssal focus in perpetuity? Perhaps we may say, as well: this "second sense of hiddenness"—whether delineated by Luther or Thacker—is the cul-de-sac of crucifixion for reason and experience. It is not the sole province of theology. It is, though, where theology begins.

Ultimately, though, whether we are speaking of the world from the perspective of the third mode of Christ's presence as body of Promise, or from the perspective of philosophy and, in this case, Thacker's "world-for-us," we are encountered by the referential instability which ensues when creation is no longer believed, and thus perceived, as Promise, as "for us." It is a minus-sign, essentially a *nihil*, an abyss, which lies not "behind" or "beyond" that which is considered *terra firma*—whether from the perspective of the body of Promise or the "world-for-us"—but in, within the *terra*, always looming exclusively as the specter of something indifferent at best and abyssal at worst. It is also a referential instability that bids us to lay claim to, to confess, again and again—hope against hope—the *nihil* as fundamental to the structure of *Promise*. And if not—according to the verdict of reason and experience—to accustom, resign, ourselves to the promise of the inevitable, interminable *nihil*.

Whether we are discussing the structure of Promise and the reality that there is no Promise who is not communicated in thoroughgoing frailty and fragility, who is not bound, identified completely with the determinate

120. Indeed, as Thacker points out, this burgeoning line of philosophy—"horror of philosophy"—studies the manner by which the genre of horror "takes aim at the presuppositions of philosophical inquiry—that the world is always the world-for-us—and makes of those blind spots its central concern, expressing them not in abstract concepts but in a whole bestiary of impossible life forms . . . " See Thacker, *In the Dust of This Planet*, 9.

structure of what *is*, or—apart from the world as promised—the naked, stark *nihil*, the abyssal silence of a world which will not categorically submit to frameworks of meaning, be they philosophical or otherwise, the brute data of time-honored experience and observation, and most certainly those of science, cannot be circumvented. So avers William Stoeger:

> Though the earth and the sun are destined for eventual destruction by the very forces that gave them existence, we might be inclined to suppose—or at least hope—that the universe as a life-generating ensemble is eternal. However, from all that we know about the evolution and dynamics of the observable universe, and about the laws of nature that govern it, this is not true. The universe itself will eventually evanesce or possibly collapse in a fiery final conflagration (the big crunch).[121]

In either case, "The universe will no longer be life-bearing."[122] The issue is not whether there is a Promise that is "undeconstructible" or not, but the whether the *Nullpunkt*[123] of what is (was) is bound to the structure of Promise, the structure of God's fidelity to creation through Jesus Christ; whether the world's *telos*, its *nihil*, is expressive of the *ex nihilo* structure of Promise. It is against the vista of this sobering observation, standing with two feet sunk deep into the soil of the empirically derived, tangible testament to its opposite outcome, that the ministry of the sacraments confesses, proclaims—hope against hope—the *ex nihilo* structure of Promise as the structure of the world's existence, the Promise of its future. To do so, such a ministry must "say what a thing is," or name *nihil* as nothing but *that*. Only in doing so may Promise be perceived and confessed.

"Accordingly," asserts Luther in his *Schmalkald Articles*, that *in nuce* of outline of his theology (1537)—his theological "Last Will and Testament,"[124] "we should and must constantly maintain that God will not deal with us except through his external Word and sacrament."[125] Certainly Luther cast this assertion against the temptation of "enthusiasm," or the perennial tendency to spiritualize and privatize the Word into a "wax nose." But such an assertion also intensifies the fundamental confession that the only Promise who can be known is a Promise communicated in, mediated by, the frail, transitory, fugacious soundwaves of preaching, the waters of Baptism, the bread and wine of the Lord's Supper, and the flesh and blood fellowship—its

121. Stoeger, "Scientific Accounts," 26–27.

122. Stoeger, "Scientific Accounts," 27.

123. Brueggemann, "Faith at the Nullpunkt," 143–54.

124. See Russell, *Luther's Theological Testament*.

125. Luther, *Book of Concord*, 313.

fleeting, ephemeral generations—of the church. The structure of Promise in all of its evanescence, fragility, mortality, and, ultimately, decomposition, belies the gifts—their infinite, unconditional, enduring nature—it bears ("life and salvation," or the promise of eternal communion with the Triune God in the new creation). There is no Word, no Promise, who does not share, is not bound to, the fragile, evanescent structure, the fate, of what *is*.

Having developed and expounded upon Luther's *communicatio idiomatum*, or the structure of Promise—a body (a text!) extended from the crucified One to creation, one bound to the created fragility, the *nihil*, of what *is*, of its communication, we have, as well, elaborated a Promise witnessed and embodied by generations whose deaths both betray the fragile, evanescent structure of Promise, and belie both the enduring, divine faithfulness that underwrites Promise and the Life it is confessed to deliver. As chapter 2 is brought to a conclusion, it is appropriate that we quote Luther,

> Therefore our life is simply contained in the bare Word; for we have Christ, we have eternal life, eternal righteousness, help and consolation. But where is it? We neither possess it in coffers nor hold it in our hands, but have it only in the bare Word. Thus has God clothed his object in nothingness.[126]

Ultimately, if this chapter began with an elaboration of the structure of Promise—according to the dictates of deconstruction—as the indeterminate, the undeconstructible, to-come, "messianic future" perpetually stirring within—but never bound to, or identified within—the contingent, then our examination of Luther's *communicatio idiomatum* has produced a Promise, a structure of Promise, diametrically different. That is, far from merely being *one* expression of life's deep, underlying, messianic structure, through Luther's *communicatio idiomatum* we have encountered a Promise who cannot be disentangled from the determinate and ephemeral, historically contingent, has-come, incarnate One, or the crucified Christ, true God and true man. He is a Promise whose ongoing communication cannot be separated from created elements: bread and wine, human flesh and sound waves, the water of Baptism. Through an elaboration of the *communicatio idiomatum*, the structure of Promise, we have learned of ourselves that we are expressions—through the third mode of Christ's presence—of that Promise, its crucified body. We, too, bear the Promise of *nihil*.

Indeed, it is a Promise inextricably bound to, and revealed by, the starting point which cannot be surpassed: the text of the crucified, mangled, exsanguinated corpse of Jesus Christ. It is a text of which we, too, are found

---

126. Luther, *Werke* 32.123, 25–29; cited in Hummel, *Clothed in Nothingness*, xii.

within his pages. We have no perspective outside of, beyond, this text, its margins. The dogmaticians of Lutheran Orthodoxy coined that text the *genus tapeinoticum;* the *nihil* which reveals Promise's *ex nihilo* creating agency.

Interlude

A Christology of God Concealed

According to Carl Braaten, in his introduction to his contribution to *Christian Dogmatics*,[1] Christology is the *sine qua non* of any dogmatics that asserts itself as Christian. Not only is the very core of the Christian faith compromised by the diminishment of Christology's centrality, what Braaten deems the "christocentric principle of theology,"[2] but indeed, he avers, "The more deeply theology probes the meaning of Jesus as the Christ of God, the more directly is it drawn to the very God of Christ."[3] Taking its bearings from the definitive revelation of God in the person of Jesus Christ, Braaten rightly asserts that Christology, far from being a determining factor in merely a handful of Christian dogmatic *loci* (say ecclesiology and the sacraments), is integral, central to understanding and articulating the order of creation and the act of redemption; central in interpreting such matters as nature, history, and human existence. Indeed, as Braaten notes, the very knowledge itself of the Triune God is predicated upon the revelation of Jesus Christ. It is through the locus of Christology, Braaten asserts, that "Christian faith

1. Braaten, "Person of Jesus Christ," 465–569.
2. Braaten, "Person of Jesus Christ," 469.
3. Braaten, "Person of Jesus Christ," 469.

looks to the apostolic witness to Jesus Christ as the final criterion of the truth concerning the nature and identity of God."[4]

Observing, as well, the plethora of gods which fill the annals of the "history of religions," that gods are a dime a dozen, Braaten simply asks, "Which God are we talking about in Christian dogmatics?" The answer: "In light of the Christocentric principle our answer is: this God is not the simple, solitary, and self-sufficient unity of radical monotheism."[5] Not only would such an answer reflect the God of classical deism and Unitarianism, but, in contrast, Braaten points out, the God of classical Christianity revealed in the person of Jesus Christ "is the self-structuring reality of Trinitarian faith, the One who antecedently differentiates the divine self as Father, Son, and Holy Spirit and is revealed as such in the economy of history and salvation."[6] Ultimately, recognizing the reality that the doctrine of the Trinity is the product of the process of theological reflection on the revelation of God in Jesus Christ, Braaten asserts, "At the heart of this development of the Trinitarian dogma was the primitive Christian kerygma of God's identification with the death and resurrection of Jesus. Where faith in Jesus as the bringer of absolute salvation is set aside, there also trinitarian theology loses the fertile soil from which it has grown into its more fully developed dogmatic and liturgical forms."[7] In short, the doctrine of the Trinity and the "principle of christocentricity" are "mutually implicative."[8] Ultimately, the "principle of christocentricity"—a quintessential expression of trinitarian monotheism—serves as a discrimen with regard to any stripe of monotheism "that would loosen the links between the identity of God and the person of Jesus Christ."[9] Briefly, though, let us ask: what is the derivation of the "principle of christocentricity"?

The "principle of christocentricity," as Braaten outlines it, is developed within the matrix of a hermeneutical process funded by the dialectical relation between Christology "from above" (the traditional Christology of the ancient church which presupposes the dogma of the Trinity and the incarnation of the Son of God; a Christology proceeding deductively from the deity of Christ to his human nature) and Christology "from below" (Christology grounded both in the kerygma of the early apostolic witness,

---

4. Braaten, "Person of Jesus Christ," 469.

5. Braaten, "Person of Jesus Christ," 470.

6. Braaten, "Person of Jesus Christ," 470.

7. Braaten, "Person of Jesus Christ," 470.

8. Braaten, "Person of Jesus Christ," 470.

9. Braaten, "Person of Jesus Christ," 471.

and Jesus of Nazareth as he is an object of historical critical evaluation).[10] Were one to ask, "How did Jesus of Nazareth, the one who proclaimed the coming of God's kingdom, become the Lord of the kingdom, the risen Christ of apostolic kerygma?" that is, were one to inquire as to the content of the "principle of christocentricity," by which Christology is conducted, any answer—according to Braaten—which fails to include any aspect of the triumvirate which includes the historical Jesus, the kerygmatic Christ, and the christological dogma of the ancient church cripples a Christology that informs everything from preaching to mission.[11] Indeed, as Braaten asserts, the gospel's fundamental thrust is not only the revealing of the identity of Jesus, but the claim that the kingdom of God has been fulfilled in his life, death, and resurrection; yet fulfilled in a such a manner that the *already* of the kingdom's arrival in Christ is held in tension with the *not yet* which is experienced amid the world's poverty and oppression, suffering and death.[12] Essentially, then, Christology encompasses the "from below" and "from above" of christological reflection (its points of departure), the historical and material transition from the "proclaimer" to the "proclaimed," and, ultimately, the "now" and "not yet" nature of the kingdom revealed in Christ as confessed by faith. But, for the sake of this project, it is Braaten's treatment of classical Christology, especially from *Chalcedon* (451) to the *Formula of Concord* (1577), that will capture our focus. Let us, as efficiently as possible, develop—through Braaten—the lead up to the formula of Chalcedon.

If the church had come to confess that the long-promised kingdom had come to fruition in the person of Jesus through his death and resurrection (the proclaimer becoming the proclaimed), then indeed not only had the kingdom entered history, but it brought the "power of God deep into the flesh and blood of Jesus the man."[13] Essentially, classical Christology is grounded on the confession that in Jesus Christ humanity is united with the reality of God in a manner "sufficient for salvation."[14] As Braaten observes, at stake in such a matter is not primarily the philosophical terms and categories employed in articulating such unity, and which would therefore ultimately be employed by Chalcedon, but rather whether such a confession of Jesus Christ would find itself wanting of "something less than a real union of the true identity of God and the final definition of humanity."[15]

10. Braaten, "Person of Jesus Christ," 477–79.

11. Braaten, "Person of Jesus Christ," 481.

12. Braaten, "Person of Jesus Christ," 492–93.

13. Braaten, "Person of Jesus Christ," 498.

14. Braaten, "Person of Jesus Christ," 513.

15. Braaten, "Person of Jesus Christ," 513.

Holding before the reader the balance, and thus the standard, of this "real union" between God and humanity, Braaten, efficiently leads the reader on a journey through signal christological heresies of the early church—from Docetism (stressing the divinity of Christ to the extent that he only "appeared" to be human) to Ebionitism (presenting Jesus as man to the exclusion of divinity altogether) to modalistic monarchianism (humanity is merely a provisional mask of an unchanging divinity) to Arianism (Jesus, though *Logos*, does not share the divine essence) to Apollinarianism (Jesus Christ is not wholly human, lacking a human spirit) to Nestorianism (Jesus Christ is truly God and truly human, yet the divinity is protected from the humanity, thus failing to affirm a complete incarnation) to Eutychianism (the divine nature overwhelms, absorbs, the human nature to the extent that Jesus Christ is "one nature." This heresy is also referred to as monophysitism). Corresponding to these christological heresies, if the Council of Nicaea (325) addressed the Arian (and similar) "logic" by affirming the *homoousios*, or the oneness of substance between Father and Son, and the Council of Constantinople (381) addressed the Apollinarian (and similar) logic by affirming the complete humanity of Jesus Christ, Braaten ultimately brings us to the Council of Chalcedon (451) which affirms the dogma of the two natures in the one person of Jesus Christ. For the sake of this project, I cite it in its entirety:

> Following, then, the holy Fathers, we all with one voice teach that it should be confessed that our Lord Jesus Christ is one and the same Son, the Same perfect in Godhead, the Same perfect in manhood, truly God and truly man, the Same (consisting) of a rational soul and a body; *homoousios* with the Father as to his Godhead, and the Same *homoousios* with us as to his manhood; in all things like unto us, sin only excepted; begotten of the Father before ages as to his Godhead, and in the last days, the Same, for us and for our salvation, of Mary the Virgin *Theotokos* as to his manhood;
>
> One and the same Christ, Son, Lord, Only Begotten, made known in two natures (which exist) without confusion, without change, without division, without separation; the difference of the natures having been in no wise taken away by reason of the union, but rather the properties of each being preserved, and (both) concurring into one Person (*prosōpon*) and one *hypostasis*—not parted or divided into two persons (*prosōpa*), but one and the same Son and Only begotten, the divine Logos, the Lord Jesus Christ; even as the prophets from of old (have spoken)

concerning him, and as the Lord Jesus Christ himself has taught us, and as the Symbol of the Fathers has delivered to us.[16]

As Braaten points out, it is necessary to note that though the formula of Chalcedon does not explain the mystery of the incarnation of Jesus Christ, it affirms the incarnation while providing "rules" by which to articulate the relationship of the two natures. Most notably, against Nestorianism the formula of Chalcedon asserts that there is no "division" or "separation" between the two natures, and against Eutychianism the creed asserts that the two natures of Jesus Christ are not to be "confused" or "changed" into the opposite nature.

Though with regard to post-Chalcedon christological development Braaten touches upon both the Council of Constantinople (553) (which affirms that the man Jesus had existence only in and through the Word, again addressing the logic of the Ebionites, adoptionists, and Nestorians), and the sixth ecumenical council of Constantinople (681) (which condemned a Monothelitism whose logic mirrored that of monophysitism), he ultimately brings us to the christological debate as it comes to expression over the teaching of the Lord's Supper during the Reformation between the Lutherans and Calvinists. With regard to this debate, it is interesting to note that both sides—Lutheran and Reformed—will claim a position from within the formula of Chalcedon, from within the logic of the *communicatio idiomatum*. So we ask moving forward: could it be that the formula of Chalcedon produced as many problems as it solved? But most importantly, let us observe: absence, the absence of Jesus Christ—initially his humanity, ultimately, his divinity—lurks on all sides of the christological debate whose trajectory is initially grounded in this controversy over the Lord's Supper. But before we arrive at the debate between the Lutherans and the Reformed, let us take up the disagreement between Luther and Ulrich Zwingli.

If, for Luther, working within a theology the cross that stresses "the grace of God in the concrete existence of the man Jesus,"[17] there is no word of God, no Logos, apart from the man Jesus, then his understanding of the Lord's Supper corresponded to just this reality. Wherever the Lord's Supper is held, Luther taught, it is precisely there that the whole Jesus Christ—divine and human natures—is present. The "flip side" of the same logic: if the humanity of Jesus Christ is absent in the celebrating of the Lord's Supper, then, for Luther, by definition the whole word of God is absent with regard to the Lord's Supper. Thus, drawing upon the formula of Chalcedon, the

16. Sellers, *Council of Chalcedon*, 210–11; cited in Braaten, "Person of Jesus Christ," 505.

17. Braaten, "Person of Jesus Christ," 510.

communicatio idiomatum, Luther was able to posit the ubiquity of Christ's humanity, or the communication of the divine nature to the human nature within the incarnational union.[18] Again, thinking from Luther's perspective, his theology of the cross: *sans* the humanity of Jesus Christ, there is no presence of the Word. Only absence.

Ulrich Zwingli would counter Luther's teaching on the Lord's Supper with his theory of *alloeosis*. That is, Zwingli asserted that such attributes as omnipotence and, in this case, omnipresence, could be ascribed to the divine nature alone; that the finite human Jesus could be present in only one location at a time (namely, now at the "right hand of God"). Corresponding with this, Zwingli's theory of *alloeosis* understood the language about the real presence—divine *and* human nature—of Jesus Christ as a figure of speech. According to Zwingli, such verbal predications apply to the divine nature alone.[19] And let us note: Zwingli, too, presumed to speak from a position within the formula of Chalcedon. But if for Zwingli the humanity of Jesus Christ could exist in only one location, then for Luther this was nothing more than a fracturing of the word of God itself, and, subsequently, a Jesus Christ who is absent at the Lord's Supper. Luther's interpretation of the *communicatio idiomatum* was an expression, corresponding to his *theologia crucis*, of his assertion that there is no word of God apart from the man Jesus. If he is present in the Lord's Supper, he is present as the God-man. And if this is the case, then *finitum est capax infiniti*, or the human nature of the Word of God, Jesus Christ, is capable of the divine attributes. Otherwise it is a meal of remembrance; better, a rite of God's absence.

As Braaten points out, moving beyond Luther's contention with Zwingli, "Starting with the Lord's Supper, the controversy on the communication of attributes exploded into a full-scale war on Christology between the Lutherans and the Reformed."[20] Perhaps the irony of such a full-scale war on Christology, though, was the fact that Lutherans and Calvinists were both working within a standard Chalcedoniasm received from medieval scholasticism upon which there was originally much agreement.[21] Thus, as Braaten observes, the list of what the Lutherans and the Calvinists agreed on with regard to the person of Christ was fairly lengthy.[22] Namely, they agreed upon the reality (1) that Jesus Christ was one person in two natures, fully divine and fully human; (2) that there was a close intercommunion

---

18. Braaten, "Person of Jesus Christ," 507.

19. Braaten, "Person of Jesus Christ," 507.

20. Braaten, "Person of Jesus Christ," 507.

21. Braaten, "Person of Jesus Christ," 507–8.

22. See Braaten, "Person of Jesus Christ," 508.

of natures within the personal union; (3) that (contra Eutychianism) these natures were not comingled, thus retaining their identities, and that (contra Nestorianism) the two natures did not exist separately as, essentially, two separate persons; (4) that the corresponding attributes of both natures were preserved; (5) that, on account of the hypostatic union, there was a communication of attributes to the person of Christ (in order that the person could utilize the attributes of both natures).[23] But it was precisely here, on this fifth and final point, as Braaten points out, that a salient point of difference arose among the Lutherans.

"[T]aking their cue from Luther's doctrine of ubiquity," Braaten notes, not only were the attributes of the two natures of Jesus Christ communicated to the person (just fine with the Calvinists!), but the "majestic powers of the divine nature" were directly communicated to the human nature in Christ.[24] The *Formula of Concord* (1577) would later systematize the *communcatio idiomatum* into three genera: (1) the "idiomatic" genus in which qualities of either nature be ascribed to the person; (2) the "apotelesmatic" genus in which the actions of the person may be ascribed to one or the other natures (in a manner commensurate with the particular nature); and (3) the "majestic" genus in which the divine attributes such as omnipotence and omnipresence, et. al., may be ascribed directly to the human nature. As Braaten rightly observes, this third genus, the *genus majestaticum*, became, for most, the "distinctive feature of Lutheran Christology."[25]

Ultimately, as Braaten observes, the Reformed-Lutheran articulations of Christology were nothing more than revivals of ancient trends of the church's Christology. If the Reformed (Calvinist) position stressed the distinction between natures, it can be said that such a position was underwritten by the "old fashioned Nestorian"[26] logic which focused on maintaining the integrity of the particular natures and the attributes peculiar to both. Likewise, if the Lutheran position stressed the unity of the person, and thus the communion of the two natures, thereby "running the monophysitic risk of mixing the two natures,"[27] it can be also be said that such a position was accused, though wrongly on both historical and theological grounds, of being a "child of Eutychianism."[28] If the Lutheran "battle formula" was "*finitum est capax infiniti*," emphasizing the assertion that the human nature of Jesus

23. Braaten, "Person of Jesus Christ," 508.

24. Braaten, "Person of Jesus Christ," 508.

25. Braaten, "Person of Jesus Christ," 508.

26. Braaten, "Person of Jesus Christ," 508.

27. Braaten, "Person of Jesus Christ," 508.

28. Braaten, "Person of Jesus Christ," 508.

Christ was capable of the divine attributes (omnipotence, omnipresence, etc.), then the Reformed "counterslogan" was "*finitum non capax infiniti*." That is, the human nature of Jesus was strictly finite, capable only of finite properties.[29] If for the Lutherans the natures were an expression of the unity of the person of Jesus Christ, for the Reformed, perhaps it could be said, the natures—the integrity of their peculiarity, ultimately, their purity—performed as a limiting function, a *de facto* rule, within which the unity could be elaborated. To say that the human nature of Jesus is present "at the right hand of the Father" and present in the Lord's Supper would destroy such a rule. What's more: if for the Lutherans there was no word of God apart from the man Jesus, the Calvinists asserted that the word of God must not endure such a limitation imposed by finitude. The *Logos*, by nature infinite, must exist *extra carnem*. Such a "loose linkage" between Logos and the man Jesus led the Lutherans to dub such a doctrine, or position, the *extra-Calvinisticum*.[30] But if such matters divided Lutherans and Calvinists, the Lutheran position certainly was no monolith, as Braaten observes.

Focused on two rival christological positions within the Lutheran camp, article 8 of the Formula of Concord (1577) sought a reconciliation of differences between the christological position of John Brenz (the Swabian side) and the position of Martin Chemnitz (the lower Saxon side). But, as Braaten suggests—no doubt a dynamic reflective of the formula of Chalcedon—every formula or creed which is elaborated to solve one set of controversies will undoubtedly open up a whole new set of debates and battle lines. According to Braaten:

> The Formula of Concord tried to find balanced language to settle the disputes among Lutherans, but with little success. It looked for middle ground, but waffled on the issue of the divine attributes during the earthly life of Jesus. Did the Formula teach a doctrine of "krypsis" or "kenosis"? Krypsis means that the divine attributes were "hidden" in the incarnation, kenosis that they had been "laid aside." The combinations of these two alternatives were endless. Did the Formula teach that the person of Christ enjoyed full possession of the attributes but used them secretly? Or did it teach full possession and voluntary abstinence from use? Or did it teach full possession and partial arbitrary use? Or did it teach partial possession and partial use? Or partial possession and abstinence from use? And in the event

---

29. Braaten, "Person of Jesus Christ," 508.

30. Braaten, "Person of Jesus Christ," 509.

of partial possession, with some degree of kenosis, which attributes were retained and which left behind in the incarnation?[31]

The questions certainly do not stop here. Instead of settling christological controversy within the Lutheran camp, more lines of debate were created. To be sure, instead of stilling controversy, the *Formula of Concord* would trigger a christological controversy that would rage into the seventeenth century and beyond between the Lutheran dogmaticians of Giessen and Tübingen.[32]

Braaten pinpoints the nub of the issue engendered by the ubiquity of the human nature of Jesus Christ:

> If the human nature of Jesus became ubiquitous, undergirding the real presence of the whole Christ in the Lord's Supper, was he also universal in an absolute sense in the whole world and in all creatures? Having started with a theology of the cross, stressing the grace of God in the concrete existence of the man Jesus, the Lutherans were drawn into a theology of glory by divinizing the flesh of Jesus, by glorifying the human with qualities of divinity.[33]

Limiting the use of the divine attributes in the person of Jesus Christ (especially with reference to Jesus in his first-century ministry), the Giessen theologians stressed Jesus Christ's state of humiliation (*status exinanitionis*). This would be considered a partial form of *kenosis*. Entertaining no truncation of the divine attributes in the person of Jesus Christ, the Tübingen theologians understood the attributes of divinity to be exercised in secret. This was affirmed as the doctrine of *krypsis*. Ultimately, as Braaten points out, a settlement to the debate would be reached—the "Saxon decision"[34]—which, setting limits on the logic of the Tübingen school, favored the partial *kenosis* of the Giessen camp.[35] But if *kenosis*, in any form, would serve as the point of departure for understanding the person of Jesus Christ for confessional Lutherans, then such a point of departure clearly either presented a new set of problems for Christology, or, simply, revisited old ones with regard to an interpretation of the *communicatio idiomatum*.

Employing as their scriptural point of departure Phil 2:6–7 ("Who, though he was in the form of God, did not count equality with God a thing

---

31. Braaten, "Person of Jesus Christ," 509.

32. Braaten, "Person of Jesus Christ," 509.

33. Braaten, "Person of Jesus Christ," 510.

34. Braaten, "Person of Jesus Christ," 510.

35. Braaten, "Person of Jesus Christ," 510.

to be grasped, but emptied himself, taking the form of a servant, being born in the likeness of men."), the kenotic theologians of the nineteenth century attempted to remain faithful to an interpretation of the *communicatio idiomatum* in the trajectory of Luther. That is, if it is the communication of attributes that concerns us within the person of Jesus, then we must elaborate a full communication of attributes. Better yet, if the Lutherans have traditionally elaborated the communication of the divine attributes to the human nature in the person of Jesus Christ, that the *finitum capax infiniti*, then why not the reverse? Could not the human attributes be communicated to the divine nature in the person of Jesus Christ, that the *infinitum capax finiti*? Is this not a communication of attributes within the priority of union of the person? Expressing just this logic, Gottfried Thomasius added a fourth genus to the traditional elaboration of the *communicatio idiomatum*: the *genus tapeinoticum* (from *tapeinos*, "humble," "lowly"). Thus, Thomasius asserted, in becoming man the Son of God jettisoned—out of a divine freedom and love which made it possible to do just such a thing— those divine attributes which revolved his "cosmological or metaphysical role,"[36] namely omniscience, omnipotence, and omnipresence. In doing so, he retained such moral attributes—also identified with God—as truth, love, and holiness. Following the lead of Thomasius, other theologians would radicalize the dynamic of *kenosis*. Braaten adduces such names as H. R. von Frank (who articulated a Jesus whose depotentiated consciousness gradually evolved into his self-consciousness as Son of God) and Wolfgang F. Gess (who asserted that the Son of God left behind all traces of his divinity in the incarnational union).[37] But kenotic Christology, driven by a return to, and faithful application of, Luther's interpretation of the *communicatio idiomatum* (indeed, an expression of his *theologia crucis*), continually gravitated to, and was forced to navigate, the subject of divine absence and a subsequent litany of questions. According to Braaten:

> If the Son of God became kenotically incarnate in Jesus in such a way that no traces of divinity were left, in what sense was Jesus really anything more than a mere man? How is a totally kenotic divinity different from no divinity at all? This could be tantamount to saying that in Jesus Christ, God had to become absent in order to be incarnate. In kenotic Christology the content of the *vere deus* seemed to disappear to the vanishing point.[38]

36. Braaten, "Person of Jesus Christ," 510.

37. Braaten, "Person of Jesus Christ," 510.

38. Braaten, "Person of Jesus Christ," 511.

Perhaps the more fundamental question is this: is the real concern of a kenotic christology within the context of Luther's *communicatio idiomatum* the disappearance of "*vere deus*" seemingly "to the vanishing point"?[39] Is the concern one of divine absence? Or, within the trajectory of Luther's *theologia crucis*, is the real concern that of insuring—through a full *communicatio idiomatum*, one involving the direct communication of natures to one another within the person of Jesus Christ—the concealment, the hiddenness, of the revealed One? Should not the *communicatio idiomatum* reflect the epistemic point of departure—the *sub contraria specie* revelation of the Word of God—of Luther's *theologia crucis*?

If underlying much of the christological debate before Luther (and certainly after him) was the ontology of Greek metaphysics and its accompanying God of impassibility and immutability, and the need to protect such a God from such adulterations as suffering and change, then, at the very least, theologians were also grappling simultaneously with an alternate, scriptural conceptualization of God. According to Scripture, "The word became flesh" (John 1:14) and "God was in Christ" (2 Cor 5:19). (Which means, as Braaten observes in a subsequent section of his locus on Christology: "The revelation of God . . . includes the negativities of Christ's human experience in this world from birth unto death.")[40] Therefore, as Braaten rightly adds, "An ontology constructed in the light of faith in the gospel will speak not of the utter impassibility and immutability of God but rather of the historicity of God and God's coming-to-be in the humanity of Jesus the Christ."[41] To be sure, as Braaten observes, it was Luther's *theologia crucis* which made the "most complete break with the hybrid system" of Greek ontology and biblical thinking. Luther's *theologia crucis* meant that the God of Greek metaphysics, the God of impassibility and immutability—impervious to the flux of finitude and the contingency of history—"would have to be radically transformed in light of the cross."[42]

If for Luther true recognition of God is in the crucified Christ, a revelation *sub contraria specie*, and that, as well, in Jesus Christ is a direct communication of attributes between human and divine natures, then the implications for Christology are fluid, in *via*. That is, according to Braaten, "Luther began the construction of a new Christology, which is still in the process of being developed."[43] He adds,

39. Braaten, "Person of Jesus Christ," 511.
40. Braaten, "Person of Jesus Christ," 533.
41. Braaten, "Person of Jesus Christ," 533.
42. Braaten, "Person of Jesus Christ," 533.
43. Braaten, "Person of Jesus Christ," 534.

The living God did not exclude but embraced the opposite in a process of exchanging qualities of nature and destiny. In exchange for death God gave life, in exchange for foolishness God gave wisdom, in exchange for bondage God gave freedom, in exchange for sin God gave righteousness, in exchange for weakness God gave power, and so on. Consequently, in exchange of God's own glory, God assumed humility; in exchange for eternity, God entered time; in exchange for God's love, God absorbed hatred.[44]

Ultimately, as Braaten avers, the incarnation of Jesus Christ is an ontological event which calls for an ontological interpretation.[45] Perhaps, according to Braaten, we can even call it an "ontological [C]hristology."[46] For not only is the "love which is the very nature of God's own being"[47] communicated in the history of the incarnational union, but "The incarnation is God's self-emptying of everything that separated the Creator from the creation, to embrace the entire cosmos as an acceptable part of the kingdom of God."[48]

Of all that could be said with regard to Braaten's thorough and adroit analysis of the development of classical Christology, there is no question that he has his fingers on the crux of the conundrum that drives, fundamentally informs, "the christological principle." Though certainly recognizing that the Creator is distinct from creation, the incarnation is "God's self-emptying of everything that separated the Creator from the creation." And certainly the formula of Chalcedon not only ably confesses "that the person of Jesus Christ unites the reality of God with humanity in a way sufficient for salvation," but does so in such a manner that "it allows plenty of room for speculative analysis, but no room at all for finding in Jesus Christ something less than a real union of the true identity of God and the final definition of humanity."[49] But, it seems, it is the "something less" that seems to disturb the christological discussion the most.

For, indeed, if it is not "something less" than a full *communicatio idiomatum* in the person of Jesus, or an incarnational union which encompasses *both* a communication of the divinity to the humanity (*finitum capax infiniti; genus majestaticum*) and a communication of the humanity to the divinity within the person of Jesus Christ (*infinitum capax finiti; genus*

---

44. Braaten, "Person of Jesus Christ," 534.
45. Braaten, "Person of Jesus Christ," 540–41.
46. Braaten, "Person of Jesus Christ," 535.
47. Braaten, "Person of Jesus Christ," 541.
48. Braaten, "Person of Jesus Christ," 541.
49. Braaten, "Person of Jesus Christ," 513.

tapeinoticum), Braaten has articulated the implications quite well. Again, he raises the matter of such a full *communicatio idiomatum* in the trajectory of Luther's *theologica crucis*: "If the Son of God became kenotically incarnate in Jesus in such a way that no traces of divinity were left, in what sense was Jesus really anything more than a mere man? How is a totally kenotic divinity different from no divinity at all?"[50]

There is no question such a conclusion—Jesus sans the *appearance* of divinity—is disturbing. But there is also no question that such a conclusion, for Luther, is unavoidable. That is, as long as we are recognizing that the issue is not one of "absence," but—commensurate with Luther's *theologia crucis*, its epistemic point of departure—"hiddenness"; a hiddenness which corresponds to the *sub contraria specie* revelation of Jesus Christ. If theology's epistemic point of departure according to Luther's *theologia crucis* is the crucified Christ, the *sub contraria specie* revelation of the Word of God, true God and true human, then Christology will reflect just this concealment. A full *communicatio idiomatum* facilitates the elaboration of just such concealment: the *genus majestaticum* concealed within the *genus tapeinoticum*.

Regardless, as Braaten has developed the matter with regard to a Lutheran formulation of Christology according to the formula of Chalcedon, certainly within the trajectory of Luther's *theologia crucis,* this point, perhaps, remains most salient: the issue of divine absence necessarily hovers, lurks, conspicuously on two wide, abyssal fronts. If the *communicatio idiomatum* affords us (originally with the context of the sacramental debates) the ability to overcome the absence of the humanity of Jesus Christ, and thus the absence of the Word of God in the Lord's Supper, then, when pressed to its full elaboration (in the intra-Lutheran debates) that same *communicatio idiomatum* ultimately expresses the *appearance* of absence. Within the trajectory of Luther's *theologia crucis* we confess that it is only appearance. Precisely, it is the Word of God who is revealed *sub contraria specie*; concealed, ultimately, within a crucified corpse. Commensurate with the theology of the cross' point of departure, it is a Christology *sub contraria specie*.

Again, the irony lies in the "something less." The "something less"—a word of God without humanity—avoided in the Lord's Supper on account of Luther's interpretation of the *communicatio idiomatum* means that the "something less"—a Jesus Christ drained of all signs and traces of divinity— is also the necessary expression of a full *communicatio idiomatum*, a Christology which reflects the Word of God whose revealing is also a concealing.

50. Braaten, "Person of Jesus Christ," 511.

Is that not precisely a Christology *sub contraria specie*, when all visual traces and clues of divinity have been drained?

But then, if "true theology and recognition of God are in the crucified Christ,"[51] then are we not merely expressing Christology's point of departure? a point of departure which cannot be disentangled from its Christology's formulations? a *sub contrario* revelation which is to be inscribed into all expressions of Christology conducted within the *theologia crucis*?

51. Luther, *Works* 31.53.

3

Promising Value beyond the Margins

Schweitzer's Window

We have already encountered Albert Schweitzer in this project. No doubt at that first meeting you were unaware of his greater significance for the sake of the "big picture." Near the end of chapter 1, above, a quotation of Schweitzer's was adduced for the sake of accentuating the unremitting indifference, as well the referential instability, of the crucified corpse of Jesus when extracted from the framework of the theology of the cross.

In this chapter we return to Schweitzer. Certainly Schweitzer is no exemplar of the "theology of the cross" and cannot be twisted and contorted to be an expression of such a manner of theology. Imagine the audacity required in venturing such an exercise in apologetics! Instead, we return to Schweitzer in order to both place his words—adduced near the end of the chapter 1—within the context of his seminal work, and, in the process, to frame the christological hermeneutic developed in chapter 4. Schweitzer's diagnosis of the so-called "historical Jesus" (in all of its expressions) as produced by the Jesus' "questers," in addition to his analysis of the "life of Jesus" as it is presented by the New Testament (in particular, the Synoptic Gospels), will serve as a framework for our task of delineating over the course of chapters 3 and 4 the manner by which Scripture conveys both the identity of Jesus Christ and the promise, or location, of value[1] for those whose gaze is

1. The manner in which the word "value" is employed, its connotation, will be clarified in the development of chapters 3 and 4.

directed at the text which presents him. As we will see, Schweitzer's redirect of the "life of Jesus" from "mirror" (of those who stand before it, their most cherished values) to "window" (through which one is to perceive the promise of a "timeless," "spiritual" mandate applicable to all "times") will both shape the current chapter, and provide a contrast to the next.[2] In the process, we will be able to discern the manner by which Schweitzer navigates the silence of the text, a silence—for Schweitzer—manifest in the seemingly inaccessible, unrepeatable, apocalyptic peculiarity of Jesus, the seams and gaps of the text which presents him, and, ultimately, the crucifixion which Schweitzer articulates so soberly.

Schweitzer's own words will be adduced liberally throughout this chapter so as to give a sense of the intellectual atmosphere, the state of biblical studies, inscribed into his observations and evaluations. Though Schweitzer's insights are dated, this by no means compromises what can be gleaned from his encounter with textual silence, its hermeneutical implications and, ultimately, its significance with regard to—for the purpose of this project—Christology, especially as text is a function, and ultimately, an expression, of Christology.

From Mirror to Window: Schweitzer and the Quest

When all was said and done, as Schweitzer observed in his seminal work which studied and evaluated—from the late eighteenth through to the late nineteenth century, "Its Progress from Reimarus to Wrede"—liberal, German theology's "Quest" for the "historical Jesus,"[3] the "Jesus" which resulted from the "Quest"—in all its expressions—was nothing more than a mirror of the scholar conducting the quest. Not only had each epoch of the "Quest" "found its reflection in Jesus; each individual created Him in accordance with his own character,"[4] but, as Schweitzer discovered,

> The Jesus of Nazareth who came forward publicly as the Messiah, who preached the ethic of the Kingdom of God, who founded the Kingdom of Heaven upon earth, and died to give His work its final consecration, never had any existence. He is a

---

2. It is worth noting for the reader that chapters 3 and 4 were originally conceived of as one—rather lengthy!—chapter. Though broken into two chapters for the sake of style and readability, chapter 4 is developed in light of chapter 3.

3. Schweitzer, *Quest.*

4. Schweitzer, *Quest,* 4.

figure designed by rationalism, endowed with life by liberalism, and clothed by modern theology in historical garb.[5]

Pressing the point that the Jesus of the "Quest" was really nothing more than a mirror of those—their most cherished values and ideals—conducting the pursuit, Schweitzer adds with regard to this "Jesus" in all of his expressions that, collectively speaking, this

> . . . Jesus who was too small, because we had forced Him into conformity with our human standards and human psychology. To see that, one need only read the Lives of Jesus written since the 'sixties, and notice what they have made of the great imperious sayings of the Lord, how they have weakened down His imperative world-contemning demands upon individuals, that He might not come into conflict with our ethical ideals, and might tune His denial of the world to our acceptance of it. Many of the greatest sayings are found lying in a corner like explosive shells from which the charges have been removed. No small portion of elemental religious power need to be drawn off from His sayings to prevent them from conflicting with our system of religious world-acceptance. We have made Jesus hold another language with our time from that which He really held.[6]

Schweitzer added,

> In the process we ourselves have been enfeebled, and have robbed our own thoughts of their vigour in order to project them back into history and make them speak to us out of the past. It is nothing less than a misfortune for modern theology that it mixes history with everything and ends by being proud of the skill with which it finds its own thoughts—even to its beggarly pseudometaphysic with which it has banished genuine speculative metaphysic from the sphere of religion—in Jesus, and represents Him as expressing them.[7]

Perhaps it may be said that Schweitzer exposed with regard to the "Quest" and its "questers"—who had been, ironically, working from within the canons of the "objective" academy and a scientifically based "historical-critical" method—the fundamental truth which Warner Sallman exploited in the realm of Christian pop/devotional art.

---

5. Schweitzer, *Quest*, 396.

6. Schweitzer, *Quest*, 398.

7. Schweitzer, *Quest*, 398–99.

That is, if for Sallman Jesus—in this case, explicitly referencing his *Head of Christ* (1940)—was no doubt a reflection of northern European ethnicity—think of the long, brown hair with golden highlights, the groomed beard cloaking a well-defined jawline, the moderately high forehead, the masculine-yet-tender appearance, and the blue eyes gazing beyond the frame, certainly an expression of some species of devout, Protestant pietism, then the "Jesus" of the "Quest" was essentially no different. That is, as Sallman artistically created a Jesus who was a mirror of mass Eurocentric Christian piety (now translated into the realm of pop/devotional art for millions of North American Christians), Jesus became for the "questers" a mirror of nineteenth-century German theology, its rationalism and liberalism and the bourgeoisie, world-affirming atmosphere and philosophy underwriting it. In each particular case—from Reimarus to Wrede—Schweitzer observed, Jesus was a reflection of each "quester's" "own modern philosophy of life."[8] Jesus had become a mirror of all that was held in high value by those questing after him. Though we do not want to get too far out in front of our project, nevertheless, we might say, mirrors—and certainly "Jesus as mirror"—are not necessarily equated with the self-knowledge of those who stand before, and gaze into, them.

But, ultimately for Schweitzer,

> The study of the Life of Jesus has had a curious history. It set out in quest of the historical Jesus, believing that when it had found Him it could bring Him straight into our time as a Teacher and Saviour. It loosed the bands by which He had been riveted for centuries to the stony rocks of ecclesiastical doctrine, and rejoiced to see life and movement coming into the figure once more, and the historical Jesus advancing, as it seemed, to meet it. But He does not stay; He passes by our time and returns to His own. What surprised and dismayed the theology of the last forty years was that, despite all forced and arbitrary interpretations, it could not keep Him in our time, but had to let Him go. He returned to His own time, not owing to the application of any historical ingenuity . . .[9]

In other words, if on one front of the "Quest" Schweitzer was all too aware of the reality that Jesus had become a mirror of those questing after him, unscrupulously wielding—especially with reference to self-awareness—their tools of historical-critical science, then, on the other front, he was keenly aware of the results of a historical-critical method that had

8. Livingston, *Modern Christian Thought*, 303.

9. Schweitzer, *Quest*, 397.

been applied with self-awareness. Applied with self-awareness, the yield of the historical-critical method was an irreducible, unrepeatable, historically particular Jesus who was the product of a Jewish apocalypticism who "saw in his own death the beginning of the long-expected apocalyptical tribulations";[10] an expression of a world-denying eschatology bound to time and place at loggerheads with the world affirmations of modernity. It is this latter Jesus—the product of a self-aware application of historical-critical method—who, in all his unrepeatable, historical particularity, "passes by our time and returns to his own."[11]

But such a conclusion, according to Schweitzer, does nothing more than—no doubt unwittingly—clear the way for the "real immovable historical foundation which is independent of any historical confirmation or justification."[12] Even though the "historical Jesus" is irretrievably lost to the sands of time, "that does not mean," according to Schweitzer, "that Christianity has lost its historical foundation."[13] That is, certainly aware of the "mirror role" to which the "historical Jesus" had been assigned by those of the "Quest," and certainly aware that the results of honest, self-aware historical-critical study produced an "apocalyptic Jesus" with "no place to lay his head" within modernity, Schweitzer presents us with a shift in perspective, a shift in what the gaze yields from the "historical Jesus." It is a shift from "mirror" to "window." The "historical Jesus" is a "window." A window unto what?

It is not the historical, particular Jesus of the first century, his Jewish apocalypticism and its anticipated tribulations and its corresponding world negation that interests Schweitzer. That "Jesus" is frozen in time and eternally inaccessible, remaining forever in contemporary eyes a "stranger and an enigma."[14] Instead, for Schweitzer, "Jesus means something to our world because a mighty spiritual force streams forth from Him and flows through our time also. This fact can neither be shaken nor confirmed by any historical discovery. It is the solid foundation of Christianity."[15] To be sure, the "truth" of Christianity after which the "questers" quested, the "foundation" of Christianity for which they sought through the "historical Jesus," was never contingent upon the Jesus who strode through history and its first

---

10. Livingston, *Modern Christian Thought*, 303.

11. As Elizabeth A. Johnson has so precisely stated with regard to Schweitzer's findings: "[T]he figure of Jesus could not be kept in the modern times but returned to his own age like a pendulum to it center of gravity." Johnson, "Jesus and the Cosmos," 141.

12. Schweitzer, *Quest*, 397.

13. Schweitzer, *Quest*, 397.

14. Schweitzer, *Quest*, 397.

15. Schweitzer, *Quest*, 397.

century in and around Jerusalem in the first place. The "truth" of Christianity had nothing to do with contingent, provisional history and its particulars. At best, for Schweitzer, empirical history in all its particular expressions, and in this case, the "historical Jesus" in all of his first-century apocalyptic strangeness, is nothing more than a window to a "spiritual force" whose veracity is not bound to historical particularity. But what does Schweitzer have to say about this "mighty spiritual force [which] streams forth from Him and flows through our time also"?

Again, Schweitzer: "But the truth is, it is not Jesus as historically known, but Jesus as spiritually arisen within men, who is significant for our time and can help it. Not the historical Jesus, but the spirit which goes forth from Him and in the spirits of men strives for new influence and rule, is that which overcomes the world."[16] The "historical foundation," we might say, for Christianity shifts from the particularity of past history to the timeless, eternal, "spiritual" force—having streamed through the Jesus of history and now released from the husk of its first-century eschatology—which flows into the present hour—now arising within us—of human activity's history. Let us develop this point a bit further.

Though it is impossible to rip the "historical Jesus" from the soil of his original historical context, especially as this pertains to his first-century apocalyptic eschatology, and mine anything meaningful and applicable for a contemporary "Christian life," it makes no difference. As Schweitzer asserts, "The abiding and eternal in Jesus is absolutely independent of historical knowledge and can only be understood by contact with His spirit which is still at work in the world. In proportion as we have the "Spirit of Jesus" we have the true knowledge of Jesus."[17] Though "Jesus" in his unrepeatable, historical particularity remains a "stranger to our time," it is "His spirit, which lies hidden in His words, is known in simplicity, and its influence is direct."[18] Peer through the window frame of the historical person of Jesus presented by Scripture long enough, and you will perceive that which endures, the "Spirit of Jesus," a "Spirit" not tethered to the times of its conveyance. Ultimately, according to Schweitzer,

> He comes to us as One unknown, without a name, as of old,
> by the lake-side, He came to those men who knew him not. He
> speaks to us the same word: Follow thou me!" and sets us to the
> tasks which He has to fulfil for our time. He commands. And to
> those who obey Him, whether they be wise or simple, He will

16. Schweitzer, *Quest*, 399.
17. Schweitzer, *Quest*, 399.
18. Schweitzer, *Quest*, 399.

reveal Himself in the toils, the conflicts, the sufferings which they shall pass through in His fellowship, and, as an ineffable mystery, they shall learn in their own experience Who He is.[19]

Although in his Jewish apocalyptic, historical particularity "He comes to us as One unknown," it is when the husk of historical peculiarity is burned away that (in opposition to the "world-accepting ethic" and "world-affirming spirit" of modernity, the premium it places on an attachment to "material and intellectual goods" and Christianity's penchant, especially Protestantism's, of making itself a "mere sociological instead of a religious force"[20]) the timeless, "world-negating spirit of Jesus"[21] can be heard again. Thus, Christ's exhortation to "Follow thou me!" becomes a call to disengage our world-affirming attachments, divesting ourselves of them in order to engage through obedient love the timeless plights and struggles known, yet unique, to every time. And it is precisely here that we discover for ourselves a Jesus whose spirit—and the "spirituality" he inspires—is timeless.

Up to this point we have elaborated Schweitzer's detection in the "Quest" of a "historical Jesus" as "mirror." And we have also observed his redirect of the "historical Jesus" as "window." But, of all that has been developed up to this point, has anything "new" really been broached? And when placed within the greater trajectory of the development of theology and biblical studies, do not Schweitzer's observations, conclusions and pronouncements—as of this writing more than 120 years in the past—with regard to the "Quest" bear a "case closed" stamp on its file? Has not this field not only been harvested but, indeed, thoroughly gleaned? Is it not time to "move on" to theologians, seminal works, and theological themes more modish? Not quite.

When we shift our focus from Schweitzer's conclusions with regard to the "Quest" to his description of the problems which beset the historical-critical method and its technicians in search of the "historical Jesus" as presented in the Gospels, and especially the Synoptic Gospels, we discover a fundamental grappling with textual silence with regard to the "life of Jesus," his person. It is this textual silence, it is safe to say, that prompted both the mirror which Schweitzer diagnosed all too clearly, and the window into the timeless, eternal "spirit" he advocated all too eloquently. It is a silence which, for Schweitzer, is threaded through the text which gives access to Jesus. In so many ways, as we will see, not only is it the silence occasioned of a crossroads between mirror and window, as Schweitzer demonstrated, but

19. Schweitzer, *Quest*, 401.

20. Schweitzer, *Quest*, 400–401.

21. Schweitzer, *Quest*, 400.

such a silence may even be the signal of a third path, namely, the beginning of "true theology."

Between the Mirror and the Window: Schweitzer and the Silence of the Text

If, as Schweitzer asserted, the conventional canons of biblical criticism, and specifically, the historical-critical method (and certainly including hermeneutical methods which fall under this category) are inadequate—"its methods not immediately applicable"[22]—to the task of constructing a "life of Jesus (an "historical Jesus"), the source of this inadequacy is inherent in the primary sources themselves. Specifically, it is not the case that the sources themselves (i.e., the biblical texts of the New Testament, and, specifically, the four gospels) are flawed, or even that their volume is paltry,[23] but it has to do with the nature of the sources themselves. It is here, according to Schweitzer, that a "twofold difficulty"[24] arises.

In the first case, though it may certainly be conceded that there are few persons of antiquity of whom so much information has been acquired, the sources—through which, Schweitzer contends, Jesus stands "immediately before us [due to being] depicted by simple Christians without literary gift"[25]—offer only a picture of Jesus' public ministry (and, by implication, not enough material "for a complete Life of Jesus"[26]). But such an assertion can only be made if we have already made a choice for the Synoptic Gospels and their funding of such a "Life." From the outset the gospels present us with a fundamental decision.

In Schweitzer's view the Gospel of John, "as regards its character, historical data, and discourse material, forms a world of its own. It is written from the Greek standpoint, while the [Synoptics] are written from the Jewish."[27] Schweitzer elaborates the irreconcilability of these sources, the Synoptic Gospels versus the Gospel of John:

22. Schweitzer, *Quest*, 6.

23. "[I]t must be admitted that there are few characters of antiquity about whom we possess so much indubitably historical information, of whom we have so many authentic discourses." See Schweitzer, *Quest*, 6.

24. Schweitzer, *Quest*, 6.

25. I strongly doubt Schweitzer's conclusion here with regard to "literary gift." Schweitzer, *Quest*, 6.

26. Schweitzer, *Quest*, 6.

27. Schweitzer, *Quest*, 6.

> And even if one could get over [these differences], and regard, as has often been done, the Synoptics and the Fourth Gospel as standing as Zenophon does to Plato as sources for the life of Socrates, yet the complete irreconcilability of the historical data would compel the critical investigator to decide from the first in favour of one source or the other.[28]

One intending to outline a "life of Jesus" is certainly—up front—forced to make a choice with regard to sources irreconcilable as to their plot, content, style, and narrative perspectives. Because of this, almost immediately, for Schweitzer, the Fourth Gospel forfeits itself as a funding source for a reliable "life of Jesus." And still: a decision to let the Synoptic Gospels fund an outline—which Schweitzer does exclusively—confines one to a narration of Jesus' public ministry, his public acts and words. It is just this dynamic which leads us to the second identified difficulty. It is this second difficulty that Schweitzer identifies with regard to the sources that will both detain us, and provide the framework for the subject of textual silence and its hermeneutical implications.

Whether one is engaged with the Synoptic Gospels—"[which] are only collections of anecdotes"[29]—or the Gospel of John—"[which] only professes to give a selection of the events and discourses"[30]—one is confronted with the problem of continuity with regard to the actual "life of Jesus." In Schweitzer's words, "The second difficulty regarding the sources is the want of any thread of connexion in the material which they offer us."[31] That is, these sources—at best—will yield only a "life of Jesus" with "yawning gaps" filled "at the worst with phrases, at the best with historical imagination."[32] How else might one arrive at the "order and inner connexion of the facts of the life of Jesus [?]"[33] Or can we assume that the tradition crystallized by—in this case—the Synoptic Gospels includes everything that occurred with reference to Jesus while he was with the disciples? If this is the case, Schweitzer thinks, certainly a "thread of connexion" will be discerned sooner or later. But, he admits, "If it is merely a fortuitous series of episodes that the Evangelists have handed down to us, we may give up the attempt to arrive at a critical reconstruction of the life of Jesus as hopeless."[34]

28. Schweitzer, *Quest*, 6–7.

29. Schweitzer, *Quest*, 7.

30. Schweitzer, *Quest*, 7.

31. Schweitzer, *Quest*, 7.

32. Schweitzer, *Quest*, 7.

33. Schweitzer, *Quest*, 7.

34. Schweitzer, *Quest*, 7.

But if it is the "inner connexion" with regard to the materials of the narrative of Jesus' public ministry as presented by the Gospels which gives us problems, then with reference to the personality of Jesus the problem is compounded. It is here that Schweitzer appears to narrow his focus to the Synoptic gospels.

As Schweitzer observes, "it is not only the [external] events which lack historical connexion, we are without any indication of a thread of connexion in the actions and discourses of Jesus, because the sources give no hint of the character of His self-consciousness. They confine themselves to outward facts."[35] He adds, "We only begin to understand these historically when we can mentally place them in an intelligible connexion and conceive them as the acts of a clearly defined personality."[36] At the same, Schweitzer points out, "All that we know of the development of Jesus and of His Messianic self-consciousness has been arrived at by a series of working hypotheses."[37] To borrow the language of Theresa Sanders (whom we engaged in chapter 1, above), Schweitzer, in his examination of the sources (and, in this case, specifically, the Synoptic Gospels and their narration of the public ministry of Jesus), has diagnosed a "death of designation," and precisely, one of "self-designation" with regard to the person of Jesus. That is, what Schweitzer perceives within the Synoptic narratives is the absence of connection between action and self-consciousness in the ministry of Jesus. Precisely, it is a lacuna between action and self-designation. On the matter of Jesus' self-consciousness, and thus self-designation, according to Schweitzer, the Synoptic narratives are silent. With regard to the implications, Schweitzer adds that

> It may be maintained by the aid of arguments drawn from the sources that the self-consciousness of Jesus underwent a development during the course of His public ministry; it may, with equally good grounds, be denied. For in both cases the arguments are based upon little details in the narrative in regard to which we do not know whether they are purely accidental, or whether they belong to the essence of the facts.[38]

What is more, Schweitzer also observes a profound contradiction within the textual silence itself between Jesus' presumed self-designation and the narration of his acts, his ministry. The sources themselves, Schweitzer adds,

---

35. Schweitzer, *Quest*, 7.
36. Schweitzer, *Quest*, 7.
37. Schweitzer, *Quest*, 7.
38. Schweitzer, *Quest*, 7.

assert that Jesus felt Himself to be the Messiah; and yet from their presentation of His life it does not appear that He ever publicly claimed to be so. They attribute to Him, that is, an attitude which has absolutely no connexion with the consciousness which they assume that He possessed. But once admit that the outward acts are not the natural expression of the self-consciousness and all exact historical knowledge is at an end . . .[39]

Do we follow Jesus' conduct and conclude that Jesus was not self-consciously the Messiah? Or do we follow the sources and conclude that Jesus was self-consciously the Messiah? In the silent gap—the death of designation, in the absence of self-designation between action and self-consciousness—the interpreter is left with two equally justifiable conclusions. What we are left with, as Schweitzer later acknowledges, is an unchallenged assertion: "That Jesus of Nazareth knew Himself to be the Son of Man who was to be revealed is for us the great fact of His self-consciousness, which is not to be further explained, whether there had been any kind of preparation for it in [what was for Jesus] contemporary theology or not."[40]

But, if Jesus' identity, specifically his messianic identity, forever stirs silently within the death of designation between his own personal self-consciousness and his public acts as narrated by the Synoptic Gospels, then perhaps—Schweitzer entertains the prospect—his messianic identity may be fished from the epoch of which he was—in this case in relation to eschatology—a product. Though Schweitzer entertains such a prospect, almost immediately he concedes its impossibility: "[W]hereas in general a personality is to some extent defined by the world of thought which it shares with its contemporaries, in the case of Jesus this source of information is as unsatisfactory as the documents."[41]

Specifically, it might be asked, what was the nature of contemporary Jewish thought at Jesus' time, especially with regard to eschatological considerations? Perhaps an answer in this area might assist in helping us to detect of which messianic "brand"—or perhaps combination of brands—Jesus was an expression. Again, no luck. Schweitzer offers his "unsatisfactory" conclusion with regard to just this problem:

We do not know whether the expectation of the Messiah was generally current or whether it was the faith of a mere sect. With the Mosaic religion as such it had nothing to do. There was no organic connexion between the religion of legal observance and

39. Schweitzer, *Quest*, 8.
40. Schweitzer, *Quest*, 365.
41. Schweitzer, *Quest*, 8.

the future hope. Further, if the eschatological hope was generally current, was it the prophetic or the apocalyptic form of that hope? We know the Messianic expectations of the prophets; we know the apocalyptic picture as drawn by Daniel, and, following him, by Enoch and the Psalms of Solomon before the coming of Jesus, and by the Apocalypses of Ezra and Baruch about the time of the destruction of Jerusalem. But we do not know which was the popular form; nor, supposing that both were combined into one picture, what this picture really looked like. We know only the form of eschatology which meets us in the Gospels and in the Pauline epistles; that is to say, the form which it took in the Christian community in consequence of the coming of Jesus.[42]

Indeed, it appears, as Schweitzer observes, that the eschatology—the messianic expectations and corresponding actions—of both Jesus and John the Baptist appear *de novo* without historical derivation or contemporary parallel.[43] So Schweitzer's conclusion with regard to Jesus' and John the Baptist's peculiar relationship to the messianic atmosphere of their time:

> The Baptist and Jesus are not, therefore, borne upon the current of a general eschatological movement. The period offers no events calculated to give an impulse to eschatological enthusiasm. They themselves set the times in motion by acting, by creating eschatological facts. It is this mighty creative force which constitutes the difficulty in grasping historically the eschatology of Jesus and the Baptist. Instead of literary artifice speaking out of a distant imaginary past, there now enter into the field of eschatology men, living, acting men. It was the only time when that ever happened in Jewish eschatology.[44]

Thus, if Schweitzer has detected a chasm of silence stirring between the actions of Jesus in his public ministry and his self-consciousness, a death of designation, then the attempt to identify Jesus' messianic identity, his self-consciousness from the at-large atmosphere of his day, produces "silence all around,"[45] or a messianism with no historical derivation and no contemporary likeness.

Presented, therefore, with an historical figure in Jesus absent a connection between public action and self-designation, combined with a messianic identity which appears to have no genetic relationship with historical

42. Schweitzer, *Quest*, 8.

43. Schweitzer, *Quest*, 367–68.

44. Schweitzer, *Quest*, 368.

45. Schweitzer, *Quest*, 368.

precedent or contemporary manifestation, all that we will ever have is a "self-consciousness [which] cannot in fact be illustrated or explained."[46] For essentially, according to Schweitzer, all that can be understood "is the eschatological view, in which the Man who possessed that self-consciousness saw reflected in advance the coming events, both those of a more general character, and those which especially related to Himself."[47] It was his duty to initiate "the eschatological development of history, to let loose the final woes, the confusion and strife, from which shall issue the Parousia, and so to introduce the supra-mundane phase of the eschatological drama."[48] It was with a view to these eschatological repercussions, the persecution and the suffering, that he chose the first disciples.[49]

Ultimately, then, we arrive full circle at the quote through which we first encountered Schweitzer near the end of chapter 1. This time with context. Or, shall we say, it is a quote now re-presented within the arena of Schweitzer's "mirror" diagnosis and his struggle with both textual silence and the absence of both historical precedent and contemporary application. This time, ultimately, it is not the silence occasioned by the narrative's perspective, or its disconnect between self-consciousness and act that stares back at us, but the abyssal, absolute silence, the complete death of designation, occasioned by crucifixion itself. For if it is—we can say from Schweitzer's perspective—John the Baptist who appears on the stage of Scripture and the history narrated by Scripture seemingly *ex nihilo*, conjured in Melchizedekian fashion, and cries out, "Repent, for the Kingdom of Heaven is at hand," quickly he is followed by a Jesus—certainly sharing the same enigmatic messianism—whose silence of self-designation occasioned by the Synoptic Gospels' narration of his life and ministry culminates in an abyssal silence, a complete death of designation, and a corresponding referential instability peculiar to death itself. Thus:

> Soon after [John the Baptist] comes Jesus, and in the knowledge that He is the coming Son of Man lays hold of the wheel of the world to set it moving on that last revolution which is to bring all ordinary history to a close. It refuses to turn, and He throws Himself upon it. Then it does turn; and crushes Him. Instead of bringing in the eschatological conditions, He has destroyed them. The wheel rolls onward, and the mangled body of the one immeasurably great Man, who was strong enough to think of

46. Schweitzer, *Quest*, 368.
47. Schweitzer, *Quest*, 365.
48. Schweitzer, *Quest*, 369.
49. Schweitzer, *Quest*, 369.

Himself as the spiritual ruler of mankind and to bend history
to his purpose, is hanging upon it still. That is His victory and
His reign.[50]

It is the abyssal silence of a mangled man shrouded in an eschatology, a
messianism, which is as foreign to our ears as it was a *de novo* reality to
Jesus' contemporaries.

All of which brings us back to Schweitzer's mirror diagnosis with
reference to those who went in search of the "historical Jesus" and found
themselves staring back in their Jesus portraits at a reflection of themselves,
the "spirit of the times," and all that was deemed of highest value according
to society and culture. All of which brings us back to Schweitzer's window,
or the manner in which the first-century Jesus, laden with first-century bag-
gage, becomes a portal to the timeless, eternal "spirit" which beckons us to
disengage our worldly attachments in order to engage the struggles known
to every time.

Whether we are speaking of the mirror which Schweitzer diagnosed in
those conducting the "Quest," or the window into the mandate of the timeless, eternal "spirit" to which he delegated the Jesus narrated by Scripture,
both options are occasioned at the crossroads of textual silence. It is the silence of its seams and gaps of narrative. It is the silence which stirs between
act and self-consciousness with reference to Jesus' public ministry. It is the
silence of an apocalyptic eschatology which seemingly refuses to transcend
the first century with regard to either form and impact. Ultimately, it is the
abyssal silence of the crucified One himself, the mangled, crucified Jesus
expressed by Schweitzer with such sober strokes.

But whether it is the mirror of Schweitzer's diagnosis or the window
of his prescription with regard to the Jesus of Scripture, both avenues of
interpretation are nothing more than attempts—in full agreement on this
point—to seek hermeneutical resolution beyond the text, its lines and letters, its margins. Both navigate the silence as if the text was not enough.
Both manage the silence as if the value the text conveys, its so-called spiritual meaning, was not contained within but stood beyond the text's own
lines and margins; as if the text really, when all is said and done, does not
reveal its own, unique subject matter, its own unique value.

Pausing for a moment, again invoking the manner by which artistic
expression conveys theological perspectives and spiritual attitudes, specifically with reference to the work of Warner Sallman, let us ask: is Sallman's
Head of Christ nothing more than a cipher beckoning us to the "spirit"
which transcends time and historical particularity, the particularity of a

---

50. Schweitzer, *Quest*, 368–69.

first-century Jesus in all his historical peculiarity? Or is it simply a reflection of that religious expression which is held in highest esteem, that combination of ethnicity and piety so many hold so dearly, and have so closely identified with Christianity, its essence? Is the *Head of Christ* mirror or window?

But if it is the case—in the trajectory of Schweitzer's window—that the value which the Jesus of Scripture reveals lies beyond the text itself, in this case in the "spirit" which beckons us to transcend Jesus' inaccessible timeliness in order to engage the timeless struggles known to all times, would not this certainly mean that Scripture is not enough? Is there another text, then, which supplements and informs our reading of Scripture? And how is such a "spiritual" hermeneutic executed? How does one arrive at such a hermeneutical level, or the level of "spirit"? And with whom do we consult about this? Shall we pray for a magisterium to guide us through this maze?

Regardless, Schweitzer was unquestionably correct in his diagnosis that the Jesus of Scripture—the raw material from which the "questers," each in their own way, crafted an "historical Jesus"—had become a mirror. His mistake was not only his inability to accept textual silence—in all the forms that have been addressed above—as having a legitimate purpose with regard to communicating the identity of Jesus Christ and the value he reveals for those whose gaze is directed at him, but, ultimately, to confuse *misuse* for *wrong device*. Observations need to be made on both points.

On the first point, let us recall: according to the dynamics of deconstruction—as developed through Derrida and Caputo (see the beginning of chapter 2, above), textual silence is the experience of undecidability, or the name given to the messianic pulse of the deep structure of existence, the promise of the unforeseeable, the undeconstructible, always to-come future, stirring within—but never identified with—what *is*, whether that *is* is the text of a scroll, the text of a crucified body, or the text of existence itself. The promise of textual silence, as presented by Derrida and Caputo, is perpetually deferred, and thus cast as a category of the future; calling from beyond the lines and margins of the text, it is a promise that cannot be identified with the text—and ultimately, the text of what *is*. On the other hand, instead of casting the promise of textual silence as a category of the "always to-come" "messianic future," Schweitzer employs the text as a window to the promise of timeless value, or a "timeless," "spiritual" mandate applicable to all times. Not only do Schweitzer and deconstruction (as presented through Derrida and Caputo) have in common the positing of a promised value which is not to be identified with the text, but what is promised is never contingent upon the particularity of what *is*.

On the second point: Scripture, and the Jesus revealed within Scripture, *is a mirror*. Schweitzer's recourse to the Jesus of Scripture as window is unwarranted (as will be developed in chapter 4, below). But a mirror is only as useful as the self-knowledge it produces in the one reflected. It must also be recognized that reflection is not synonymous with self-knowledge. A mirror may become an instrument of self-justification just as easily as it may become the medium of self-knowledge. As will be developed, it is the self-knowledge unveiled in such a reflection—the unveiling of one's value— that separates purely academic and hermeneutical flights of fancy from the beginnings of "true theology."

It is to this self-knowledge—the christological function of the text— and the "true theology" which ensues that we now turn.

4

Being Exegeted

Christological Existence

Unveiling Value: The Beginning of True Theology

It is not difficult, given the place of theology within the academy, to picture a
theologian—perhaps with an eye to guaranteeing that one's theology remains
modish, relevant, and published, or perhaps to justify theology's place among
humanities curricula—as dabbling a little in the social sciences, a little in
some branch of philosophy, a little in some field of psychology, and a little in
some field of biology. No doubt more of one than the others. Perfectionism
and dilettante-ism make for tough co-habitants in the same mind. When
the issue is theology's relevance among the humanities curricula, then any
knowledge about humanity that creates a new angle is welcome.

From this perspective, Martin Luther's delineation of theology's subject matter may seem at best parochial and pessimistic, at worst startlingly
and suffocatingly reductionistic, and thus highly unpromotable, unmarket-
able. Specifically, Luther asserts, "[a] the theologian discusses man as a sinner." He continues,

> In theology, this is the essence of man. The theologian is con-
> cerned that man become aware of this nature of his, corrupted
> by sins. When this happens, despair follows, casting him into

hell. In the face of the righteous God, what shall a man do who knows that his whole nature has been crushed by sin and that there is nothing left on which he can rely, but that his righteousness has been reduced to exactly nothing?[1]

Such self-knowledge is far from speculative, far from theoretical in its observation and elaboration. Corresponding with an understanding of life which suffers God's work, whose relationship to God's agency is purely receptive, the *vita passiva*, such a self-knowledge is derived "completely of practice and feeling."[2] It is a self-knowledge grounded less in science (*scientia*) and cognitive faculty than wisdom (*sapientia*) and experience.[3] Indeed, "A man hears and learns what grace and justification are, what God's plan is for the man who has fallen into hell, namely, that He has decided to restore man through Christ."[4] Such a knowledge is a "twofold theological knowledge" whose *simul* focus is "the theological knowledge of man and also the theological knowledge of God."[5] Thus, as Luther famously asserted, the "proper subject of theology is man guilty of sin and condemned, and God the Justifier and Savior of man the sinner. Whatever is asked or discussed in theology outside this subject, is error and poison."[6] Again, in Luther's words:

> Therefore this theological knowledge is necessary: A man should know himself, should know, feel, and experience that he is guilty of sin and subject to death; but he should also know the opposite, that God is the Justifier and the Redeemer of a man who knows himself this way. The care of other men, who do not know their sins, let us leave to lawyers, physicians, and parents, who discuss man differently from the way a theologian does.[7]

But if Luther is able to state, regarding the source of such self-knowledge, that "All Scripture points to this, that God commends His kindness to us and in His Son restores to righteousness and life the nature that has fallen into sin and condemnation,"[8] then "all" of Scripture does what only Scripture is able alone to do: *sola Scriptura*. *Sola Scriptura*—one of the three

---

1. Luther, *Works* 12.310–11.
2. Luther, *Works* 12.311.
3. See Bayer, *Theology the Lutheran Way*, 21–32.
4. Luther, *Works* 12.311.
5. Luther, *Works* 12.311.
6. Luther, *Works* 12.311.
7. Luther, *Works* 12.311–12.
8. Luther, *Works* 12.311.

famous *solas* employed since at least the nineteenth century by English-speaking Protestants to summarize Luther's theology[9]—is the confession that theology does not begin, and therefore is not conducted, or even sanctioned, before or beyond Scripture—the text—but in it, within its lines and margins, its letters and spaces. Indeed, if Scripture's authority is bound to the reality that it alone "pushes Christ"—"*Was Christum treibet!*"—then *sola Scriptura* is essentially a christological assertion.[10] The *sola Scriptura* assertion is an expression of the christological priority.

And if Christology begins in the "pushing" of Christ—that it "does God" to us[11]—then this "pushing" is at once a fundamental shift in what is meant by "interpretation." Specifically, Christology begins with a hermeneutical reversal sanctioned within the lines and letters of Scripture itself, a reversal between interpreter and interpreted; a reversal that both blocks the window to extra-textually derived meaning, and fractures the reflection of self-affirmation in order to unveil the text for its true usage, namely, as mirror of self-recognition. It is the christologically grounded self-recognition that signals the beginning—for Luther—of "theology." In short, as Lutherans have traditionally asserted, "Scripture interprets us."[12] Christology, one conducted from the cross in the trajectory of the *theological crucis*, is not fundamentally something theologians "do" or "study," but is indeed a subject matter theologians "experience," "suffer," in their being interpreted by Scripture alone. But it is precisely here, as Vítor Westhelle has pointed out, that there is a bit of ambiguity to unpack, one that helps to clarify Scripture's agency.

Though, as Westhelle observed, Luther's thesis that "[S]cripture interprets itself" (*scriptura sui ipsius interpres*)[13] is well known and understood with reference to the hermeneutical reversal which takes place, namely that Scripture interprets its alleged interpreters and not vice-versa, it is the mechanics of a such a reversal that have traditionally been a bit ambiguous.[14] Indeed, Westhelle observes, the traditional English translation, or "[S]cripture interprets itself," is both imprecise—missing the sharpness of the literal translation—and suggests that a correct meaning arises when selections of Scripture have been employed against one another. Instead, in its

9. See especially Wengert, *Reading the Bible*, 1–21.

10. See Wengert, *Reading the Bible*, 8–11.

11. See especially Forde, *Theology Is for Proclamation*, 2–8.

12. See Paulson, "Lutheran Assertions Regarding Scripture," 373–85; Westhelle, "Luther on the Authority of Scripture," 373–91.

13. Luther, *Werke* 7, 97, 20–22.

14. With regard to this dynamic. I am completely indebted to Westhelle for this insight. See Westhelle, "Luther on the Authority of Scripture," 377–79.

place, he provides a more literal, precise translation: "the Scripture is in itself the interpreter."[15] It is this rendering that clarifies the mechanics of such a hermeneutical reversal.

Recognizing that the word *interpres*, a Latin noun, "designates that which stands between two values or 'prices' (*inter-pres*)," Westhelle elaborates,

> The etymology of the word points to the exchange of merchan-
> dise in markets of antiquity. It was often the case that because of
> difference in the languages or dialects spoken by the merchants
> bargaining for the value of goods there was a need for an in-
> terpreter to convey the value or the price asked by a merchant
> to another in the process of negotiating an exchange. That the
> Scripture interprets itself has the precise meaning that it is not
> interpreted, but is the interpreter itself. The Scripture stands
> between two "values" and allows for the exchange to happen.[16]

But if Scripture is the interpreter itself which stands between two values, what are they?

Those values, for Luther, combine to provide the "proper subject of theology," or "man guilty of sin and condemned, and God the Justifier and Savior of man the sinner"; *homo peccator et Deus salvator*. Scripture is the interpreter of this *mirabilis mutatatio*,[17] this happy, or marvelous exchange,[18] Christ in our place and we in the place of Christ; Christ's value becomes ours and ours becomes Christ's. Ultimately Westhelle adds, and I quote him at length,

> As our interpreter, the Scripture makes intelligible to us a lan-
> guage that for us is foolishness (*moria*, 1 Cor 1), because we
> come to the "market" with the notion that we can barter with
> the valuables we think we have. And the interpreter tells us that
> it is worth nothing and yet the other party is giving even himself
> to us in this foolish and scandalous exchange: nothing for all, all
> for nothing. If we try to do something, even that little we sup-
> pose we retain (*facere quod in se*) in this exchange, we destroy
> the gift, and the happy exchange turns into a miserable deal.[19]

15. Westhelle, "Luther on the Authority of Scripture," 378.

16. Westhelle, "Luther on the Authority of Scripture," 378.

17. Luther, *Werke* 31/11, 435, 11; Luther, *Works* 17.225.

18. In the words of Robert Bertram, as Kurt Hendel has passed them along to me, the "sweet swop."

19. Westhelle, "Luther on the Authority of Scripture," 378.

But if in this exchange Scripture serves as the interpreter of values, "nothing for all, all for nothing," the interpreter of an infinitely asymmetric exchange of value, in so doing, for Luther, it becomes simultaneously—as our interpreter—the mirror of theological knowledge, or more precisely, self-knowledge. Scripture becomes the mirror of zero-value, the *nihil* standing before it, gazing into it, and, in the process, the beginning of a theology—a Christology—from the cross. To be sure, if the authority of Scripture—*sola Scriptura*—is bound to the recognition that it alone "pushes Christ," then "pushes" (*treibet*) is a euphemism for "crucifies," or the reality that Scripture is the only document, the only text, known to humanity which, if used properly, crucifies its readers and hearers, its interpreters. And, as the mirror of self-knowledge, the zero-value, the *nihil* of the one gazing into it, Scripture is clear, crystal-clear. Too clear. The only problem, as will be developed, is the veil which gets draped over it. But, before we move forward—risking both redundancy and prolixity—let us pause briefly for some perspective, namely, in order to reflect on both Albert Schweitzer's "diagnosis" and his "prescription" in light of what has been just developed with regard to Scripture's authority.

If Schweitzer was able to diagnose the phenomenon that the Jesus of Scripture had become nothing more than a mirror of the one—the "quester"—attempting the Jesus portrait, then his prescription with regard to the Jesus of Scripture laid bare in all his first-century, apocalyptic peculiarity according to the results of the historical-critical method was to assign his significance as a window to the "spiritual" meaning, or value, promised beyond the text; to a timeless, "spiritual" meaning which calls us to relax our grip on worldly attachments in order to engage the "timeless" struggles known to every time. But whether one takes the hermeneutical road of Schweitzer's diagnosis (the mirror) or journeys the path of Schweitzer's prescription (the window), both routes of interpretation amount to be nothing more than attempts to seek hermeneutical resolution—a decision with regard to the value the text promises—beyond the text, its lines and letters, its margins. Both hermeneutical options navigate the text—and ultimately its silence—as if the text was not enough, as if the value promised by the text can only be found before or beyond the text, and hence its value—what the text promises—was not mediated by the text itself. But if its value, its life-giving, salvific significance, lies outside of the text itself, its letters and lines, its spaces and margins, is never to be identified with them, then how is one to ever know their interpretation to be the correct one? Better, who sanctions the correct interpretation? And how is it decided who sanctions correct interpretations? Again, is a magisterium in order?

As Gerhard Forde has pointed out, the problem with such a method of interpretation practiced by folks like Schweitzer lies in its presuppositions. As Forde observed, the folly of such a logic practiced by Schweitzer and folks like him was to think

> that "life-giving Spirit" was a level of *meaning* that could be got-
> ten at by interpretation. But interpretation does not yield *spirit*,
> it only yields more letter. Even if the Holy Spirit himself, in the
> Scriptures, inspires an interpretation beyond the original literal
> or historical meaning, that is still only more *letter*. Interpreta-
> tion does not give life.[20]

But behind the assumption that one can hermeneutically move through the letter—text—to the eternal, "spiritual" meaning behind it can also be found two more assumptions. These include, namely, the "freedom" of the interpreting subject who stands before the text-as-object, who presumes the freedom of transit between "text," or "letter," and "spirit," or even the freedom to recognize "spirit," and the corresponding idea that the text is a mere point of departure for such a freedom of movement. That is, according to Forde

> "Spirit" means the intelligibility one arrives at by the interpre-
> tive process. The anthropological presupposition accompany-
> ing such moves is that the human spirit as "rational" and "free"
> can—indeed, must—make the move from the letter to "spirit"
> if there is to be salvation. The text is the jumping-off place, the
> exercise ground, the symbolic "map," for the human spirit and
> its flight, the material upon which it works in its freedom.[21]

Thus, when we consider Schweitzer's hermeneutical prescription for han-dling the Jesus of Scripture as presented by the results of the historical-critical method against the hermeneutical reversal sanctioned by "proper subject of theology" which *sola Scriptura* works upon its subjects, the as-sumptions of such a prescription are voided.

If the text, the *interpres*, determines the values which comprise the "proper subject" of theology—*homo peccator et Deus salvator*—and thus mirrors the zero-value, the *nihil*, of the one gazing into it, then the implica-tions corresponding to such a determination are profound: the recognition of the loss of one's agency as an interpreting subject, the rendering of the "freedom" to access "spirit" becomes an illusion, and the recognition that the text—far from being a "window," or "jumping-off place" to the realm of

20. Forde, "Law and Gospel," 245.

21. Forde, "Law and Gospel," 245.

eternal "spirit"—is, in reality, a mirror of what or who lies dead in its tracks. The problem is not fundamentally about interpreting one's way into life or "Spirit," but instead the reality that one cannot interpret their way out of death. In its autonomy, Scripture, the *interpres*, reveals both the illusion of any freedom of agency required for such a movement, and the absence of any value required to negotiate such an exchange, or life for death. To lift the veil on such a reality lies not within the realm of hermeneutics.

Even though Luther expressed in his debate with Jerome Emser over 2 Cor 3:6 ("The letter kills, but the Spirit gives life")[22] that Scripture has one, proper "grammatical, historical meaning,"[23] such an assertion must be qualified. That is, one can argue that even Schweitzer, on account of a thoroughgoing application of historical-critical method and a resulting "historical Jesus," arrived here. Only, to be sure, to seek the "life-giving Spirit" beyond him.

Instead, as Luther asserted, the transit from literal meaning, or "killing letter," to spiritual meaning, or "life-giving Spirit" is not an interpretive move—"St. Paul does not write one iota about these two meanings"[24]—but one of proclamation, or "two kinds of preaching or preaching offices."[25] One of the letter. One of the Spirit. Though, we might say, one cannot interpret their self out of death, it is from death—its location and recognition—that one is authorized to proclaim the Promise and await its life-creating agency.

The [office of the] letter," according to Luther,

> is nothing but divine law or commandment which was given in the Old Testament through Moses and preached and taught through Aaron's priesthood. It is called "letter" because it is written in letters on stone tablets and in books. It remains letter, and does not yield more than that, because no man improves through the law; he only becomes worse . . . [The law] only commands and orders something done which man is neither able nor willing to do.[26]

22. See Luther's *Answer to the Hyperchristian, Hyperspiritual, and Hyperlearned Book by Goat Emser in Leipzig* in Luther, *Works* 39.143–203.

23. Luther, *Works* 39.181. A position contrary to that of Emser's. For Emser, the "life giving Spirit" is an expression of the reality, according to Luther, that "Scripture has a twofold meaning, an external one and a hidden one, and he calls these two meanings 'literal' and 'spiritual.'" It is the literal meaning that kills and the spiritual one (no doubt allegorical in nature) that gives life. See Luther, *Works* 39.175.

24. Luther, *Works* 39.182.

25. Luther, *Works* 39.182.

26. Luther, *Works* 39.182.

The [office of the] Spirit, on the other hand, Luther explains, is one of "the divine grace, grants strength and power to the heart; indeed, [the Spirit] creates a new man who takes pleasure [in obeying] God's commandments and who does everything he should do with joy."[27] If through the "ministry of the Spirit" "God's Spirit and grace are offered"[28]—for "everything that is not Spirit or grace is death"[29]—then through the "ministry of the letter" it is demonstrated that "the letter can do no more than kill a man, that is, show him what he should do and yet cannot do. Thus he recognizes that he is dead and without grace before God and that he does not fulfill the commandment, which, however, he should fulfill."[30]

To be sure, if the text, the letter, was once treated as a passive medium through which the realm of the Spirit was hermeneutically stormed and the pretense to its life-giving and value-bestowing authority usurped, for the Luther the text, the letter, is now suffered as the active agent by which one is crucified of all claims to life-giving agency, especially, in this case, as that pretense revolves around hermeneutical agency. One cannot hermeneutically storm the realm of Spirit through the lines of the text. One can only await the Spirit's life-giving agency within the text itself. One can only suffer the Promise whom the text mediates, both the Word's crucifying and resurrecting agency. As well, it should be noted—now explicitly—that "if everything that is not Spirit or grace is death," then Schweitzer's "spiritual meaning" derived through historical Jesus-as-window is nothing more than cold, dead letter. "[I]t is a crude misunderstanding to call allegories, tropologies, and the like 'Spirit,' since all of them are contained in letters and cannot give life."[31]

But if biblical interpretation and its expressions—allegory, tropology, etc.—are in no way Spirit-attaining, and thus life-giving, it may also be said that they have traditionally served a greater illusion, or as the veil to a fundamental truth about the interpreter herself. In so doing it has veiled the proper subject of theology, thus covering its proper point of access, disguising its proper methodology, no doubt under the guise of some species of neutral, detached, academic objectivity, or even an insulated, orthodoxy-inspired triumphalism. We can say that the signature of the "ministry of the letter" lies in its "unveiling." According to Luther, further elaborating the "ministry of the letter,"

27. Luther, *Works* 39.182.
28. Luther, *Works* 39.183.
29. Luther, *Works* 39.184.
30. Luther, *Works* 39.183.
31. Luther, *Works* 39.184.

[The Apostle Paul] wants us to preach and make the letter clear and to lift the veil from Moses' face. This is how it happens: he who understands the law of God correctly and looks it in the face—without the veil—will find that the works of all men are sin and that there is nothing good in them unless the grace of the Spirit enters into them.[32]

Luther adds, "[the law] wants to show us our misery, our death, and our merit, and lead us into true knowledge of ourselves."[33] By lifting the veil on the illusion that the Scripture is either mirror of self-affirmation or window to "spiritual meaning," the "ministry of the letter" proclaims the proper use of the text, that in it "[M]an recognizes himself in the *mirror* and in the face of the letter or the law—how dead he is and in what disgrace he is with God. This knowledge makes him afraid and drives him to seek the Spirit, who makes him good, godly, holy, spiritual, brings all things into accord with the law, and leads him to God's grace."[34] The "ministry of the letter" unveils the mirror of self-knowledge and, through it, the Promise of Life, of Spirit, which it presupposes and to which it drives; a Life, a Spirit, the dead can only await and trust as Promise.

The crucified Christ of Scripture is the crescendo of such a self-knowledge, its zero value, its *nihil*; the reflection of the abyssal, crucified silence for which there are no hermeneutical loopholes. Theology begins and is sustained precisely here, amid the self-recognition of zero-value, one's death, or *nihil*, and its subsequent praying, awaiting, hoping for the Promised Life-giving Spirit. It begins with a theologian who has suffered the unveiled letter, the proper function of the law, and the corresponding experience—the mirror—of self-knowledge. The proper function of the law reveals the necessity of theology's proper subject, and, ultimately, the humanity God intended from the beginning, namely, one whose existence—called-out *ex nihilo*—is animated in their *nihil* by Promise alone.

The "ministry of the letter" rips off the veil of the long-held illusion harbored in hermeneutics which covered the text, the letter, its mirroring of zero-value and the *nihil* of the one whose gaze is arrested by it. By pulling the veil from Scripture, from the text, the "ministry of the letter" exposes the face of the text mirroring the truth to the one who stands before and gazes into it. In doing so, the "ministry of the letter" reveals all prior hermeneutical attempts to achieve "spiritual meaning" before and beyond the text to be nothing more than fledgling attempts at self-preservation, even

32. Luther, *Works* 39.185.
33. Luther, *Works* 39.185.
34. Luther, *Works* 39.188. Italics are mine.

a self-justification, before the world and the Word. In the context of this project, we might say that Schweitzer diagnosed one veil only to prescribe another veil, one dead letter for another. Hermeneutics—even hermeneutics which are called "biblical" by their practitioners—may flourish without theology ever commencing.

But, even here, it must be made clear that the "ministry of the letter"—as well as the corresponding "ministry of the Spirit"—is not simply a testament to an incomplete hermeneutical reversal, to a bit of hermeneutical autonomy, along with its discretion and agency, held in abeyance, or "up the sleeve," to be unleashed—in this case in the form of the "killing letter"—on some and not others. To the contrary. The preaching of the "ministry of the letter" is necessitated by the interpreter who has suffered the autonomy of Scripture, its ability to unilaterally interpret the value, the *nihil*, of its interpreters and the lifelessness of their extra-textually derived "meanings" and "allegories," crucifying them in such a fashion that Spirit and Life can only be awaited as a category of God's Promise. One is crucified as an interpreter and raised—interpreted by the text—as minister of the letter and the Spirit.

When the autonomy of letter and Spirit are properly experienced and applied as offices, as "ministries," then it becomes impossible to manipulate the text into a launching pad, a window, for a meaning, an allegory, of one's own making. "Rather," as Forde, asserts,

> The sacred text is at work to change us, incorporate us into its story: the story with a future, not 'the soul's death.' The 'killing' function of the law cuts off every 'metaphysical' escape, every defense mechanism against the text, every self-justification, in order to save, to put us back in time before the God of time, to make us historical beings, to wait and to hope.[35]

As the text through the "ministry of the letter" ceases to be both mirror of affirmation, and thus self-justification, and a portal—window—to timeless meaning, so it restores its hearers to the only time they experience, the time they cannot hermeneutically transcend, or *this* Promise-created-time of trusting and hoping, waiting and praying; of Promise-worked crucifixion and resurrection. The autonomy, and ultimately the authority, of Scripture lies in its unilateral ability to create of its hearers those who are extensions of its text, its story, or those who, in their self-recognition of *nihil*, are raised to live by the Promise of God's Spirit, God's Life.

If, following Luther, Scripture alone has ultimately—in its interpretation of the exchange between *homo peccator et Deus salvator*—provided a mirror of the zero-value, the *nihil*, of the humanity standing before it,

---

35. Forde, "Law and Gospel," 249.

gazing into it, it has also, simultaneously, articulated the "proper subject of theology." A theology working from such a "proper subject" will outline the implications of a life lived—a theological existence—before such a "subject," or a God incarnated into the zero-value, the *nihil*, of God's people. Luther's *theologia crucis* is such a theology. We now move from text as Scripture, interpreter of humanity's zero-value, its *nihil*, to text as crucified Christ, the incarnation of that same zero-value and *nihil*.

Theologia Crucis and the Incarnate Text of Zero Value

If, as was developed above, Scripture's authority is bound to the reality that it alone "pushes Christ," then not only is *sola Scriptura* a christological assertion, but a kenotic one as well. Scripture's authority is expressed through the divestment of its own. As the text which interprets the christological exchange of value—*homo peccator et Deus salvator*—thus revealing the proper subject of theology, it also pushes the text of the incarnate God—the God of the exchange—to whom it points. Scripture gives way to the God incarnated without remainder into the zero-value, *nihil* of humanity; text recedes before crucified text.

The point of departure of Luther's *theologia crucis* is just this God, the incarnate God of humanity's zero-value, its *nihil*. Thus it must needs bear repeating: "[I]f true Theology and recognition of God are in the crucified Christ,"[36] then, for the theologian of the cross, Christianity is fundamentally a religion whose text is a crucified body, mangled and silenced of the Promise which once coursed through its words and gestures; ultimately a corpse in the repose of abyssal silence. This point of departure, articulated in the parlance of Lutheran Christology, is also termed the *genus tapeinoticum* (the humble, lowly genus). To be sure, this point of departure expresses the communication of the human attributes to the divine attributes in the person of Jesus Christ. It is a crucified text analogous to the currency—let us say—issued by the *Weimarer Republik*: now simply a piece of paper drained of value (save, perhaps for a little of the nostalgic variety) and siphoned of all signs of its issuing source, an issuing source nowhere to be evidenced. But if "God can be found only in suffering and the cross,"[37] that "apart from this man [Jesus] there is no God,"[38] then Luther's *theologia crucis*, with its epistemological point of departure a crucified text—silent, exsanguinated of divine designation, and suspended according to the calculations of reason

36. Luther, *Works* 31.53.

37. Luther, *Works* 31.53.

38. Luther, *Works* 37.218.

and experience in referential instability—corresponds to his understanding of Scripture's authority.

Let us recall that *sola Scriptura* is the confession that theology does not begin, and therefore is not conducted, before or beyond—outside—Scripture, the text. It involves the assertion that Scripture's authority is bound to the reality that it alone "pushes Christ," and therefore that it both determines the proper subject of theology—*homo peccator et Deus salvator*—and simultaneously interprets, mirrors, humanity's zero-exchange value, its *nihil*. In corresponding fashion, Luther's *theologia crucis*—specifically as elaborated in his *Heidelberg Disputation* (1518)[39]—delineates the confession, the reality, that there is no text outside of the crucified Christ—the corpse of Jesus Christ with its cuts and bruises, the viscous streaks of blood, a decomposing body reposing in abyssal silence—that mediates both the knowledge of God and the structure of Promise. The crucified Christ as text both mirrors humanity's zero-value, its *nihil*, and becomes the locus of the paradigm of God's agency, or the manner by which the dead letter reveals—*sub contraria specie*—the Life-giving Spirit. The crucified Christ reveals the manner by which Promise—of life, of new creation—is bound to the crucified text, to the structure of what *is*, ultimately "a corpse in a crypt." Again, there is no Promise that is not bound to crucified body. Promise is crucified body.

How does Luther, in the course of his twenty-eight theological theses in his *Heidelberg Disputation*, articulate such a dynamic, delineate an existence before a God incarnated into humanity's zero-value, its ultimate *nihil*? Though it is beyond the scope of this project to offer a thorough—thesis by thesis—treatment of Luther's *theologia crucis* as it is presented in the *Heidelberg Disputation*, a brief presentation of its significant points and major contours, its trajectory, will be helpful for the purpose of this project.

If, as Luther asserts in thesis one, "The law of God, the most salutary doctrine of life, cannot advance man on his way to righteousness, but rather hinders him,"[40] let us also note: Luther's intention is to relocate the agency of such righteousness' attainment—the righteousness of God, or better, righteousness before God—from humanity to God. But here let us pause, before we go any farther, to swap-out terms for the purpose of this project and the consistency of its language.

Recollecting that, for Luther, the "proper subject of theology" is "man guilty of sin and condemned, and God the justifier and Savior of man the sinner," Christ's value becoming ours and ours becoming Christ's, then

---

39. The *Heidelberg Disputation* is this project's primary text for delineating Luther's *theologia crucis*. See Luther, *Works* 31.35–70.

40. Luther, *Works* 31.42.

"righteousness"—the "righteousness before God"—is swapped out for "value." Restated: Luther's goal is to relocate and redefine the manner, the agency, by which *value*—traditionally spoken of as the "righteousness of God," or "righteousness before God"—is both articulated and attained. Therefore, if Luther is able to assert in thesis eighteen, "It is certain that man must utterly despair of his own ability before he is prepared to receive the grace of Christ,"[41] then such an assertion is nothing more than an exclamation-point placed at the end of the seventeen theses coming before it, or the step-by-step unveiling of the illusion of where that ability to attain righteousness, or value before God—*coram Deo*—has traditionally been located, namely, "law," "works," and "free will."

Analogous to Luther's understanding of Scripture's authority, *sola Scriptura* and its hermeneutical reversal of "interpreter" and "interpreted," the *Heidelberg Disputation* elaborates a hermeneutical reversal with reference to one's righteousness, or value before God; with reference to *who* interprets its reality, and who *is interpreted* by it. Thus, regarding the first seventeen theses of the *Heidelberg Disputation*, Deanna Thompson observes that Luther "peels away layer after layer of illusion, demonstrating how every possible avenue of human effort fails to achieve righteousness before God."[42] She adds, "[Luther] begins by expressing how the sinful human being can never fulfill the law. Luther then shows how the law is based on the illusion of the effectiveness of good works, and he concludes that trust in good works springs from yet another illusion: a will free to choose good."[43] Within the framework of this project, based upon our substitution of language—"value" for "righteousness"—we may say it this way: through the first seventeen theses—of which thesis 1 deals with the "law," theses 2 through 12 deal with "works (derived from the law)," and theses 13 through 17 deal with "free will"—the manner by which value is attained by human agency before God through such value-enhancing dynamics as "law," "works" based on the "law," and "free will," all working in consort to fund one's ability for "doing that which is within you" (*"facere quod in se est"*)—certainly recognizing that God rewards the imperfect outcome of such a project with "justifying grace"—is revealed as illusion.

But it is not simply the illusion of value and its attainment that is revealed, but, along with it, so is the illusion of a certain manner of doing theology. It is the illusion of a certain type of theologian, or the "theologian of glory." That illusion, and the one whose methodology is dictated by such an

41. Luther, *Works* 31.51.
42. Thompson, *Crossing the Divide*, 17.
43. Thompson, *Crossing the Divide*, 17–18.

illusion, ultimately, is articulated by Luther in thesis nineteen. It is here that he asserts "That person does not deserve to be called a theologian who looks upon the invisible things of God as though they were clearly perceptible in those things which have actually happened [Rom 1:20]." Such an illusion is grounded, ultimately, in the misuse of another a text, so to speak, namely, the text of creation itself.

Analogous to the manner by which Schweitzer located Scripture's significance, or value, beyond the text, ultimately presenting Scripture as a window to the "spiritual" value beyond the prison of unrepeatable, historical particularity (Lessing's "accidents of history"!), the theologian of glory operates under the assumption that creation is a text whose meaning, far from being bound to its lines and letters, lies outside and beyond the text itself. As if creation, perhaps, in all of its mundane contingency and particularity is unable to mediate within its own lines and contours divine truth; its tidy meaning to be found nowhere within its text.

In corresponding fashion, the theologian of glory—and Luther is being generous here in his application of the sobriquet "theologian," for they have not arrived yet at the "proper subject" of theology"!—is a philosophizing sleuth who works backward from the text of creation (no doubt wielding some species of analogy) in order to discern (or might we say "project"?) the manner by which God—in God's invisibility (according to the theologian of glory)[44]—bestows timeless value on God's subjects, a.k.a., "righteousness before God."

With reference to the crucified Christ—text as crucified corpse of Christ—the theologian of glory operates in a similar, predictable fashion. That is, the crucified Christ, too, is a window, a transparency to the meaning, the value, which lies beyond him, behind him. Perhaps the crucified Christ is essentially a portal by which is affirmed the timeless truth of redemptive—and, no doubt, inspirational!—suffering. Perhaps the crucified Christ provides the direct line of sight through which the cosmic struggle between good and evil has been waged and won (by whom does the evidence suggest?). Perhaps the crucified Christ is a transparency to divine justice, transactional in nature. What kind of "god" worthy of our devotion, worthy of such an appellation, would not desire a pound of flesh to satisfy his honor? What kind of "god" of "old time religion" would not require a good coat of blood for our Scapegoat?

For the theologian of glory the crucified Christ bears no significance, no value, unless there is a general "theory" (read: extra-textually derived

44. Let us be reminded: for Luther, God is visible in God's hiddenness; the revealing is a concealing. The word "invisibility" is employed here in reference to the theologian of glory's usage.

meaning or value informing the text, one certainly vying either for acceptance by the gatekeepers of orthodoxy or the voices of activism, but not both!) beyond it, informing us of its "contemporary meaning" and the "timeless" divine logic underwriting it. Recognizing that, for theologians of glory, the visible things of creation never bear within themselves transcendent meaning, but remain windows, transparencies, to the transcendent behind it all, Forde reminds us, "If we can *see through* the cross to what is supposed to be behind it, we don't have to *look at* it!"[45] It is this seeing, a seeing whose gaze is arrested *at* the cross, that distinguishes the theologian of glory from another kind of theologian.

"He deserves to be called a theologian, however, who comprehends the visible and manifest things of God seen through suffering and the cross."[46] So asserts Luther in thesis 20. With the layers of value-attaining illusion—"law," "works," and "free will," or all the key components which allegedly permit one "to do that which is within them" to attain value *coram Deo*—having been stripped away, the theologian of the cross begins to perceive in the crucified One not a window to transcendence and "timeless" meaning behind the "accidents of history," but a very "timely" mirror of self-knowledge, a reflection of one's possibilities and capabilities, especially with reference to the combination of agency and value (righteousness!) before God. No longer a transparency, the cross becomes one's story,[47] the crucified One becomes one's identity. "We see in the death of Jesus our death," Forde observed, "and we remember that we are dust."[48] "The cross alone [becomes one's] theology."[49] Such a theologian's gaze is now locked on to the fundamental text of theology, or the crucified body of Jesus Christ. The body of the crucified Christ becomes the text in which both creation and its Creator, the nature of their relation, are perceived by the theologian of the cross. Revealed in the crucified One for the theologian of the cross is both one's own death, or *nihil*, and the Word's *ex nihilo* life-creating agency. And it is only here, in the infinitely asymmetrical relation between the two, that a theologian's value can be assessed. A theologian of glory, we may say, attempts to attain value apart, and thus divorces it, from the point of its unconditional, *ex nihilo* conferral, a conferral one can never arrange or anticipate, only await "hope against hope" (Rom 4:18). The theologian of glory will not take

45. Forde, *On Being a Theologian of the Cross*, 76.

46. Luther, *Works* 31.52.

47. See Forde, *On Being a Theologian of the Cross*, 8.

48. Forde, *On Being a Theologian of the Cross*, 9.

49. *Crux sola est nostra theologia.* Luther, *Werke* 5, 176, 32; quoted in Forde, *On Being a Theologian of the Cross*, 3.

ownership of, to say the least endure, the *nihil*, the text, where divine value is awaited and received—without condition, without distinction—*ex nihilo*.

The theologian of the cross, denuded of all illusions of seeking value behind the text of cross and creation, now "sees" in the crucified corpse of Jesus the manner by which God has always dealt with and recognized value. Or as Luther asserted,

> Just as God in the beginning of creation made the world out of nothing, whence He is called the Creator and the Almighty, so His manner of working continues unchanged. Even now and to the end of the world, all His works are such that out of that which is nothing, worthless, despised, wretched, and dead, He makes that which is something, precious, honorable, blessed, and living. On the other hand, whatever is something, precious, honorable, blessed, and living, He makes to be nothing, worthless, despised, wretched, and dying. In this manner no creature can work; no creature can produce anything out of nothing. Therefore His eyes look only into the depths, not to the heights . . .[50]

If the theologian of glory "does not want to be that nothing out which the Lord can create,"[51] the theologian of the cross confesses God's Promise of life, the communication of such a Promise, is bound to the structure of *nihil*. The Life-giving Spirit is bound to body.

Thus, if according to Luther in thesis 21, "A theologian of glory calls evil good and good evil," while, on the other hand, "A theologian of the cross calls the thing what it is actually is,"[52] then such a distinction is *not simply* grounded in an epistemic point of departure shaped by a crucified God, but the knowledge borne of experience that life's *nihil*—whether expressed with regard to value before God, or the dust from which we are created and will return—is the medium by which God unilaterally conducts God's "proper work," namely creating value (before God) and life (in this creation and in the new one). To "call a thing what it actually is" not only "takes away from theology the pretense of saving God from death and humiliation,"[53] but allows the theologian of the cross to inhabit the gaze of a God whose "eyes look only into the depths,"[54] thus experiencing a God who "dwells in the darkness of faith."[55] To "call a thing what it actually is" means one "sees,"

---

50. Luther, *Works* 21.299.

51. Luther, *Works* 25.158.

52. Luther, *Works* 31.53.

53. Westhelle, "Enduring the Scandal," 112.

54. Luther, *Works* 21.299.

55. Luther, *Works* 21.304.

"names," the *nihil* in order to confess it as fundamental to the *ex nihilo* structure of God's Promise of life, of new creation.

As a theologian who sees mirrored in the text of the crucified body of Jesus their own story, a theologian of the cross ultimately arrives at—what for Luther is the aim of the *Heidelberg Disputation*, thesis 28—"The love of God [which] does not find, but creates, that which is pleasing to it."[56] As people of faith who recognize in the crucified text, in the crucified body of Jesus, their own story, their own existence, theologians of the cross are ultimately cast with the crucified Christ upon the love of a God whose creating agency, whose life-giving ways, are concealed *sub contraria specie*, who creates *ex nihilo*. In such a fashion one is delivered, by faith, to the God of creation; to the God who creates from love.

A theologian of the cross constantly comes to terms with a God who does not restlessly ransack the kingdom of being—the academy of Somebodies and Somethings—seeking to confer adulation on those deemed deserving, but instead enters into the formless void, the anti-hierarchy of Nobodies and Nothings, in order to lovingly, deliberately, intimately, mold and breathe life into the vessels of God's love. The theology of the cross' epistemic point of departure will always appear to the Somebodies of this world as an infernal void, a Rubicon-like abyss, below the plane of being and advancement.

Translated into the terms of classical Christology: if the subject of theology for a theologian of the cross is the incarnate, crucified Christ, true God and true man, then—as we have seen—it is a Subject who both mirrors humanity's zero-value, its *nihil*, and reveals God's *ex nihilo*, life-giving presence and agency. With that being the case, the crucified corpse of Christ, or the *genus tapeinoticum*—in the repose of abyssal silence, mangled and exsanguinated of all clues and traces of divine- and self- designation—is the primary text, the primary point of departure, for a theologian of the cross. As the text of Promise's body, Word of God, true God and true man, it is a text—drained of divine designation, suspended in the ambivalence of referential instability according to the calculations and judgments of reason and experience—which reveals the Word's life-creating agency, the *genus majestaticum*, within its lines and margins. It is a text which mirrors the *nihil* of one's existence, one's story; an existence which, perhaps more often than not, appears to reason and experience as one both threaded with ultimate *nihil*, and bounded by an abyss on all sides. It is also the text from which the theologian of the cross is permitted by faith to confess the *nihil* as both fundamental component of Promise's structure, its body, and mask

56. Luther, *Works* 31.57.

of its life-giving agency. A theology whose point of departure is this text—the *genus tapeinoticum*—affords one a location beyond which there is no advance in this life, or one of trusting that the crucified Christ is the revelation of God's life-giving agency. It is a theology which cannot move beyond faith's prayer: "I believe; Help thou mine unbelief!" (Mark 9:24) With regard to elaborating the nature of theological existence the implications are enormous. Ultimately, as we will see, Christology *is* christological existence.

Theological existence is one situated between the revelation of Promise and the experience of the structure, the *nihil*, in which it is hidden. Which means: theology is thoroughgoing Christology, or an existence of comprehensive cruciformity. If the proper subject of theology is *homo peccator et Deus salvator*, or Scripture's unveiling and mirroring of humanity's zero-value, its *nihil*, and the Promise of divine value exchange (all for nothing!), then such a christological framework—a God incarnated into that same zero-value and *nihil* without remainder, or Luther's radical interpretation of the *communicatio idiomatum*—also permits us to articulate the theologian of the cross as one who suffers the incarnate Word's *sub contraria specie* life-giving agency. The experience of theologian of the cross is one of being suspended with the crucified Christ from the cross, confessing, praying, "hoping against hope" (Rom 4:18), that their crucified humanity is the *genus tapeinoticum*, or the mask within which God's life-giving agency, the *genus majestaticum*, is present. Restated: theological existence is one pinned to the cross and thus situated between the revelation of the *ex nihilo* Promise of life and new creation, and the experience of the structure of its communication—its concealment, the *nihil* to which it is bound.

But the subject of Christology is not exhausted here. The subject of Christology is not depleted at the foot of Jesus Christ's cross—his story having become ours, cast in a theological existence with Jesus upon the love of a God whose creating agency is concealed *sub contraria specie*, who creates *ex nihilo*. Christology's subject is not complete until it moves beyond the *with* to include the *in*.

The One, Plural Cross

As Gerhard Forde recognized all too well, the question (observation? Accusation? Lament?) exhaled in abject despair from the cross, "My God, My God, why have you abandoned (*egkatelāpō*) me?" (Mark 15:34) can only be answered, awaited, suffered, in the first person. It can only be awaited within the lines and margins of one's own existence, cast upon the only dynamic which (who!) animates creation, or the love of God who creates *ex nihilo*. "We can only die *with him* and await God's answer in him."[57]

But here a correction is issued. Better, an extension. More than this: *in*; humanity *in* Christ, Christ *in* humanity. Picking up from chapter 2, above, or the development of Luther's Christology, let us recall the discussion of the three modes (at least)[58] of Christ's presence elaborated on the basis of Luther's radical interpretation of the *communicatio idiomatum*.

If the first mode of Christ's presence is his corporeal presence as the historical man Jesus of Nazareth, and the second mode is best exemplified by the place of the "real presence" in the bread and cup of the Lord's Supper, then the third mode places Jesus beyond a circumscribable, recognizable location. It is by means of the third mode of Christ's presence, a necessary expression of the direct communication of the two natures within the person of Jesus Christ, that humanity—in its manifold diversity—may be considered as an expression of the structure of Promise, or the first mode of Christ's presence; a presence which is essentially the matrix and mirror of that same humanity in all of its expressions.

As extensions of the first mode of Christ's presence—as per the third mode of Christ's presence—humanity in its manifold particularity is both a reflection, and expression, of a Promise bound to the fragility and ephemerality, the suffering and death, the *nihil*, of what is. The crosses of humanity—far from being reduced to signifiers, windows, and transparencies of the cross of Jesus Christ—*are confessed* to be the masks of God's ubiquitous, life-giving creativity; the body of Promise. Such a reality was captured by Regin Prenter when he asserted that "The deep truth of Luther's theology

---

57. Forde, *On Being a Theologian of the Cross*, 3.

58. Following Luther's elaboration of the third mode of Christ's presence Luther asserts, "*I do not wish to have denied by the foregoing* [elaboration of the modes of Christ's presence] *that God may have and know still other modes whereby Christ's body can be in a given place.* My only purpose was to show what crass fools our fanatics are when they concede only the first, circumscribed mode of presence to the body of Christ although they are unable to prove that even this mode is contrary to our view. For I do not want to deny in any way that God's power is able to make a body be simultaneously in many places, even in a corporeal and circumscribed manner. For who wants to try to prove that God is unable to do that? Who has seen the limits of his power? The fanatics may indeed think that God is unable to do it, but who will believe their speculations? How will they establish the truth of that kind of speculation?" Luther, *Book of Concord*, 610–11. Italics mine. Essentially, the point is this: Luther's Christology, the expression of his radical interpretation of the *communicatio idiomatum*, is only limited by one's understanding of God's agency. As radical as "three modes of Christ's presence" may be for many Lutherans, this number may only be "scratching the surface" of Christology's subject matter.

of the cross is that it views the cross of Golgotha and the cross which is laid upon us as *one* and the same."[59]

But with the *communicatio idiomatum* elaborated as to its logic and implications, perhaps, as has been demonstrated throughout this project, theological points are conveyed more profoundly, their impressions made more vivid, in the medium of art than they are in the tedious, prosaic medium—the words—of the theologian. It is this reality which will now be exploited for the sake of the project.

To the left of the desk at which I write hangs a print.

Matthias Grünewald, *Crucifixion* (1512–1516)
Unterlinden Museum, Colmar, France

It hangs adjacent to Holbein's *The Body of the Dead Christ in the Tomb.* At the center of the print is the crucified Christ. He is hanging from a cross, its transverse bar slightly bent, indicating the pull of his—now—dead weight, which appears to be planted on a river bank. Crowning a tilted, slack-jawed head which rests on a chest that bears the outline of its bones— eyes half open and mouth frozen in a post-mortem yawn—is a wreath of

59. Prenter, *Luther's Theology of the Cross*, 18.

thorns that appear more like a cluster of spikes. The arms, unnaturally elon-
gated, appear to sprout into spasmed hands which have been hammered-
through with nails whose appearance is that of railroad spikes. The fingers
expressing the—now crystallized—full bloom of pulsating pain, a flowering
upward frozen in death. The shoulders appear to be dislocated, perhaps,
as well, giving credence to the bowing of the transvers bar, perhaps as well
testifying to the agony of a body from which the inhabitant could not twist,
turn, and contort in order to tear himself to freedom. The feet, right on top
of left, bear a spike that runs through them to the vertical beam. Both traced
down the right side of his chest and emanating from the feet are trails of
blood now viscous in post-mortem ebb. The flesh of the toes and toenails
appear rotten, resembling large chunks of Roquefort.

It is a print of Matthias Grünewald's *Crucifixion*. The original painting
itself is part of a much larger work, or the Isenheim Altarpiece, which is a
wooden polyptich consisting of nine panels mounted on two sets of fold-
ing wings. The Isenheim Altarpiece was created between 1512 and 1516 by
artists Niclaus of Haguenau (in charge of the sculpting) and Grünewald (in
charge of the painting) to serve as the focal point of devotion in the Isenheim
hospital which was established and run by the Brothers of St. Anthony.[60]

It was at the Isenheim hospital that the Brothers of St. Anthony committed themselves to the treatment of ill and dying peasants. Though the
Brothers of St. Anthony treated sufferers of the plague, it is also said that a
great many of the peasants who were treated were afflicted with a disease
common to the Middle Ages, popularly known as "St. Anthony's fire," called
ergotism. This illness from which many languished and died excruciating
deaths is now known to have been caused by the consumption of rye flour
contaminated by a fungus—ergot—which grows on rye grass. The ergot
fungus contains a chemical that was not only responsible for hallucinations
and the compromised central nervous systems of its victims resulting in
death, but a profound skin infection manifested by the appearance of gangrenous, pox perforated appendages—hands and feet—brought about by a
constriction of blood flow to the extremities.

But of all that can be said regarding a description of Grünewald's
ghastly crucified Christ, the wounds, the viscous streams blood, the traces
of an abject suffering frozen by death, perhaps the most salient affliction
and theologically significant features depicted in Grünewald's crucified
Christ is the gangrenous-green tinted body and the corpse beaded with pox
marks. For if it is the crucifixion—the cross with its vertical and horizontal

---

60. See Hickson, "Grünewald, *Isenheim Altarpiece*"; Musee Unterlinden, "Isenheim
Altarpiece."

beams, its horrific nail and spear wounds and grotesque manner of death, a body exsanguinated of all sign of divine reference—that expresses the once-for-all-ness, the historical particularity of the first-century crucifixion of Jesus Christ, and with it—according to the theology of the cross—the epistemological locus of God's presence and activity among God's people, it is through the gangrenous-green tint of the corpse and the body-covering pus-filled pox marks that that crucified Christ transcends his historical particularity. In this case it is a transcendence which expresses—mirrors—the cruciformity of God's people at Isenheim. In the gangrenous corpse and the pox-dotted flesh the sufferers of Isenheim, those entrusted to the Brothers of St. Anthony, would have seen reflected in the crucified Christ's corpse their own illness and suffering, their own crucifixion, their own horrific end. Grünewald's *Crucifixion* captures the horrific reality of both the crucifixion's historical particularity, and manner by which the crucifixion mirrors the cruciformity of God's people: the cross not simply "for us," but "in us." Grünewald's work manages to express both the locus of God's recognition in the crucified Christ, and the manner by which that same cruciformity extends beyond its first century particularity, ultimately expressing the structure, the body, of Promise writ-large.

And if it is the case that Grünewald's *Crucifixion* was intended both as a "point of identification" and as a thaumaturgic (for those whose gaze rested on the image of the crucified Christ) for the afflicted residents of Isenheim,[61] then certainly it may be proper to speak of that thaumaturgical dynamic according to which Promise—its structure—has been articulated throughout this project: in the image of the crucified Christ their community found themselves reflected as expressions of the life, the new creation, his crucified corpse conceals; extensions of a Promise bound to the fragility and ephemerality, the affliction and suffering, the *nihil*, of existence, of who they are.

Could it be that Grünewald simply "beat to the punch" with paint and brush what Luther's theology, and thus Christology, implied, yet left for a more fuller development? What this project—working within the trajectory of Luther's *theologia crucis* and his corresponding Christology, or his radical interpretation of *communicatio idiomatum*—has labored to birth through ink and paper? There is no historical justification for drawing such a conclusion, namely, one beyond that of Grünewald rendering the crucified Christ in solidarity with the suffering of the community, as a mirror in whom members of the community saw their condition reflected. Regardless, recognizing that expressions of truth—especially theological truth—are often

---

61. See Hickson, "Grünewald, *Isenheim Altarpiece*."

not tied to conscious intention, perhaps are we able—with christological justification!—to perceive as expressed on Grünewald's canvas the reality this project has labored to delineate, namely: the plurality of the one cross of Christ, the diversity of expression of the crucified One.

Conclusion

Chapter 3 began before the text of the New Testament, its Jesus, especially as expressed by the Synoptic Gospels, with Albert Schweitzer's detection of textual silence, its gaps of narration with regard to the life of Jesus, its seams of redaction, the seemingly *de novo* historical derivation of Jesus' eschatological expression, and ultimately the abyssal silence of the crucifixion itself. All of which caused Schweitzer to appropriate the text, its narrative of Jesus, as a "window" to the "timeless" value to be discovered beyond it. Ultimately—in chapter 4—Luther's *theologia crucis* and his corresponding Christology have permitted us to delineate a dynamic diametrically different.

Through a development and application of Luther's *communicatio idiomatum*, and specifically by means of the third mode of Christ's crucified presence, we have been able to perceive that humanity in its manifold particularity is, as well, an expression of this body of Promise. The text of such a Promise—the incarnate Word of God, true God and true man—is the *genus tapeinoticum* writ-large. The *genus tapeinoticum* writ-large is the text of the third mode of Christ's presence, the body of Promise. Mirrored in the crucified body of Christ, it is also an extension, an expression, of that same body of Promise. As the *genus tapeinoticum* writ-large, this crucified text—the One, Plural Cross—is the revelation of Promise's *ex nihilo*, life-giving agency, or the *genus majestaticum*. Within the crucified body of Promise, the incarnate One, true God and true man, is both humanity's *nihil* and humanity's destiny, its life, with the Triune God.

To be sure, the *genus tapeinoticum* and the *genus majesticum* are not merely outdated categories of an ancient Christology substantially delineated, or only terms to be theoretically navigated and esoterically related. Instead, they are the categories of christological existence determined by the structure, the body, of Promise, its unity perceived by the eyes of faith created from the cross. It is a christological existence, an expression of the *genus tapeinoticum* writ-large, which is the mask of Promise's *ex nihilo* creating presence, or the *genus majestaticum*. Indeed, as has been developed within this project, Christology—what Luther's radical interpretation of the *communicatio idiomatum* should be freed from the province of dogmatism and arid confessional orthodoxy to express—is ultimately an existence suffering the concealment of Promise's revelation. It is an existence of praying against the temptation born of reason's calculations and experience's judgments and conclusions that within the *nihil* stirs the presence of Promise's *ex nihilo* creating agency, that they are an inseparable unity as the Word of God, the body of Promise, an incarnate, crucified Word expressive of the Triune God's commitment to this creation. Christological existence is one which suffers the *sub contrario* creating agency of the body of Promise.

A Christology which reflects the concealed revealing of its Subject, the crucified Christ, the Word of God, true God and true man, will issue in a faith, a christological existence, concealed *sub contrario*, as well. So Luther asserted,

> Hence in order that there may be room for faith, it is necessary that everything which is believed should be hidden. It cannot, however, be more deeply hidden than under an object, perception, or experience which is contrary to it. Thus when God makes alive he does it by killing, when he justifies he does it by making men guilty, when he exalts to heaven he does it by bringing down to hell.[62]

The revelation of God's life-giving agency through the Word, or proper work, must be believed against what experience registers and reason judges to be abandonment, divine absence, or better God's wrath, or strange work.[63] Faith is a constant flight, a movement, from the hidden God of reason and experience's assessment to the life-giving Word of God revealed *sub contraria specie*. That one is able to confess the strange work of God, indeed that one is an expression of the *genus tapeinoticum* writ-large, means that faith has apprehended the revealed Word, that it has apprehended the presence of Promise's life-creating agency, the loving agency through whom one's life is created and sustained; that it has apprehended its existence within the body of Promise. Christological existence is one that confesses its cruciformity to be the experience and expression of the body of Promise.

If, as Vítor Westhelle asserted, "Theology is properly done *in usu passionis*, at the foot of the cross,"[64] then ultimately we can confess that the untold, countless number of humanity's narratives—its sufferings, its deaths, the ultimate, abyssal silence of its graves, its *nihil*—are not merely the "foot of the cross," but indeed the crucified body of Christ itself. With him. In him. Him in us. This body of plurality—we pray, we confess, we "hope

62. Luther, *Works* 33.52.

63. See Luther, *Works* 21.301. For a description of the "strange" and "proper work" of God, see Steinmetz, "Luther and the Hidden God," 23–31.

64. Westhelle, "Enduring the Scandal," 120.

against hope" (Rom 4:18)—is the body of Promise; the Promise of *nihil*. It is the Text of Promise.

Experience understands the suspended struggle involved in such a confession. It is a christological existence, a Christology suspended from the cross.

We are left with both life's sober experiences and observations and faith's breakthrough, or confession, always a mixture, both converging on a single truth:

there is one Crucified, and he is plural.

Moving to chapter 5, we will observe this dynamic, this christological existence, this *christologia crucis*, narrated by Luther through the media of both proclamation and lecture.

Interlude

A "Heaven-storming" or "Creation-bound" Christology?

Heinrich Schmid, in his seminal textbook on classical Lutheran theology entitled *The Doctrinal Theology of the Evangelical Lutheran Church*, presents the doctrine of the two natures, their relationship, of Christ—the *communicatio idiomatum*—according to a taxonomy consisting of three genera (see Introduction, above).[1] Let us, briefly, rehearse that taxonomy.

According to Schmid's outline the first genus is the *idiomatic* genus which refers to the ascription of attributes of both natures—divine and human—to the person of Jesus Christ. The second genus, the *genus majestaticum*, refers to the human nature's participation in the divine attributes within the person of Jesus Christ. The *genus apotelesmaticum* is the third genus in Schmid's taxonomy of the two natures of Christ. The *genus apotelesmaticum* refers to the genus in which operations of the person of Christ may be ascribed to either of the two natures in a manner peculiar to their respective nature. Indeed, the *genus majestaticum* became the distinctive feature of classical Lutheranism and the funding source for the sacramental rally cry *"finitum est capax infiniti"* (the finite bears/is capable of the infinite).

---

1. This taxonomy can be traced back to the *Formula of Concord* (1580), and before that, to Martin Chemnitz.

120

For Karl Barth, though, it was just this distinctive feature of classical Lutheranism that became enigmatic for contemporary theology, blurring the lines—to say the least, for Barth—between Christology and anthropology. Although much ink has been spilled on Barth's theology in general, and Christology in particular, it is his criticism of classical Lutheranism's *communicatio idiomatum* that will be developed here.

To be sure, having elaborated in his *Church Dogmatics*, specifically, paragraph 64 ("The Exultation of the Son of Man"),[2] "the Lutheran doctrine of the so-called second genus of the *communication idiomatum*—the *genus majestaticum*—a name which it owes to the fact that the *Filius Dei majestatem suam divinam asumptae carni communicavit*,"[3] Barth raises the question as to the "real meaning and intention" of this "special Lutheran theory," this "remarkable train of thought." Never vacating his sympathetic capacity even amid the wind-ups of his most profound criticisms, Barth asserts

> We have to realise that for all its curious and alien features the reality of the high grace of the reconciliation of the world with God, the perfection of the fellowship established between God and man, and the presence and efficacy of God in our human sphere, are all taken with final and total seriousness. An attempt is made to think out to the very last the fact and extent that all this did and does take place in Jesus Christ the one Son of God and Son of Man. If we, too, take this seriously, if we, too, think it out to the end, and if we are clear that the decisive word must be spoken in Christology, and particularly in an understanding of the humanity of Jesus Christ, we cannot keep our distance from at least the intention of this theologoumenon, which is so closely akin to the distinctive Eastern Christology and soteriology of the Greek fathers.[4]

No amount of sympathetic consideration for this "special Lutheran theory," though, could dissuade Barth from his conclusion that "when all this has been said, it has also to be perceived and said that this intention cannot be executed as attempted along these lines."[5] That is, such "train of thought," the Lutheran *genus majestaticum*, though unquestionably originally an expression of the attempt to hold the unity of Christ's person in general, and the humanity of Christ in particular, in high regard, was perceived by Barth only to reinforce the transformation of Christology into

2. Barth, *Church Dogmatics*, 4.2.3–377.

3. Barth, *Church Dogmatics*, 4.2.77.

4. Barth, *Church Dogmatics*, 4.2.78–79.

5. Barth, *Church Dogmatics*, 4.2.79.

anthropology, a transformation Barth had diagnosed from F.D.E. Schleiermacher through Ludwig Feuerbach. In the process, such a formulation
seemed, for Barth, to dissolve the objective, particular revelation of Jesus
Christ in AD 1–30 into something less objective and historically particular;
into something more amorphous and indissoluble and indistinguishable
from Christian existence.

With the once-for-all, objective, historical, particular revelation of
Jesus Christ in mind, Barth adds,

> But does not a recognition of the reality of the atonement as
> it has taken place in Jesus Christ, of the perfection of the new
> fellowship established in Him between God and man, and of the
> presence and efficacy of God in the human sphere as guaranteed
> by Him, imply that the look which we direct at Him, and at the
> act of God which has taken place in Him, should be not merely
> openly but totally directed at Him and Him alone, as a look at
> the Victor and His victory, to use our earlier expression, or at
> His giving and our corresponding receiving, at the history as
> such takes place between God and man in Jesus Christ?[6]

Thus, for Barth, the "Lutheran" *communicatio idiomatum* as it came to expression in the *genus majestaticum* not only detracted from the *illic et tunc*
history of what took place between God and man in the revelation of Jesus
Christ, but also muddled and compromised what was meant by the "true
deity" and the "true humanity" of Jesus Christ. So again, Barth:

> [D]id they look only at the given happening as such, the victory
> which took place in the history, looking away from the event of
> the divine giving and human receiving to what is given to the
> human essence of Jesus Christ in this event, to a status mediated
> to Him in this event? What is really meant by the humanity of
> Jesus Christ as it is appropriated and illuminated and inter-pen-
> etrated by His deity—loaded, as it were, with His deity, because
> participant in all its attributes? The objection can obviously
> be brought at once against this view that it is a strange deity
> which can suddenly become the predicate of human essence,
> and a strange humanity to which all the divine predicates can
> suddenly be ascribed as subject. Does not this compromise both
> the true deity and the true humanity of Jesus Christ? Does it not
> involve either a deification of the creature or humanization of
> the Creator, or both?[7]

6. Barth, *Church Dogmatics*, 4.2.79.
7. Barth, *Church Dogmatics*, 4.2.79.

But, if Barth has detected in the "Lutheran" *genus majestaticum* a detraction from the *illic et tunc* history of what was accomplished in the revelation of Jesus Christ, abstracting the "humanity" of Jesus from this once-for-all, objective history—this event—of revelation, in addition to compromising "true deity" and "true humanity," Barth's criticism of this "special Lutheran theory" has yet to reach a crescendo.

If Barth's theology, in so many ways, was critical of, and developed in reaction to, the transformation of Christology into anthropology which he had detected from Schleiermacher to Feuerbach, then Barth detected in the *genus majestaticum* something insidious. To be sure, in the *genus majestaticum* Barth detected the Rubicon beyond which this transformation would become complete. With the ubiquity of Christ's humanity, or the "Lutheran" *genus majestaticum*, in his crosshairs, Barth asserts, "[W]hen it speaks of a divinization of human essence in Jesus Christ, and when this divinization of the flesh of Jesus Christ is understood as the supreme and final purpose of the incarnation . . . a highly equivocal situation is created."[8] Though Barth recognizes that such a "train of thought"—the *genus majestaticum*—is articulated only within the sphere of Christology, and thus only with reference to the humanity of the one Jesus Christ, the trajectory from Schleiermacher to Feuerbach for contemporary theology, and thus Christology, begs the question: "But how are we to guard against a deduction which is very near the surface, which once it is seen is extremely tempting, and once accepted very easy to draw, but which can compromise at a single stroke nothing less than the whole of Christology?"[9] Elaborating his point, Barth asks, "For after all, is not the humanity of Jesus Christ, by definition, that of all men? And even if it said only of Him, does not this mean that the essence of all men . . . is capable of divinization? If it can be said in relation to Him, why not to all men?"[10] If such is the case, then Barth asserts, "[I]n Christology a door is left wide open . . . from the very heart of the Christian faith" itself.[11] Barth adds (quoting the rest of his assessment of the *genus majestaticum* liberally):

> And through this door it is basically free for anyone to wander right away from Christology. Who is to prevent him? For, as we have seen, what is said is not said strictly and exclusively in relation to Jesus Christ Himself, but with a side glance at the abstraction of the "human nature" of Jesus Christ, at what the

8. Barth, *Church Dogmatics*, 4.2.81.

9. Barth, *Church Dogmatics*, 4.2.81.

10. Barth, *Church Dogmatics*, 4.2.81.

11. Barth, *Church Dogmatics*, 4.2.81.

union with the divine nature in Jesus Christ means for it. The reservation with which its divinization was asserted was, of course, that it is that of *His* human nature. But the reservation itself was and is quite unable to set aside the suspicions which necessarily arise against the concept of this divinized human nature as such. And quite obviously it cannot meet the question whether the christological bracket in which the divinization is asserted may not be dissolved, and everyone be free to stride through the door opened by this concept, and away from the christological centre. But where does the way through this door lead? It obviously leads smoothly and directly to anthropology: and not to a dull naturalistic and moralistic anthropology, but to a "high-pitched" anthropology; to the doctrine of a humanity which is not only capable of deification, but already deified, or at any rate on the point of apotheosis or deification. If the supreme achievement of Christology, its final word, is the apotheosized flesh of Jesus Christ, omnipotent, omnipresent and omniscient, deserving of our worship, is it not merely a hard shell which conceals the sweet kernel of the divinity of humanity as a whole and as such, a shell which we can confidently discard and throw away once it has performed this service?[12]

Thus, in the footnote following, Barth presses the point of the *genus majestaticum* opening, from the center of Christology (this Trojan Horse of all Trojan Horses!), wide the door to a "high pitched anthropology" when he offers this line of questioning:

Is not its characteristic inversion of above and below, heaven and earth, God and man, a realization, at bottom, of the possibility which as the apotheosis of human nature had long since been prefigured by the Lutheran form of the doctrine of the *idiomata*, although still enclosed in this christological shell? Was Hegel so wrong after all when he thought that he could profess to be a good Lutheran? Was it mere impudence that L. Feuerbach usually liked to appeal to Luther for his theory of the identity of the divine with human essence, and therefore of God's becoming man which is really the manifestation of man become God?[13]

To be sure, Barth asserts in his footnote,

It is far from our purpose to suggest that Luther and Lutheranism ever intended all this. But it can hardly be denied that with

12. Barth, *Church Dogmatics*, 4.2.81–82.
13. Barth, *Church Dogmatics*, 4.2.82–83.

their heaven-storming doctrine of the humanity of the Media-
tor they did actually prepare the way for the distinctive modern
transition from theology to a speculative anthropology.[14]

If the Lutherans argued that the *communicatio idiomatum* highlighted
the absolute uniqueness of God's revelation in Jesus Christ, then, ultimately,
Barth drew another set of conclusions. For Barth the "Lutheran" *communicatio idiomatum*, and, specifically, the *genus majestaticum*, not only detracted, diminished the once-for-all, objective and particular event of God's
revelation in Jesus Christ (perhaps even, in the trajectory of Schleiermacher,
to an element of inward experience, thus making Jesus and humanity only
quantitatively different by degrees), but put in place the "final nail" for the
"coffin" of the complete inversion of theology's subject matter, apotheosizing
humanity in the process. Though its development is beyond the scope of this
project, Barth would respond by elaborating the *communicatio gratiarum*.

To be sure, the "bone to be picked" with Barth does not concern his
critique of "Lutheranism's" doctrine of the two natures, as such. The reader
will notice that the present interlude began with Schmid's taxonomy of the
two natures of Jesus Christ in order to provide a point of reference for
Barth's analysis. Indeed, within the parameters of this project the Christology of "Lutheranism" (referred to earlier in the Introduction, above, as
"classical Lutheran theology") warrants a severe critique. But whether or
not it contributes—when ripped from its original christological context—
to a "heaven-storming" Christology is up for debate. That is for another
project. Rightly or wrongly, Barth was interpreting "Lutheran" Christology
through a powerful set of lenses: the inversion of theology's subject matter
from Schleiermacher through to the liberal, German theology of such folks
as A. Ritschl and W. Herrmann. One could argue that he was practicing
eis-egesis with regard to "Lutheranism's" two natures doctrine on this point,
pulling it from the context of its original christological intention in order
for it to fit snugly within the trajectory of Schleiermacher and Hegel and
Feuerbach.

The fundamental matter, though, involves the distinction which
Barth failed to make with regard to Luther and "Lutheranism." If it was the
taxonomy of the relationship of the two natures presented in the manner
of Schmid—the *idiomatic* genus, the *genus majestaticum*, and the *genus
apotelismaticum*—that funds Barth's analysis of "Lutheranism's" *genus
majestaticum*, then, from Luther's perspective, such a presentation is a
mischaracterization. Such a delineation of the two natures both omits the
fundamental point of departure of his *theologia crucis*, one which determines

14. Barth, *Church Dogmatics*, 4.2.83.

his whole Christology—the crucified man Jesus, or the *genus tapeinoticum*, and also errs in the manner by which the two natures are related. From Luther's perspective it is an elaboration of the *communicatio idiomatum* that is only partial, incomplete at best.

There is no question that a comparison of Luther's and Schmid's taxonomies elaborating their respective understanding of the two natures, their relationship, of Jesus Christ reveals fundamental differences. To be sure, with reference to Schmid's taxonomy—one consisting of the *idiomatic genus* (the attributes of both natures ascribed to the person), the *apotelesmatic genus* (the attributes/operations of the person ascribed to the either of the two natures in a manner respective of their nature; natures mediated by the person of Jesus Christ, thus protecting the immutability of divinity), and the *genus majestaticum* nestled in between—Luther's taxonomy is simpler, more direct.

A taxonomy of Luther's *communicatio idiomatum* would simply entail, on the same line, the *genus tapeinoticum*—as 1A—and the *genus majestaticum*—as 1B. Adjacent one another, directional arrows could be drawn which extend from each in the direction of the other in order to depict direct communication (perhaps with a circle enclosing the two terms to indicate the priority of the personal union).[15] Again, let us be reminded: the *genus tapeinoticum* is the name given to the communication of the human attributes to the divine nature in Christ, while the *genus majestaticum* is the name given to the communication of the divine attributes to the human nature in Christ. If the *genus majestaticum* permits the theological slogan "*finitum capax infiniti*," then the *genus tapeinoticum* permits one to assert that "*infinitum capax finiti*." They are merely necessary expressions of the double, simultaneous transit of natures within the one person of Jesus Christ. The *genus tapeinoticum* expresses the reality that, for Luther, the *theologia crucis*, its point of departure, remains inextricably inscribed into his christological formulation. If "true theology and recognition of God are in the crucified Christ,"[16] then the *genus tapeinoticum* reflects a Christology—commensurate with Luther's *theologia crucis*—*sub contraria specie*.

Whereas Schmid's delineation of the relationship of the two natures, expressed in his taxonomy, attempts to protect an immutable "divinity" from flies, from death, Luther's theology, and thus his *communicatio idiomatum*, not only begins precisely there, in a crucified Christ, but refuses to move beyond such a point of departure. Indeed—in christological terms—such a point of departure, or the crucified humanity of Christ, is communicated to

15. See Luther, *Works* 41.98–103.
16. Luther, *Works* 31.53.

the divine nature in the person of Jesus Christ. The only "divinity" Luther knows is the one that has been crucified, one that attracts flies. To leave such a theological point of departure behind implies that the theology of the cross is merely an initial stage in theological thinking and existence, perhaps one from which, ultimately, more mature, more developed theologians and their christologies are able to press forward.

To be able to leave such a point of departure behind, or a Word of God revealed in the concealment of crucifixion, exsanguinated of all divine reference, would perhaps amount to turning the *theologia crucis* into the first step of a systematized mysticism (could this be just another name for orthodoxy?) in which the recognition of a crucified God is vacated as one grows and evolves in their relation to, and knowledge of, God. To be sure, to vacate such a point of departure will result in the stripping of christological formulations of the methodology from which they originated, or a theological existence suspended between Promise and experience, one of meditation, prayer, and *Anfechtung*. There is, to borrow a phrase from Lessing, a *garstiger breiter Graben* between the theologian who exclusively associates the "faith" (*fides quae creditur,* "faith which is believed") with that which is to be defended, protected (certainly from a perspective of confident, insulated orthodoxy), and one who experiences the "faith" (*fides qua creditur,* "faith by which it is believed") as that which, grounded in a *fides quae* revealed *sub contrario* in the crucified Christ, expresses the discrepancy between Promise and its opposite. The experience of such faith will always consist of as many parts unbelief as it does belief.[17]

Again, recognizing that, for Luther, the *communicatio idiomatum* consists of a double transit of natures within the personal union, to admit only a *genus majestaticum* would be the same as conceding that there is only a partial, incomplete *communicatio idiomatum*. But not only does such an understanding of the *communicatio idiomatum* both render it incomplete and suggest that the theology of the cross is merely an initial phase in theological knowledge, one to be jettisoned when *Anfechtung* falls away, but—ominously—such an incomplete *communicatio idiomatum* would mean that Promise is not underwritten by God's irrevocable death; that the second person of the Trinity, God the Son, really did not die, that God really never had "skin in the game." A testament cannot go into effect unless the testator dies completely.

17. Perhaps it will become clear from a reading of chapter 5 and the final interlude that, for a "Christology from the cross" in the trajectory of the *Heidelberg Disputation*, the *fides qua creditur* and the *fides quae creditur* are, though both concealed *sub contraria specie*, simultaneous realities.

That Barth clearly conflated "classical Lutheran theology's" *communicatio idiomatum* with Luther's is the issue. Such an oversight, such a conflation is unfortunate, even disappointing, especially given the incredible theological acumen and discernment of Barth; especially given his ability to present other theologies—even Schleiermacher's!—so sympathetically. But his conflation does leave us with questions.

To be sure, it is certainly worth asking what conclusions Barth would have made with reference to Luther's delineation of the *communicatio idiomatum*. Would he have concurred with many of those in the intra-Lutheran debates (see the Interlude above) that the *genus tapeinoticum* would have left us with the absence—or at least the appearance of its absence—of divinity? Or would he have concluded that the *genus tapeinoticum* would have left us with a Christology commensurate with its starting point in the *theologia crucis*, a *theologia crucis* whose paradigm of God's unveiling and veiling is so critical to his understanding of revelation, especially as elaborated in paragraph 4 ("The Speech of God as the Mystery of God") of his *Church Dogmatics*?[18] Let us note: Luther is not able to divorce the *modus operandae* of revelation—its hiddenness/revealedness, unveiling/veiling—from its christological substance. Or was the *communcatio idiomatum*—a *genus majestaticum* with or without a *genus tapeinoticum*—from Luther forward simply an enigmatic concoction to begin with, something to be left behind entirely? Was the rehabilitation of *communicatio gratiarum* always, immovably part of Barth's agenda due to his concerns with regard to contemporary theology? At the same time, a "Lutheran" note of caution must be sounded: the *genus tapeinoticum* should never be considered apart from the personal union of Jesus Christ, true God and true. *That* would result in pure anthropology.

Ultimately, were Barth *not* to have conflated Luther with "Lutheranism" on the matter of the *communicatio idiomatum*, would his analysis of Luther's *communicatio idiomatum*, considering its true intention and context—considering Luther's *theologia crucis*, its epistemic point of departure, his refusal to encounter the Word of God apart from the humanity of Christ—have at least gotten within the rubric of his criticism the direction of the movement right? That is, would he at least have declared regarding Luther's Christology that—far from being considered "heaven-storming"— it is "creation-bound"; indeed, a Christology expressive of the Triune God's complete, self-less commitment to creation? Even Barth asserted that one does not know the Word of God apart from its secularity, its twofold

---

18. Barth, *Church Dogmatics*, 1.1.163–86.

indirectness.[19] To criticize Luther's Christology on the terms of its being "creation-bound" would have been sympathetic and accurate. The nature of such a criticism, the distortions such a powerful mind may have uncovered from this perspective, will always beg an answer.

Is it fair to say that Barth's theological agenda—the agenda which conflated Luther with "Lutheranism"—was simply too powerful and blinding to offer a criticism of Luther's Christology from such a "creation-bound" perspective, or that of the *theologia crucis*?

19. Barth, *Church Dogmatics*, 1.1.168.

5

Promise Concealed and Suspended

Luther Narrating Christology

Deeply Buried under the No

> Jesus left that place and went away to the district of Tyre and
> Sidon. Just then a Canaanite woman from that region came out
> and started shouting, "Have mercy on me, Lord, Son of David;
> my daughter is tormented by a demon." But he did not answer
> her at all. And his disciples came and urged him, saying, "Send
> her away, for she keeps shouting after us." He answered, "I was
> sent only to the lost sheep of the house of Israel." But she came
> and knelt before him, saying, "Lord, help me." He answered, "It
> is not fair to take the children's food and throw it to the dogs."
> She said, "Yes, Lord, yet even the dogs eat the crumbs that fall
> from their masters' table." Then Jesus answered her, "Woman,
> great is your faith! Let it be done for you as you wish." And her
> daughter was healed instantly. (Matt 15:21–28)

The woman had heard the report about Jesus. It is on the merit of such a
report, the Promise it harbors, that she approaches Jesus. "What kind of report?" Luther asks in his sermon.[1] Quickly he informs his hearers, "Without

---

1. As far as Martin Luther's sermons go, this 1525 *Lent Postil* on Matt 15:21–28

doubt a good report and reputation that Christ was a godly man and gladly helped everybody. This report about God is a true Gospel and word of grace."[2] Luther adds, "This is the source of the woman's faith, for if she had not believed, she would not have run after him."[3] Following a short digression from the Gospel narrative in which Luther elaborates the relationship between self-knowledge and one's receptivity for Christ, in this case, the way in which "humbled" self-knowledge promotes the latter, and having prepared the sermon's hearers as to the manner by which "Christ drives and pursues faith in His people so that it becomes strong and firm,"[4] Luther digs into the "blow-by-blow" of the interaction between the Canaanite woman and Jesus.

Having approached Jesus on the merit of the report about him, "with sure confidence that He would deal graciously with her according to what was reported about Him,"[5] she experiences the antithesis of what she anticipates. So Luther observes, "But Christ pretends to be completely different, as if He would let her faith and good confidence be wrong and what was reported about Him be false."[6] What the Canaanite woman experiences is a Jesus—according to Luther—who "is as silent as a stump."[7] Luther then conveys—commiserating with his hearers—such an experience: "It is a very hard blow when God appears to be so stern and angry and hides His grace so very deeply. This is well known by those who feel and experience it in their hearts and think that He will not do what He has said and will let His Word be false."[8]

But how does the woman react to the deafening, divine silence? Is she deterred, driven-off? "She turns her eyes away from His unfriendly appearance, is not misled by all of that, does not dwell on it, but clings steadily and firmly to her confidence in the good report she had heard and grasped about Him, and does not cease."[9] Indeed, we may say, Luther presents her as a theologian par excellence, or one whose existence is situated between Promise ("the good report") and the experience of that Promise; a Promise concealed within the silence of the very One who is confessed to mediate it.

("The Canaanite Woman's Faith" according to the NRSV subheading) is by no means long, a mere four-and-a-half pages in the American Edition of Luther's *Works*. Yet, for the purpose of this project its implications are rather profound. See Luther, *Works* 76.378–82: "Gospel for the Second Sunday in Lent."

2. Luther, *Works* 76.378.

3. Luther, *Works* 76.378.

4. Luther, *Works* 76.378.

5. Luther, *Works* 76.379.

6. Luther, *Works* 76.379.

7. Luther, *Works* 76.379.

8. Luther, *Works* 76.379.

9. Luther, *Works* 76.379.

In the discord between Promise and experience, Luther asserts, she brackets out experience and clings only to the "good report," the Promise she has heard, the Promise which has driven her to Jesus.

At this point Luther the pastor pauses the story to press the point for his hearers. That is, we must do likewise, learning "to cling firmly to His Word alone, even if God with all His creatures would act differently than this Word says about Him. How it hurts nature and reason when, in destitution, she takes off, and leaves behind everything she senses, and clings to the bare Word alone,"[10] even when she senses the opposite. Though "experience alone makes a theologian,"[11] one—a theologian of the cross—does not confuse experience as the guarantor of the Promise. The experience which makes one a theologian is the undergoing of the discrepancy between the Promise heard and what the self sees and experiences.

"Second," Luther continues, "when her outcry and faith do not help, the disciples step forward with their faith and plead for her; they think that they will certainly be heard [Matt 15:23]."[12] Luther adds, "When they think that He should become gentler, He becomes all the more harsh and lets both their faith and their plea miss their goal, as she sees and senses. He is no longer silent and does not let them doubt, but rejects their plea and says, 'I was not sent except to the lost sheep of the house of Israel' [Matt 15:24]."[13] According to this interpretation of the text, as Luther points out, "This blow is still harsher, since not only our own person is repudiated but also that comfort is rejected which we still have, namely, the comfort and intercession of godly and holy people."[14] Jesus will not even consider the plea of his own associates with regard to this woman. But the core issue is named, and it is one of eternal alienation. Luther speaking for Christ: "Yes, it is true. I hear every plea, but I have made that promise to the house of Israel."[15] Again, Luther pauses the Gospel narrative to convey the woman's experience of the alienation to his hearers, to existentialize the narrative, so to speak:

> What do you think? Is that not a thunderbolt that dashes both
> heart and faith into a thousand pieces, when we feel that God's

10. Luther, *Works* 76.379.

11. Luther, *Works* 54.7.

12. This section of the sermon does not reflect the Gospel narrative in v. 23 in which the disciples come to Jesus urging him, "saying, 'Send her away, for she keeps shouting after us.'" One can argue on solid grounds that Luther has inserted the matter of the deficiency of intermediaries in order to eliminate intercession as a category of evangelical theology, a theology grounded in justification by faith.

13. Luther, *Works* 76.379.

14. Luther, *Works* 76.379.

15. Luther, *Works* 76.380.

Word, on which we build, was not spoken to us but applies [only] to others? Here all saints and intercession are at a standstill, and the heart must abandon the Word, if it would stick with its own perceptions.[16]

But the woman, against experience, remains with the priority of the report about Jesus. She will not be driven off. "She clings to the Word, even though it is being forcefully torn out of her heart. She does not turn away from His stern answer, but still trusts firmly that His goodness is still hidden behind it."[17] The Canaanite woman does what any theologian of the cross would do: she doubles down on the "good report," the Promise about Jesus, against the contrary experience, or the experience of the Promise of life concealed under the form of its opposite (*sub contraria specie*), whether that be silence or a resounding *no*. A theologian of the cross doubles down on Promise against the experience of its absence, clinging like a vice-grip to the One reputed to have uttered such a Word.

But the woman is relentless. "Third," Luther continues, "she runs after Him into the house . . . perseveres, falls down before Him, and says, 'Lord, help me!'"[18] And it is precisely here that the crescendo of judgment hits its highest pitch. For it is here that "she gets the final deathblow, when He says directly to her . . . that she is a dog and unworthy to share the children's bread [Matt 15:26]. What will she say to this? He simply asserts that she is one of the damned and lost, who is not to be numbered among the elect."[19] So, Luther tells his hearers, "That is an answer that can never be contested, one that no one can get past. Yet she does not cease, but concedes His judgment and grants that she is a dog."[20] Conceding his judgment, she asks for no more than a dog's allotment, or the crumbs that fall from their master's table.

"Is not that a masterpiece?"[21] exclaims Luther. Such is the beauty of the narrative. Not only does she defiantly hold the "good report," the Promise, up to Jesus, clinging to it against the experience of its absence, employing the Promise against Jesus himself, but this time—Luther quickly adds—"She clutches at Christ's own words. He compares her to a dog; she grants that and asks nothing more than that He would let her be a dog, as He Himself

16. Luther, *Works* 76.380.
17. Luther, *Works* 76.380.
18. Luther, *Works* 76.380.
19. Luther, *Works* 76.380.
20. Luther, *Works* 76.380.
21. Luther, *Works* 76.380.

had judged her to be."[22] You have judged me a dog? Then let me receive the Promise as it befits a dog.

Luther steps back from the narrative with only a verse or two yet to be expounded and declares to his hearers regarding this story, that it "was written for all our comfort and instruction, so that we may know how deeply God hides His grace from us, so that we would not consider Him according to our perception and thinking but strictly according to His Word."[23] But it is also here that Luther connects the story to the "real time" of his listeners' lives.

That is, having asserted that, "Here you see that though Christ pretends to be harsh, yet He gives no final judgment when He says, 'No.' Rather," Luther elaborates, "all His answers sound like no, but they are not no—they are undecided and pending."[24] The closed Gospel narrative is opened out by Luther, its closure suspended, in order to implicate his hearers into the discrepancy, experienced by the Canaanite woman as narrated by the Gospel story, between Promise and the experience of its absence, or a *no* which comes first in the form of divine silence and subsequently as divine judgment. He adds, "He does not say, 'I will not listen to you,' but is silent and says neither yes nor no. So also He does not say that she is not of the house of Israel, but that He was sent only to the house of Israel [Matt 15:24]. Thus He leaves it undecided and pending between *no* and *yes*."[25]

It is this "undecided and pending" experience, this as of yet outstanding answer—*yes* or *no*—which casts one into the chasm, the discrepancy, in which true theology begins, armed with a Promise and no experience, no sensory-derived data to back it up. Not only has Luther the preacher suspended the story's ending, inviting his hearers into the woman's discrepancy, but he refuses to give his hearers the closure they have not experienced for themselves; he will not relieve his hearers of their own suspendedness within the chasm between God's *yes* and *no*. Though the suspension of the answer, its undecidedness and the experience of its undecidability, seems to argue more for a *no* than a *yes*, Luther asserts the contrary is, in fact, at work. "In fact, *there is only yes there* [cf. 1 Cor 1:19–20], but it is very deep and secret, and it looks only like no."[26]

In summary fashion Luther asserts, "This points out the condition of our heart in temptation. As it perceives, so Christ acts. [Our heart] thinks

22. Luther, *Works* 76.380.

23. Luther, *Works* 76.380.

24. Luther, *Works* 76.380–81.

25. Luther, *Works* 76.381.

26. Luther, *Works* 76.381. Italics are mine.

there is nothing else but only no, and yet that is untrue. Therefore, it must turn away from this perception and with a firm faith in God's Word grasp and hold onto the deep, secret yes under and above the no, as this woman does."[27] The Word's life-creating *yes* (Gospel) remains deeply concealed within the Word's life-crucifying *no* (Law) to sinners. The life-giving, or proper work, of God's Promise must always be believed against what experience registers and reason judges to be abandonment, or better, God's wrath, or strange work.[28] If, in Luther's words, faith can be considered a movement in which one "flees from and finds refuge in God against God,"[29] the refuge is one that remains concealed to experience and reason. But as Luther points out, faith is more than embracing the epistemic irony of its object—the *yes* concealed in the *no*, the proper work concealed in the strange work. Fundamentally it begins with the embrace of judgment.

As Luther asserts, "When we grant that God is right in His judgment against us, then we have won and caught Him in His own words."[30] Luther elaborates:

> We certainly say with our mouths that we are sinners, but when God Himself says this in our hearts, then we no longer stand, and we desperately desire to be godly and regarded as the godly, as long as we would be free from His judgment. But it must be so: if God is to be just in His words [Ps. 51:4] that you are a sinner, then you can make use of the right which God has given to every sinner, namely the forgiveness of sins. Then you not only eat the crumbs under the table like the dogs, but you also are a child [of God] and have God as your own, just as you want.[31]

At the core of faith's movement, within the trajectory of its epistemic point of departure—a crucified God—is the acceptance of God's judgment, the *no*, which categorically crucifies all anthropologically initiated

---

27. Luther, *Works* 76.381.

28. For a description to the "strange" and "proper work" of God, see Steinmetz, "Luther and the Hidden God," 23–31.

29. "*Ad deum contra deum confungere.*" Luther, *Werke* 5, 204, 26–27.

30. Luther, *Works* 76.381.

31. Luther, *Works* 76.382. Iwand asserts, "For the righteousness of God is the categorical precondition for faith. Faith means to take God's judgment on oneself: to trust in his promise and to accept his forgiveness. When we give God justice, we act on the first condition of faith even when we don't know where this step will lead. Both are inseparable from one another and interpreted in terms of the other. So it is clear that the concept of giving God justice conveys the condition that in faith a person takes a decisively judging position *for* God *against* himself." Iwand, *Righteousness of Faith according to Luther*, 21.

avenues—whether they be epistemologically or emotionally commandeered or funded by some combination of law, works, and free will—of demanding, laying-claim to, what will only be gifted. The *yes*, the Promise—concealed deeply in the *no*—will not be taken, only patiently awaited and received. Acceptance of the *no* justifies the life-giving agency—wisdom!—of God, an agency whose *ex nihilo* manner both obviates all direct seizures of Promise's content, and reveals the *nihil* for what it is apart from God's agency.

Christology Narrated in the First Person

Though, at first blush, Luther's sermon on the Canaanite woman may be employed to express the manner by which he describes the movement of faith, its paradigmatic experience which corresponds to the hiddenness of its object, something more fundamental is being expressed. Indeed, Luther is—in the medium of sermon, proclamation—articulating a Christology whose content—a Promise buried deeply *sub contraria specie*; one suffered and now proclaimed—uniquely permits narration, and thus the addressing of the real-time experiences of his listeners. Shaped by its point of departure, or the *sub contraria specie* revelation of God's Promise, God's *yes*, is a Christology—now in narrative form—whose divine content remains concealed, suspended between an undecided *yes* and *no* for the lives—the narratives of Luther's listeners, the manifold narratives of humanity—that are encompassed by the scope and agency of the Promise it conveys. Ultimately this suspendedness, as with the case with the Canaanite woman, is resolved for the person of faith who has come to perceive through the Holy Spirit God's strange work as the revelation of God's proper work.

If Luther's radical interpretation of the *communicatio idiomatum* ultimately permitted us to translate its genera—the *genus tapeinoticum* and the *genus majestaticum*—into categories of christological existence within the body of Promise, the former—humanity understood through the third mode of Christ's presence as the *genus tapeinoticum* writ-large—confessing that it is the mask of the life-giving agency of the latter, then by means of the medium of the sermon Luther is also able to expound this same Christology existentially, this time in narrative form. To be sure, Luther's Christology, as evidenced by his short *Lent Postil* of 1525, above, uniquely mirrors, and thus narrates, the experiences of its listeners, the suspendedness and undecidedness of those who exist between the "good report," or the Promise, and the experience of its silence, its absence in real-time; of those situated between Promise and world, between *yes* and *no*. It is a waiting existence which, experiencing what seems to be an interminable *no*, trusts that God's *yes* has been decisively revealed in the crucified Christ.

Needless to say, theology, for Luther, cannot be reduced to an academic vocation. Instead, the circle of theology's practitioners, for Luther, reflects the breadth his Christology permits, or the scope of Promise's confessed structure and agency. To be sure, as the Canaanite woman's story indicates, theology is practiced by those who are able discern God's strange work in service of God's proper, life-giving work; by those who are able to double down on God's *yes* against the experience of God's *no*.

Taking our bearings from the Canaanite woman in Luther's sermon, there is no *theology per se*, only a theological existence whose narration is suspended between the "good report" about Jesus, and—amid the experience of this world, its adversities, its despair, its suffering, its dying, its deaths—an experience of God which runs the gauntlet from God's deafening silence to God's *no* to, ultimately, the experience of a world drained of divine reference.

Theological existence, as instantiated by the Canaanite woman in Luther's sermon, is a relentless, tireless clutching of the Promise, unabashedly holding it up to God's face, doubling down against the experience of its opposite, its absence. As there is no *theology per se*, she embodies its proper location and thus *usus*, or between Promise and *opus alienum*; clinging to the reputation of Jesus against the experience of Jesus himself. To be sure, because there is no *theology* in abstraction, only a theological existence suspended—narrated in the first person—within the structure and scope of Promise's body and agency, respectively, there are only *theologians*. As Gerhard Forde observed, "Luther does not talk about theology in the abstract but rather about the different kinds of theologians and what they do, and the way they operate."[32] Suffering the abyssal chasm between Promise and Jesus, holding the Promise against Jesus—his indifference, his judgment, the experience of his silence and seeming absence, his ultimate cruciformity—the Canaanite woman is a theologian *par excellence*. She is a theologian from the cross. Hers is an undecidedness stilled when faith breaks through from the experience of *no* to *yes*.

As Luther observed, "God deals strangely with His children. He blesses them with contradictory and disharmonious things, for hope and despair are opposites. Yet His children must hope in despair . . . And these two things, direct opposites by nature, must be in us, because in us two natures are opposed to each other, the old man and the new man."[33] For the theo-

---

32. Forde, *On Being a Theologian of the Cross*, 11.

33. Luther, *Works* 14.191; Luther, *Werke* 18, 518.

logian of the cross—this side of the resurrection of the dead—this duality is never diminished. For those who cling to the Promise, "their whole life is one trusting and hoping in God and a relying on, and waiting for Him[.]"[34] "[N]o matter how [long He] be delayed."[35] Indeed, to be a "true Israelite" is to be a "wrestler with God" (corresponding to the meaning of "Israel," the people of God), or one—suspended between Promise and the experience of its delay, hope and despair—"who wait[s] for the Lord so firmly they wrestle, as it were, with God[.]"[36] A theologian of the cross suffers the experience of this suspendedness and undecidedness, this vacillation between *yes* and *no*; the seemingly ephemeral triumph of Promise and the punishing struggle with the experience of its abyssal silence. There is no reference point beyond this location. Amid our waiting we trust, we double down, against the experience of suspendedness and undecidedness that God's *yes* to us has already been revealed to us in the crucified Christ.

But such a confrontation—between Promise and experience—and the existence which issues from it—waiting, despairing, praying, wrestling with God—has profound implications for theological methodology. That is, asserting that at the core of Luther's theology sit the dual *foci* of Promise and faith, Oswald Bayer observed, "By experiencing the confrontation of the heard promise with his experience of the world and the self, everyone comes upon that temptation for which one can only be sustained by prayer."[37] Indeed, "Faith in this promise is nothing more than prayer."[38] Prayer corresponding to Promise as point of departure is conducted in the key of lament. It is this temptation, together with the prayer by which it is grappled, that, for Luther, comprised a reworking of theological methodology, a fundamental restructuring and reordering of its traditional conceptualization, the one he inherited.

Noting the manner by which Luther translates his *theologia crucis*—his "doing theology at the foot of the cross"[39]—methodologically, Vítor Westhelle develops the background against which Luther's translation was conducted. According to Westhelle,

> During the Middle Ages theologizing was largely accepted as comprising three steps: *lectio, oratio,* and *contemplatio.* Luther changes the order of the first two. He starts with *oratio* and then moves to *meditatio* (which includes *lectio*). But what is more

34. Luther, *Works* 14.193; Luther, *Werke* 18, 520.
35. Luther, *Works* 14.192; Luther, *Werke* 18, 519.
36. Luther, *Works* 14.193; Luther, *Werke* 18, 520.
37. Bayer, "Luther as an Interpreter of Holy Scripture," 77.
38. Bayer, "Luther as an Interpreter of Holy Scripture," 77.
39. Westhelle, "Luther's *Theologia Crucis*," 165.

significant and relevant for our topic: He totally changes the last step from *contemplatio* to *tentatio*. His choice of inserting these in Latin in the midst of a German text underscores his intention of making clear where the difference lay between his way of doing theology and the dominant one in the Middle Ages. The radical difference finds itself in the explanation where he presents his choice for a German translation: 'Third, there is *tentatio, Anfechtung*. This is the touchstone that teaches you not only to know and understand, but also to experience how right, how true, how sweet, how lovely, how mighty, how comforting God's word is, wisdom beyond all wisdom.'[40]

Westhelle adds, "*Anfechtung* means being in trial, probation, and tribulation, spiritual or otherwise. This is the 'touchstone' because you cannot do theology without experiencing cross and suffering persecution."[41]

A theology which corresponds to the epistemic point of departure of an incarnate, crucified God will necessarily reflect at the core of its methodology—inscribed even into its christological formulations—temptation, *tentatio, Anfechtung.* Theologians suspended in the real-time narrative of Christology's subject matter and agency, between Promise and the experience of its absence, understand the unretractable and pervasive nature of *Anfechtung* for theological existence and expression. It is the *sine qua non* of theological existence and expression. To build upon Westhelle's insight: *Anfechtung* is the expression of an existence dangling in undecideness and suspendedness between the "good report about Jesus" and Jesus; between the hearing of Promise and an encounter with a world which is neither transparent to, nor mirrors, that same Promise. It is not an element of theological methodology that can be contrived, only endured, experienced (or, shall we say, contrived as much as a theological identity can be acquired by adopting your middle name—reducing your first one to an initial, donning a flat cap, circular lenses, a theological couture scarf wrapped just right, a Tweed jacket, and learning how to drink Scotch!).

Such a methodology is not the instantiation via human faculty of a bridge to divine knowledge, but the beginning of a wisdom suffered by divine action; suffered by the agency and medium of a Promise whose presence does not yield to acquisitive knowledge—whether grounded in affect or intellect—of that very presence. *Anfechtung* is the theologian of the cross' constant reminder that theological methodology is suffered, not mastered. There is no *theology* of the cross *per se*, only *theologians* of the cross, or those

40. Westhelle, "Luther's *Theologia Crucis*," 165.
41. Westhelle, "Luther's *Theologia Crucis*," 165.

who suffer the agency and medium of Promise. Just as theirs is an existence located—in temptation, prayer, and biblical reflection upon the Promise—in the discrepancy between Promise and the experience of its absence, a world seemingly opaque to its presence, so there is no Christology *per se*, only theologians molded—"clay in the potter's hand"! (Jer 18:6)—by the structure and agency of Christology's subject matter, or Promise. Theologians of the cross are those whose christological formulations are grounded in the epistemic point of departure of the crucified Christ, and thus inscribed with, and therefore expressive of, the methodology of struggle from which they emanated.

If throughout the course of this project we have been able to both translate the genera (the *genus tapeinoticum* and the *genus majestaticum*) of Luther's radical interpretation of the *communicatio idiomatum* into categories of christological existence expressive of *the body of Promise*, and—employing the media of Luther's sermons and (as we will see) lectures—*narrate that same Promise*, the experience of its real-time suspendedness, then there is also a concomitant contention threading this project. It is an argument grounded in the methodology of Luther's *theologia crucis* itself.

To be sure, this project also contends that theological existence from the cross, and thus the methodology of a theologian of the cross—its epistemic point of departure (a crucified God, exsanguinated of all divine reference), concomitant temptation (as it comes to expression in a theologian's undecidedness and suspendedness, *Anfechtung*), and countering prayer (clutching Promise against experience of its absence)—cannot be siphoned from its christological formulation. Precisely: stripping the *genus tapeinoticum* from Promise's structure, or Luther's *communicatio idiomatum* (a fundamental betrayal of Luther's theological point of departure), and abstracting from that same Christology the narratives which have suffered the agency of Promise, are symptoms of just this disconnect. They are symptoms of the desiccation of theological existence from theological formulation. Luther's radical interpretation of the *communicatio idiomatum* and his narration of Christology through sermon and lecture express the theological existence, the methodology, from which they originated. The christological formulations of a theologian of the cross will be indelibly inscribed with the theological existence—the temptation, the prayer, the humility—of which they are an expression. It is the originating context—the Promise of *nihil* and temptation of Promise, prayer animating both sides—from which a theologian from the cross cannot move beyond.

"And this is the reason," Luther asserted, "why our theology is certain: it snatches us away from ourselves and places us outside ourselves, so that we do not depend on our own strength, conscience, experience, person, or works but depend on that which is outside ourselves [*extra nos*], that is, on the promise and truth of God, which cannot deceive."[42] The certainty of faith is grounded in the reality that what the Triune God gives—life, righteousness, new creation—will only come in the form of Promise, as categorical, *extra nos* gift. Such giving is concealed in the crucifixion of all combinations of human capabilities and works designed to take the gifts of God, to allocate the righteousness of God, apart from the Triune God's unilateral giving. A Christology from the cross is formulated in just this context, in just this experience.

What grows in the disconnect between christological formulation and existence, the struggle from which it emanates, is the siren song of a self-manufactured certitude which has either simply forgotten the structure and agency of Promise, or never experienced it. If faith's certainty is grounded in the *extra nos* Promise, then not only is faith concealed in prayer uttered from the context of abject temptation, but, ultimately, there is no formulation of a Christology from the cross which is not an expression of this *coram Deo* struggle, which is not an expression of its prayer. It only returns—heard as Promise in Proclamation—to become the foundation of a new prayer which commences anew both theological existence and its expression. Perhaps, we may say, the confession, the formulation, of Christology is one of the most profound forms of repentance there is. All theology is sustained by a Promise it can only authenticate through its own perpetual crucifixion. Indeed, suffering the crucifixion of one's agency, faith is the crucified mask of Promise's life-giving agency.

Christology Suspended in Struggle

> *The same night he got up and took his two wives, his two maids, and his eleven children, and crossed the cord of the Jabbok. He took them and sent them across the stream, and likewise everything that he had. Jacob was left alone; and a man wrestled with him until daybreak. When the man saw that he did not prevail against Jacob, he struck him on the hip socket; and Jacob's hip was put out of joint as he wrestled with him. Then he said, "Let me go, for the day is breaking." But Jacob said, "I will not let you go, unless you bless me." So he said to him, "What is your name?" And he said, "Jacob." Then the man said, "You shall no longer be called Jacob, but Israel, for you have striven with God and with humans, and have prevailed." Then Jacob asked him, "Please tell me your name." But he said, "Why is it that you ask my name?"*

42. Luther, *Works* 26.387.

> *And there he blessed him. So Jacob called the place Peniel, saying,*
> *"For I have seen God face to face, and yet my life is preserved." The*
> *sun rose upon him as he passed Penuel, limping because of his hip.*
> *Therefore to this day the Israelites do not eat the thigh muscle that*
> *is on the hip socket, because he struck Jacob on the hip socket at*
> *the thigh muscle.*—Genesis 32:22–32

From the initiation of the struggle forward there is no question for Luther as to the identity of the one who has thrust himself upon Jacob in the dark of the night at the Jabbok. During the course of his narration of the struggle Luther, at least at four different points, wants his lecture-hearers[43] to be certain "that the wrestler is the Lord of glory, God Himself, or God's Son, who was to become incarnate and who appeared and spoke to the fathers."[44] Again: "Without any controversy we shall say that his man was not an angel but our Lord Jesus Christ, eternal God and future Man, to be crucified by the Jews."[45]

At the same time, what is also clear for Luther—and therefore his lecture audience—is the reality that the identity of his adversary—at all points during the struggle—remains opaque to Jacob. For if Jacob had "no idea who it is who is wrestling with him"[46] at the beginning, by the time the grappling is finished "the wrestler conceals his identity and leaves him in uncertainty and doubt."[47] Again: "Jacob did not know who the man was, and his reason would come to no conclusion or take counsel . . ."[48] Nevertheless, Luther asserts, "although Jacob does not know who this man is, he . . . feels that he has been forsaken by God or that God is opposed to him and angry with him."[49]

Juxtaposing Luther's narration of the account with the biblical text and its economy of verbiage, the liberty Luther takes with regard to the narrating the text is fascinating. For if Scripture narrates that "a man wrestled with [Jacob] until daybreak" (Gen 32:24), shrouding in textual silence the particulars of the struggle, Luther inserts into the textual silence of this nocturnal contest a shouting match. As the unidentified assailant assaults Jacob with such terrifying threats as "You must die, Jacob, for you are not the man to whom God gave the promise,"[50] and "You must perish, Jacob, you are in for it!"[51] so

---

43. See Luther's *Lectures on Genesis*; Luther, *Works* 6.122–55.

44. Luther, *Works* 6.130.

45. Luther, *Works* 6.144.

46. Luther, *Works* 6.130.

47. Luther, *Works* 6.143.

48. Luther, *Works* 6.135.

49. Luther, *Works* 6.134.

50. Luther, *Works* 6.135.

51. Luther, *Works* 6.135.

Jacob counters the terrifying onslaught with such shouts as "No! that is not God's will. I shall not perish!"[52] To be sure, Jacob, for Luther, is suspended in nocturnal combat between Promise and God. As theological existence is one of clutching Promise in the face of experience, indefatigably holding God's face to God's Promise, so obviously priority is given to Promise in this combat at the Jabbok. The extent of such a priority given to Promise is articulated by Luther near the beginning of his narration of the actual struggle and, as such, provides the lens through which Luther unfolds the struggle. So Luther declares, "I shall cling to the Word of God and be content with that. By it I shall die, and by it I shall live."[53] But such a clinging, Luther observes, must be prepared to not only defy Godself if need be, but accept the reality of enduring an existence stripped of everything except a Promise for which one must even be prepared to suffer punishment if need be.

> Or, if God Himself appeared to me in His majesty and said: "You are not worthy of My grace; I will change My plan and not keep My promise to you," I would not have to yield to Him, but it would be necessary to fight most vehemently against God Himself. It is as Job says: "Though He slay me, Yet will I hope in Him" (cf. Job 13:15). If He should cast me into the depths of hell and place me in the midst of devils, I would still believe that I would be saved because I have been baptized, I have been absolved, I have received the pledge of my salvation, the body and blood of the Lord in the Supper. Therefore I want to see and hear nothing else, but I shall live and die in this faith, whether God or angel or the devil says the contrary.[54]

As we have seen, not only does one suffer the agency of Promise, but one must be prepared to suffer a God who refuses to be held accountable, to underwrite, such a Promise. In such a case one flees to, and clings all the more to, the Promise, or the *sub contrario* revelation of Jesus Christ.

With experience registering divine wrath, even unto abandonment, amid this nocturnal assault, and reason's judgment rendered ineffectual with regard to ascertaining either the assailant's identity or an ultimate resolution to the situation—"in such a struggle all the senses are disturbed, and reason is confused"[55]—Jacob is left with only one recourse. It is faith which can only assert against experience: "I have the promise."[56] It is this faith, for Luther,

52. Luther, *Works* 6.135.
53. Luther, *Works* 6.131.
54. Luther, *Works* 6.133.
55. Luther, *Works* 6.135–36.
56. Luther, *Works* 6.134.

always holding to Promise against the experience of divine *no* and forsaken-ness, which "conquers God"[57] in that it clings to God where God has concrete-ly surrendered Godself, namely, "in His Word, promise."[58] But such a "faith" is no unambiguous reality. To be sure, Luther calls it the "weakness of faith."[59]

Although Luther clearly understands "faith" as that dynamic which clings to the Promise—"faith in the Promise"[60]—in the face of experience, whether it is experience of the divine *no* or the experience of a world drained of Promise, that "faith" also appears to never surpass an inchoate status; an experience beyond the "weakness" of trial and temptation in which a con-clusive judgment of finality may be reached regarding the solidity of Prom-ise. For if, as Luther maintains throughout his narration of Jacob's struggle, "nature and a weak faith"[61] cannot abstain from questioning whether or not the Promise is still valid, that "weakness of faith"—at times appearing as a faith worn to the thinnest of threads, seemingly negligible—is enough to "conquer God." It is a conquering veiled by faith's own diminishment, the crucifixion of a prowess once attributed to faith and now transferred by Luther to Promise and its agency. Obviously then, never at any point, for Luther, does Jacob move beyond the "uncertainty and doubt"[62] of the "weak-ness of faith," even after the "wrestler reveals himself as God and man,"[63] the God bound to God's Promise. Any final resolution of uncertainty as to the man's identity remains suspended in vacillation between *yes* and *no*, a continual flight from the God of experience to the God of Promise. It is a suspension, an undecidedness, as we will see, which Luther opens unto his listeners under the heading "church."

Indeed at times it appears, for Luther, that the clutching of Promise by which God is "conquered" belongs to an existence beyond "faith." It ap-pears as a "faith" stretched so "weak," so thin, as to become seemingly im-perceptible and inconsequential, having acquiesced into a praying beyond faith—a prayer more of unbelief and despair than belief and hope?! a prayer whose unbelief is the mask of faith?!—animated and suspended purely by a motivation and persistence generated by Promise itself which works unilaterally in spite of human faculty or agency.[64] For ultimately, as Luther

---

57. See Luther, *Works* 6.140–41.

58. Luther, *Works* 6.141.

59. Luther, *Works* 6.142.

60. Luther, *Works* 6.134.

61. Luther, *Works* 6.133.

62. Luther, *Works* 6.143.

63. Luther, *Works* 6.143.

64. Luther, *Works* 6.154.

indicates, to "conquer God" appears to center more upon the shear given-ness of Promise, or "having the Promise," and the persistence—no matter its motivation—of prayer and its relentless seeking, knocking, and petitioning to validate it against experience of its absence. It can even be said that the ability to "conquer God" appears to emanate from a third party—the agency of Promise—alongside the grapplers. Or as Luther puts it, God is conquered

> Not with the strength or weapons of your flesh and nature but with confidence in the cause that intervenes between you and God, namely, that He has promised and sworn that He will be your God. With this confidence you will conquer, *inasmuch as it arises not from nature but from promise.*[65]

Faith is the crucifixion of one's agency by which Promise is experienced. Faith is the expression for one's existence becoming a veil for the agency of Promise; the transfer to Promise's agency which faith, now crucified, once attributed to itself. It is an agency of which faith is now a mask. Such an experience—in thought and feeling—will never register as anything more than loss: of agency, of meaning and value, of righteousness.[66]

❖ ❖ ❖

Excursus: "To be Justified by Faith"

As Luther asserted, "justification is the article by which the church stands and falls."[67] On this point Oswald Bayer elaborates, *"Justification is not a separate topic apart from which still other topics could be discussed. Justification is the starting point for all theology and it affects every other topic."*[68] Indeed, as Bayer observes,

> "[Luther] understood the event of justification in its social and cosmic breadth just as profoundly as he perceived it in its existential depth. To him as biblical interpreter, particularly as the Old Testament scholar he primarily was, it was precisely the social and cosmic breadth of justification that was disclosed to him by its existential depth. Not only is our relationship to God and ourselves made new through justification by faith, but at the same time our relationships with all creatures are renewed. Even a new perception of space and time is included in our new relationship to God and the world.[69]

---

65. Luther, *Works* 6.154. Italics are mine.

66. The death by which one suffers the *vita passiva*.

67. Quoted in Bayer, "Justification as Basis and Boundary of Theology," 288.

68. Bayer, "Justification as Basis and Boundary of Theology," 274.

69. Bayer, "Justification as Basis and Boundary of Theology," 274.

With this said, let us also note that justification is grounded in, is the expression of, the person and work of Jesus Christ. To be sure, as Kjell Ove Nilsson asserted, "for everything depends on the matter that Christ—who is the truly united, divine-human one—has accomplished the work of redemption *pro nobis*. And because the unity of the action itself is connected with the unity of person, in which the *communicatio* doctrine is the center, therefore the *communicatio* comprises the core of Luther's theology."[70] For Luther the *communicatio idiomat*um and justification are "flip sides of the same coin" so to speak, the latter expressing the effect of the Triune God's unreserved, complete self-giving through the Son of God by which the promise of life and salvation is given apart from human input or merit, or the justification of sinners, and the former, the *communicatio idiomatum*, expressing the communication of that Promise, or the incarnate, crucified One, true God and true man. Luther's radical interpretation of the *communicatio idiomatum* is the elaboration of a Jesus Christ whom Luther will not entertain apart from his *pro me, pro nobis* revealing. Which also means: justification is a "justification *by faith*." It is by faith that the crucified Christ, the *sub contrario* revelation of Promise's life-giving agency, is apprehended, received, *pro me*. Which means: "faith," in one way or another, has informed this project in one way or another from beginning to end. To be sure, the fundamental nature of faith for Luther's theology is unquestionable. Indeed, faith's power, for Luther, is profound. That is, according to Luther in his 1535 *Lectures on Galatians*, "faith is something omnipotent . . .its power is inestimable and infinite; for it attributes glory to God, which is the highest thing that can be attributed to Him. To attribute glory to God is to believe in Him, to regard Him as truthful, wise, righteous, merciful, and almighty, in short, to acknowledge Him as the Author and Donor of every good. Reason does not do this, but faith does. It consummates the Deity; and, if I may put it this way, it is the creator of the Deity, not in the substance of God but in us. For without faith God loses His glory, wisdom, righteousness, truthfulness, mercy, etc., in us; in short, God has none of His majesty or divinity where faith is absent. Nor does God require anything greater of man than that he attribute to Him His glory and His divinity: That is, that he regard Him, not as an idol but as God, who has regard for him, listens to him, shows mercy to him, helps him, etc. When he has obtained this, God retains His divinity sound and unblemished; that is, He has whatever a believing heart is able to attribute to Him. To be able to attribute such glory to God is wisdom beyond wisdom, righteousness beyond righteousness, religion beyond religion, and sacrifice beyond sacrifice. From this it can be

70. Nilsson, *Simul*, 228.

understood what great righteousness faith is and, by antithesis, what a great sin unbelief is. Therefore faith justifies because it renders to God what is due Him; whoever does this is righteous."[71] Later, in those same lectures on Galatians, Luther asserts that "this is the reason why our theology [read: "faith"] is certain: It snatches us away from ourselves and places us outside ourselves [*extra nos*], so that we do not depend on our own strength, conscience, experience, person, or works, but depend on that which is outside ourselves [*extra nos*], that is, on the promise and truth of God, which cannot deceive."[72] And certainly one would be remiss to omit Luther's famous explanation of the third article of the Apostles' Creed in his Small Catechism: "I believe that by my own understanding or strength I cannot believe in Jesus Christ my Lord or come to him, but instead the Holy Spirit has called me through the gospel, enlightened me with his gifts, made me holy and kept me in the true faith [. . .]"[73] At the same time, Luther asserts, "For it happens, indeed it is typical of faith, that often he who claims to believe does not believe at all; and on the other hand, he who doesn't think he believes, but is in despair, has the greatest faith."[74] To be sure, thinking of Luther's response to Valentine Hausmann's chronic unbelief (see Preface, above), unbelief has as much to tell us about the presence of faith, its concealed nature and the agency of God's Promise, than anything. Joseph Sittler's "theological precision begotten of deprivation" appears to be the description of this same faith, or one that is concealed by unbelief (or, let us say, that struggle and unbelief are contained within the life of faith, its movement). But, all of this prompts a line of questions: what is it that faith refers to in Luther's theology, i.e., the *fides qua* (faith by which) or the *fides quae* (faith which)? Who is the source of faith? Who is the subject of faith? Does it refer to the agency—no matter how "weak" and inconsequential—of the one who is "justified by faith"? Who does faith "belong" to? As well: how does one unknowingly give glory to God? How can a believing subject be unaware of faith's presence? As New Testament scholar Ernst Käsemann observed, no doubt echoing Luther, though faith is a creation of the Word, the Word's address, faith is also the description of complete passivity before God. It is a passivity analogous to the creation story in Genesis 2, or, specifically, the soil from which Adam is molded: "For Paul faith is not the same as piety . . . he does not view faith as a human capability and therefore it also cannot be defined in terms of mankind. To define faith, he has to say who God is. He does this in his

---

71. Luther, *Works* 26.227; Luther, *Werke* 40, 360–61.

72. Luther, *Works* 26.387; Luther, *Werke* 40, 589–90.

73. Luther, *Book of Concord*, 355.

74. Luther, *Works* 40.241.

doctrine of justification by speaking of the *creator ex nihilo*. Faith is the Yes to the message of this God. It is thus confession that this God always and only makes the ungodly righteous."[75] He adds, "The word also creates faith, since we continually come out of an existence and world of superstition and are thus incapable of true hearing on our own. Only in the address of grace does faith achieve its knowledge, trust, certainty, hope, and task. Apart from this word, which sets faith at once both in contradiction with the world and also under the assault of its fleshliness, there is no guarantee of salvation for it."[76] But, Käsemann adds, faith—though not a human capability—does have a corresponding experience, or "is a condition as poverty is, or waiting for blessing. [Faith] is the place where the Creator alone can and will act as such."[77] This is the *vita passiva*. Faith is the suffering of one's location *coram Deo*, or the creative agency of Promise. In the words of Hans Joachim Iwand, "Faith is really born in us; and the emptiness of life, the nothingness in the collapse of all worth, is the reverse side which we perceive and which we feel in this birth. In the moment of faith's breakthrough we can know ourselves only as fallen away, doubting, despairing. There is nothing to be seen in the place where we know of ourselves."[78] Such "poverty," or "waiting" (Käsemann), such "doubting" and "despairing," the experience of "nothing to be seen in the place where we know of ourselves" (Iwand), permits us, in a manner commensurate with Luther's employment of the term elsewhere in his writings, to consider, to call, faith itself a "mask" of Promise's *sub contrario*, life-giving agency. Ultimately, then, if, as Bayer points out, "Faith in this Promise is nothing more than prayer,"[79] then prayer itself—an expression of *simul*'s reality, one's existence between Promise and experience—is a "mask." With this being the case, another perspective opens up on the methodology of Luther's *theologia crucis*. Recalling Luther's reshaping of theological methodology—from his late-Medieval inheritance—to *oratio, meditatio, tentatio (Anfechtung)*, it should also be noted that, when one examines Luther's "Preface to the Wittenberg Edition of Luther's German Writings"[80] in which he famously elaborates his theological methodology from the cross, the word "faith" is conspicuously absent. It can be argued that "prayer" (*oratio*) better corresponds to the experience of the crucifixion of one's agency with reference to Promise. Regardless, faith—always

---

75. Käsemann, *Commentary on Romans*, 112.

76. Käsemann, *Commentary on Romans*, 110.

77. Käsemann, *Commentary on Romans*, 111.

78. Iwand, "Theology of the Cross," 6.

79. Bayer, "Luther as an Interpreter of Holy Scripture," 77.

80. Luther, *Works* 34.279–88.

reminding ourselves that we are not discussing an assent to historical data, or facts (*fides historica*)—is the experience, and thus suffering, of the Triune God's unilateral giving; an expression of the reality that what the Triune God gives—forgiveness, righteousness, life itself—will only come in the form of Promise, or categorical gift. Faith, then, is the expression of this crucifixion of one's agency by which Promise is experienced, the experience of the transfer to Promise's agency of what was once attributed to one's self, one's capabilities, even if previously considered under the term "faith." Faith's definition, we can say, will always be inscribed with, and bear the reflection of, the Word of God who authors life completely, even trust in the author of life, the Word of God, itself. Though God creates faith, we may ultimately say that faith belongs to the believer, is the active force within the believer. Perhaps the best way to elaborate such a dynamic within the scope of this project is through an application of Luther's *communicatio idiomatum* itself. If the subject of faith itself—as Luther indicates explicitly in his explanation to the third article of the Apostles' Creed—is God (the Holy Spirit), then faith can be considered a communication of the divine, the *genus majestaticum*, to the human within the person of Jesus Christ. In this case, within the scope of this project, we may say that the faith is concealed within the *genus tapeinoticum* writ-large, the body of Promise.

Nearing the end of his lecture on the text, Luther opens out the narrative of Jacob's struggle at the Jabbok upon his listeners. If the undecidedness and suspendedness for Jacob remains unrelieved by the end of the biblical narrative for Luther, it only corresponds to the experience of his audience, one which he assigns under the rubric of "church." In this case, the church, according to Luther, is an extension, a continuance, of the narrative. "For," as Luther relates to his listeners,

> we are reminded [in Jacob's struggle with Jesus Christ at the Jabbok] that in our life we should prepare ourselves in the same manner and learn to recognize the church of God in that picture of Jacob's struggle. For God hides the church and also our salvation under a dark and horrible cover, to which we must become accustomed so that we do not despair or fall into unbelief even in the greatest danger and adversities which are thrown in our way by Satan, the world, or God Himself.[81]

81. Luther, *Works* 6.146–47. Earlier in his Genesis lectures Luther asserts regarding the perpetual hiddenness, the suspended and undecided nature of Promise's relation to experience, "Would that we all could bestow it on Him, that is, conclude with certainty that

Indeed, Luther observes, Jacob's struggle with Jesus Christ at the Jabbok not only dovetails with the real-time narratives of his listeners, but yields a wisdom which can be applied seamlessly to the narratives of those same listeners. So, Luther prepares his listeners,

> when you think that our Lord God has rejected a person, you should think that our Lord God has him in His arms and is pressing him to His heart. When we suppose that someone has been deserted and rejected by God, then we should conclude that he is in the embrace and the lap of God. So Jacob feels and thinks nothing else but that he will be destroyed. But when he takes stock of matters, he is held fast in the embrace of the Son of God.[82]

But though Luther knows he can convey the knowledge of the cross from the biblical narrative, he also understands that he cannot provide the wisdom which is born of an experience with Promise, a Promise whom his listeners can only experience for themselves. Knowledge of Promise's agency, its *modus operandae*, is not to be confused with the wisdom which arises from doubling down on the Promise amid the experience of its opposite, better, its absence. The latter requires a classroom the academy's lecture hall and seminar circles cannot provide. That is, not only is such a wisdom *not* theoretical, but, when practiced, will never—in this life—escape the suspendedness and undecidedness created by a *sub contrario* Promise whose scope and agency envelopes his listeners, or, in this case, the church which confesses it. Thus, as Luther ultimately observes,

> If you ask where the church is, it is nowhere in evidence. But you must not pay regard to external form but to the Word and to Baptism, and the church must be sought where the sacraments are purely administered, where there are hearers, teachers, and confessors of the Word. If the church is still not in evidence, you should remember that our blessings are hidden and that their magnitude cannot be perceived in this life. Man is still wrestling . . .[83]

He has regard for us and cares for us, especially when He seems to have forgotten us, when we think we have been forsaken by Him. For he who can say in affliction: 'God sees me' has true faith and can do and bear everything, yes, he overcomes all things and is triumphant." Related to the church, which, for Luther, is a real-time extension of the biblical narrative and the Promise's scope and agency, Luther asserts, "For the entire church symbolizes eternal damnation, since it is cruelly afflicted and slain by its enemies. Yet is not abandoned." See Luther, *Works* 2:70. An ecclesiology inscribed with the methodology of the cross, the experience of Promise's agency is, to say the least, always an interesting development.

82. Luther, *Works* 6.149.
83. Luther, *Works* 6.149.

If Luther can say with regard to the Christian church that "it is nowhere in evidence," let us be reminded that, for Luther, the seventh—and final—mark of the Christian church is "the holy possession of the sacred cross."[84] Such a mark is Luther's "application of the consequences of the theology of the cross to ecclesiology."[85] The Christian church is the *ecclesia crucis*. The *ecclesia crucis* confesses its forsakenness and despair, its cruciformity, to be the revelation of God's life-giving agency, to be the text of God's body of Promise. In so doing the *ecclesia crucis* serves, ministers to, that same forsakenness and despair wherever it is recognized with its newly created eyes. They are eyes which, inhabiting the gaze of God, "look only into the depths."[86]

As the cross story is our story, Christology ultimately comes to expression, is experienced, in the first person as christological existence. Which means: suspended from the cross, we can only await the life-creating agency of God's Promise, trusting that God's *yes*, God's life-giving presence has already been revealed in the crucified Christ. We may confess that we are an expression of that body of Promise, its *sub contrario*, life-creating agency. In that confession is the experience of both God's judgment, and the gift of God's mercy; the recognition of both our *nihil*, and, within it, God's categorical, *ex nihilo* gifting of life.

Such a Christology, one suspended from the cross, cannot *not* be inscribed with the temptation and prayer, the wrestling, by which its wisdom is experienced, suffered, and ultimately confessed. Concealed within such a wrestling is the certainty of salvation from which it is formulated, the Promise who is always prior.

---

84. Luther, *Works* 41.164. In his *On the Councils and the Church*, Luther outlines seven marks or holy possessions of the Christian church. They are: Word, Baptism, Lord's Supper, Confession and Forgiveness, the Office of Ministry, Public Worship, and "possession of the sacred cross," or, let us call it, Cruciform Existence. See Luther, *Works* 41.3–184 (specifically, 148–66).

85. Westhelle, "Luther's *Theologia Crucis*," 166.

86. Luther, *Works* 21.299.

Interlude

A Presence Suffered, Not Sought

The Heidelberg Disputation and the Subject of Theology

At the beginning of his virtual smorgasbord of contemporary christologi-cal development, assessment, and insight, renowned theologian Michael Welker, in the expanded version of his 2004 Edinburgh Gunning Lectures[1] asserts that "Christology's task is to elucidate that the proclamation and confession 'God revealed himself in Jesus Christ!' does genuinely offer a reli-able *insight* of faith."[2] That task, for Welker, is promptly given contemporary context and navigational orientation by what he has coined Dietrich Bon-hoeffer's "First Legacy" and "Second Legacy"—both legacies drawn from Bonhoeffer's famous letters written from incarceration. Ultimately, these legacies raise questions which, in so many ways, frame Welker's wrestling with the significance for contemporary theology of Luther's theology of the cross, especially as delineated in the *Heidelberg Disputation* (1518). Let us unpack, employing Welker's words liberally, both what is meant by these two "legacies" and Welker's analysis of Luther's theology of the cross for contemporary theology. Again, in so many ways, these two "legacies" pro-vide the lens by which he analyzes Luther's theology of the cross.

---

1. Welker, *God the Revealed.*
2. Welker, *God the Revealed*, 12.

Who Is Jesus Christ for Us Today?
Bonhoeffer's Double Legacy

In order to explicate Bonhoeffer's "First Legacy," Welker adduces Bonhoeffer's question, one posed from prison in late April, 1944: "What keeps gnawing at me is the question, what is Christianity, or who is Christ actually for us today?"[3] Welker subsequently paraphrases Bonhoeffer's answer: "Jesus Christ reveals the God who is powerless and suffering in the world."[4] Immediately he offers Bonhoeffer's famous words written from his prison cell: "God consents to be pushed out of the world and onto the cross; God is weak and powerless in the world and in precisely this way, and only so, is at our side and helps us."[5] Welker refers us to Bonhoeffer's profound trust in "the God of the Bible, who gains ground and power in the world by being powerless."[6] To be sure, Welker observes, "This trust in the weak and suffering God has deeply moved many people. Bonhoeffer's words have been repeated again and again—almost devoutly: '. . . only the suffering God can help.'"[7] But, Welker asks, can Bonhoeffer's words remain persuasive in the long run, persuasive when exposed to contexts beyond those from which they originated?

Indeed, as Welker notes, the context from which Bonhoeffer spoke these words informing his "First Legacy" was one of all-encompassing threat: to his life and the lives of fellow prisoners, to his family in a city being bombed by the Allied Forces, to his friends serving on the front lines, to his relatives involved in the conspiracy to kill Hitler. And more than this: he had observed Nazi ideology poison not only the fabric of German society and the lives of its people, but indeed the fabric of the church itself, a poison permeating even the church's official confessional documents. Welker notes the Scylla and Charybdis-like situation in which Bonhoeffer lived and ministered: "The future appeared dark: either the war would be lost and Germany would be ostracized the world over, or—but such was unfathomable—the world would come under Nazi rule."[8] "Was it," Welker asks, "this hopeless, desperate situation that made Bonhoeffer trust solely in the suffering God?"[9]

3. Welker, *God the Revealed*, 16.
4. Welker, *God the Revealed*, 16.
5. Welker, *God the Revealed*, 16.
6. Welker, *God the Revealed*, 16.
7. Welker, *God the Revealed*, 16.
8. Welker, *God the Revealed*, 16.
9. Welker, *God the Revealed*, 16–17.

No doubt the focus on a God revealed in suffering and crucifixion was nothing new, as evidenced by Tertullian's reference to such a God as early as 200 C.E. And, certainly, the crucified God was not merely a central point for Luther and the Reformation, but indeed provided a point of orientation for such significant philosophers as G. W. F. Hegel and Martin Heidegger. And Jürgen Moltmann, among others, would help to imbue popular theological discourse with the legacy of the crucified God for the latter half of the twentieth century. But still, for Welker, a God who "gains ground and power in the world by being powerless," a crucified God, is met by doubt. It is a doubt which begs, for Welker, the line of questioning which follows:

> Why is God—whom, after all, we call "the Almighty"—not rather called into question precisely through suffering and death? Why does God's presence not become unrecognizable in suffering and death? Why and how should, of all things, the suffering and dying Jesus on the cross reveal God? If, however, Bonhoeffer's assertion that "only the suffering God can help" could be explained by his desperate situation, then the question arises how this obscure discourse about the "crucified God" is supposed to speak to and persuade people living in less oppressive or even peaceful and pleasant times?[10]

But, as Welker observes, when one emphasizes in the question "Who is Jesus Christ for us today?" the prepositional phrase "for us today," the dilemma is intensified. "What," Welker asks, "will the answer be if 'for us' no longer means 'Bonhoeffer's situation' or 'a situation full of affliction and despair?"[11] Do not different contexts require—even demand—completely different answers to the question "Who is Jesus Christ *for us today*?" It is this matter of contextual diversity that issues, for Welker, in a short litany of questions:

> Will the answers in what we call Christian and post-Christian societies in Europe and in large parts of North America today not be completely different than in societies shaped by non-Christian religions, societies unfamiliar with Christianity, or in those that may even fear and loathe it? Will the religiously tied and theologically sleepy mainline churches of western industrialized nations and information societies not provide different answers than countries in Africa, Asia, and Latin America with currently extremely dynamic churches and rapidly growing movements of faith? Across all these different contexts, can we

10. Welker, *God the Revealed*, 17.

11. Welker, *God the Revealed*, 17.

really claim that God would have us know that we must live as those who manage their lives without God. The same God who is with us is the God who forsakes us . . . Before God, and with God, we live without God"?[12]

But, Welker observes, those who speak of a crucified God are also confronted with an unremitting tension. Welker asks, "Does God remain withdrawn from human beings even when he is near to them? Is God thus absent even in his presence? This tension confronts all who confess the revelation of God in the human being Jesus Christ and speak of the 'crucified God.'"[13] It is a tension, Welker observes, which "continues to produce a peculiar fascination arising particularly from the suggestive depictions of the beginning and end of Jesus' earthly life: the baby in a manger in Bethlehem and the dying Jesus on the cross at Golgotha—so close does God come to humanity!"[14]

Essentially, this God who is difficult to grasp in his nearness—most poignantly at crib and cross—has been artistically depicted as an "iconic presence" which has informed significant expressions of Christian piety throughout the centuries. With reference to the birth narrative of Jesus artists have expressed that iconic presence through various combinations of a humble setting—stable, ruins, or cave—with a birth at dawn or dusk in order to capture in Jesus' birth the unity of vulnerability and magic. The iconic presence of the cross has been expressed most notably by means of the "triumphal cross" (erected in churches from the eleventh century onward) and a cross-focused piety, one focused on the sufferings of Jesus, which is still dominant today. But whether that iconic presence, that aura, comes to expression at crib or cross of Jesus, as Welker points out,

> it is the proximate, poor, powerless, and suffering God who reveals himself. Though he may perhaps be "difficult to grasp" as God, he still touches human beings in a somehow consoling manner, strengthening them emotionally and even in their compassion. Thus does he come close to them in this fascinating way.[15]

At the same time, as many biblical witnesses attest, that vulnerable nearness rendered artistically and piously as an iconic aura also masks an abject reality. That abject reality takes the form, as Welker observes, of the

12. Welker, *God the Revealed*, 17–18.
13. Welker, *God the Revealed*, 19.
14. Welker, *God the Revealed*, 19.
15. Welker, *God the Revealed*, 20.

powerlessness of Jesus in the face of the "powers of this world" (1 Cor 2:8); the collusion of Roman political power with Jewish religion and public sentiment which culminates in a miscarriage of justice. That abject reality also takes the form of a birth narrative endangered at every point: from the vulnerability of a delivery with no assistance in less than adequate conditions to the provocation of a child massacre in the area of Bethlehem. To be sure, the iconic aura which was meant to depict the emotionally and devotion-inspiring presence of a suffering God also conceals the stark reality of an abject vulnerability and powerlessness which begs the question: "Why and in what way should God reveal himself in this particular man, of all people? And how should God bring help and salvation through this particular man and this revelation?"[16]

Finally, as Welker notes, the Old Testament makes it unambiguously clear that the nearness of God was not be reduced to aesthetically dictated moods. Instead, enthusiasm for the nearness of God was translated into a recognition of the Law's primacy and its demand for the propagation of justice and mercy among the population. "In accordance with the Law, in piety, and following their fundamentally moral guiding beliefs," Welker notes, "Israel lived and continues to live in community with God. According to the Old Testament, this is the community with God that is owed to revelation."[17] But, ultimately, if such community expression affirms the proximity of God, then in what manner does God's revelation of God's community with human beings in Jesus Christ shape life in general and community in particular?

According to Welker, "One is inclined to think first of the power of the church, its institutions, worship services, seminaries, hospitals, homes, and worship in liturgy, confession, and proclamation."[18] All of which leads him to ask, "In extolling the enormous legal, political, educational-historical, and charitable impact of Christian religiosity and churches can we thus speak of a genuine triumphal procession of the revelation of God in human history?"[19] But Welker counters such consideration with a darker, sobering realization with regard to the Christian religion's impact upon the world.

When one considers the countless ways in which the Christian religion has been involved in the mistreatment and persecution of various populations throughout history—Crusades, witch-burnings, missions under the cover of colonialism; such manifestations of "Christianity" as the German Christian Church of the 1930s and 1940s and the contemporaneous

---

16. Welker, *God the Revealed*, 21.

17. Welker, *God the Revealed*, 22.

18. Welker, *God the Revealed*, 22.

19. Welker, *God the Revealed*, 22.

Westboro Baptist Church in Kansas, et al.—one begins to understand the danger of aligning God's presence, God's revelation too closely, too directly, with ecclesiastical expression and authority. The aura of divine presence, really nothing more than a cosmetic, all too easily becomes the exploitation of power's stamp of approval.

The "burning question"[20] for Welker then becomes one of how to differentiate legitimate ecclesiastical expressions which correspond to God's immanence, God's revelation in Jesus Christ, from expressions which are merely exploitations of that alleged presence. Were this distinction not to be made, asserts Welker, between an ecclesiastical expression that corresponds to God's revelation in Jesus Christ and one that is an exploitation for sinister ends, then a "disastrous suspicion"[21] would remain stamped on Christianity's expressions: is any appeal to God's revelation, God's presence "nothing more than a dangerous illusion"?[22] One gilded with the contrived aura of iconic presence at that.

Having examined Bonhoeffer's "First Legacy"—"only the suffering God can help"—against the bar of experience, its misuse, Welker ultimately asks,

> Is common sense correct when it states that we speak either of an obviously powerful God or of a powerless human, but that the claim that God is revealed and present in this man Jesus is simply completely unbelievable? Are the other monotheistic religions justified in complaining that Christianity steps shockingly out of line with its assertion that God revealed himself in Jesus Christ? It abandons any sensible notion of and faith in God. Talk of the powerless and crucified God simply dissolves all talk of God.[23]

Regardless of whether one agrees that common sense is correct to accept this binary reality; of whether one agrees that other monotheistic religions are justified in their assertion of the incarnation's misalignment with the monotheistic status quo, discussion of the "powerless and crucified God" abrogates all sensible notions of faith in, and talk of, God. Pressed by such an examination of Bonhoeffer's "First Legacy"—the inquests and impeachments of a God who is near in powerlessness—Welker turns to Bonhoeffer's "Second Legacy," or the God who wants to be revealed in "the polyphony of life."

---

20. Welker, *God the Revealed*, 22.
21. Welker, *God the Revealed*, 22.
22. Welker, *God the Revealed*, 22.
23. Welker, *God the Revealed*, 23.

Providing the point of departure from which to consider Bonhoeffer's "Second Legacy," Welker cites a portion of Bonhoeffer's letter to Eberhard Bethge dated May 29th, 1944:

> I often notice hereabouts how few people there are who can harbor many different things at the same time. The bombers come, they are nothing but fear itself; when there's something good to eat, nothing but greed itself; when they fail to get what they want, they become desperate; if something succeeds, that's all they see. They are missing out on the fullness of life and on the wholeness of their own existence . . . Christianity, on the other hand, puts us into many different dimensions of life at the same time; in a way we accommodate God and the whole world within us. We weep with those who weep at the same time as we rejoice with those who rejoice. We fear . . . for our lives, but at the same time we must think thoughts that are much more important to us than our lives . . . Life isn't pushed back into a single dimension, but is kept multidimensional, polyphonic. What a liberation it is to be able to think and to hold on to these many dimensions of life in our thoughts . . . One has to dislodge people from their one-track thinking—as it were, in "preparation for" or "enabling" faith, though in truth it is only faith itself that makes multidimensional life possible . . .[24]

As Welker observes, it is from such a consideration that Bonhoeffer comes to the conclusion that Christians—again he quotes Bonhoeffer—"recognize God not only where we reach the limits of our possibilities. God wants to be recognized in the midst of our lives."[25] The "kingdom" of such a faith, according to Bonhoeffer" is a "Kingdom stronger than war and danger, a kingdom of power and might, a kingdom that is eternal terror and judgment for some and eternal joy and righteousness for others. It is not a kingdom of the heart but reigns over the earth and the whole world . . . a kingdom for which it is worth risking our lives."[26] Faith in the God revealed in Jesus Christ depends on both the suffering and powerlessness of God and a kingdom from which no aspect of human life is exempted.

Considering the scope of such a reign—seemingly still nascent in its elaboration for Bonhoeffer, as Welker observes—Bonhoeffer conceived of a *"multidimensional, polyphonic life"*[27] corresponding, and becoming vis-

---

24. Welker, *God the Revealed*, 24.
25. Welker, *God the Revealed*, 24.
26. Welker, *God the Revealed*, 24.
27. Welker, *God the Revealed*, 25.

ible, to faith which includes and incorporates the adversities and dangers continually present to human life. Indeed, according to Welker,

> On the basis of the revelation of God in Jesus Christ who is "the center of life," we must, according to Bonhoeffer, counter a cultural and religious development that pushes God increasingly far away and turns him into an increasingly marginal figure, a God of boundary situations and at the boundaries of knowledge. We must take seriously that God wants to be encountered precisely in the multidimensionality of our lives.[28]

But, Welker asks, does not such a God—recognized in the center of life, its fullness—contradict a suffering and powerless God pushed out of the world? Does not such a God present in the fullness and totality of life by definition militate against a suffering and powerless God? Does not the "Second Legacy" render obsolete the "First Legacy"? "Only when we look at the correlation between Bonhoeffer's two messages," asserts Welker, "can we participate in his search for convincing language about God and for a sustainable Christian faith."[29]

At the same time, the examination of this correlation yields an understanding of Bonhoeffer's "critique of religion" and his observation of a "religionless age." That is, essentially, if God wants to be recognized in the fullness of human life, this fullness no doubt addresses—and now encompasses—the abstract foundations by which God was heretofore understood. If God is present in the fullness of existence, then "religion"—our understanding of it—should correspond to this fullness. Bonhoeffer, following his theological mentor Karl Barth, criticizes conceptualizations of religion that attempt to "save some room for religion in the world or over against the world."[30] These conceptualizations can be categorized into two groups, namely abstract theism and metaphysics. While the former harbors the assumption "of an entity that from within 'transcendence' determines everything," the latter is grounded in a conceptualization of a God emanating from one's "innermost subjectivity."[31] Not only does Bonhoeffer deem as "intellectually dishonest" those who "defend these religious bastions exclusively 'in an afterlife' or in the 'most interior depths,'"[32] but included in the attack is the appeal to a "religious apriori," or "that form of intellectual piety that, by referencing a religious core inhering in every person

28. Welker, *God the Revealed*, 25.
29. Welker, *God the Revealed*, 25.
30. Welker, *God the Revealed*, 26.
31. Welker, *God the Revealed*, 26.
32. Welker, *God the Revealed*, 26.

and preceding all experience, [appeals] to each person's inwardness and conscience."[33] Far from being an unconditioned foundation for religious experience, the "religious apriori" itself is an expression of the contextual nature of human existence.

Thus, as Welker, points out, Bonhoeffer is critical of both the God pushed to the boundary and the conceptualizations of God which resort to abstract foundations. Over and against all attempts to confine God to a "metaphysical beyond" or the "deepest interiority preceding all experience"—to abstract foundations, it is Bonhoeffer's intention to speak of God concretely at the center of human existence's whole range of experience. Thus, summarizing and reinforcing Bonhoeffer's "double legacy," Welker asserts, "At the center of our lives, in the polyphony of life, we encounter the living, but at the same time powerless God who does not simply efface the power of the world and of people, but instead allows himself to be pushed out of their world—even onto the cross."[34]

"But how is Bonhoeffer's double legacy to be understood today?"[35] To be sure, as Welker observes, Bonhoeffer's "double legacy" leaves more questions for Christology than answers. For one, Welker asks, "Has the world at the beginning of the third millennium really left behind the metaphysical supports and religious invocation of inwardness as religious foundations and supports of Christian faith?"[36] No doubt, one cannot expect a monolithic answer to such a question. But it is his next question that, in so many ways, provides the lens through which he analyzes Luther's *theologia crucis*, especially as delineated in his *Heidelberg Disputation* (1518): "How does God encounter us in multidimensional, polyphonic reality—in the suffering and in the inconspicuousness of the coming reign?"[37]

Whether or not Bonhoeffer presents us with a "double legacy" is certainly open to robust discussion. (Could it be that both of these so-called "legacies" are simply "flip sides of the same coin" with regard to a world experienced *etsi deus non daretur*? Could it be that both of these "legacies" are two poles on the continuum of theological existence oriented by what Karl Barth articulated as a revelation profoundly veiled in the "mystery of its secularity,"[38] and thus a theological existence in which all false conceptions of God are crucified so that the world in its irreducible secularity—*sans* a

---

33. Welker, *God the Revealed*, 26.

34. Welker, *God the Revealed*, 27.

35. Welker, *God the Revealed*, 27.

36. Welker, *God the Revealed*, 27.

37. Welker, *God the Revealed*, 27.

38. See Barth, *Church Dogmatics*, 1.1.163–65.

deus ex machina or a God of interiority—becomes the context for the Christ hope?) But, let us ask, how is Luther's *theologia crucis* able to lend an answer Welker's question? As well: if, as was iterated by Welker at the beginning of this interlude, Christology's task is to elucidate that the proclamation and confession "God revealed himself in Jesus Christ!" does genuinely offer a reliable *insight* of faith, then what "reliable insight of faith" can be gleaned, from Welker's analysis of Luther's theology of the cross, especially as it is delineated in his *Heidelberg Disputation*?

Luther's Heidelberg Disputation (1518): Analysis and Analysis of the Analysis

Asserting both its "revolutionary" nature and the perspective by which its full dimensions may be grasped, or the life of Jesus and the power of the resurrection, Welker rightly asserts that Luther's theology of the cross

> directs itself against any understanding or idea of God that is developed solely within abstract speculation and as such is ac- cessible solely to an intellectual elite, and against those forms of religiosity that would ignore God's concern with suffering, distress, and the diverse self-endangerment of both the world and human beings. The theology of the cross respects not only God's presence in a creation that is radically different from God, but also the seriousness and the judging, saving power of this same presence.[39]

Elaborating the epistemological point of departure for Luther's theol- ogy of the cross, grounded in John 14:6b ("No one comes to the Father except through me."), Welker observes that

> Luther radically objects to the notion that God's revelation in Jesus Christ can in any way be perceived or grasped through some "absolute speculation" concerning God that ignores the humanity of Christ. God's revelation simply cannot be grasped through metaphysical speculation. Nor, for that matter, is it intended solely for small groups of scholars and ecclesiastical leaders. Instead, it pleased God to reveal himself in his Son—in his Son's life and thus also in his impotence and suffering—and

---

39. Welker, *God the Revealed*, 144.

it is with *this* fact that both faith and theology, and all scholars and all ecclesiastical and secular dignitaries, must become
engaged.[40]

Welker observes, continuing to provide the revolutionary implications
of Luther's theology of the cross, that Luther's focus upon the humanity of
the Christ set in motion an educational revolution—one whose foundation
was already being set in the late Middle Ages—analogous to the revolution
commenced by the empirical orientation of the natural sciences.[41] Not only
did this exclusive focus upon the humanity of Christ involve a renewal of
theology and piety, but, as well, a reorientation for society and education, in
general. Together with his colleagues in the Reformation—Georg Spalatin,
Andreas Bodenstein von Karlstadt, and Philip Melanchthon, among others—Luther was involved in a university reform in which scholastic methods were preempted by a return to both the original sources of theology and
Scripture and the reintroduction of Greek and Hebrew philology. Indeed,
the goal—commensurate with his theology's concrete point of departure—
was the disintegration of thinking grounded in "speculation and philosophizing." Stemming from this reform, Welker notes, was the expansion of
biblical education, the improvement of biblical translation, and the exploitation of the printing press for the sake of the written Word's proliferation
to a wider population.

Having provided background with regard to Luther's dispute with
Rome over the practice of indulgences, as methodically elaborated in the
Ninety-five Theses (1517), noting the explosive atmosphere created by Luther's indictment in the *Ninety-five Theses* of the church's abuse of power,
Welker introduces us to the theses which were presented by Luther on April
26, 1518 at the Augustinian monastery in Heidelberg at the behest of his
superiors. Through these theses, the *Heidelberg Disputation*, Luther would
take issue with the scholastic theology of his day. It is to Welker's brief analysis of these theses that we now turn.

Initiating his analysis of the *Heidelberg Disputation* by citing thesis 1
("The law of God, the most salutary doctrine of life, cannot advance man
on his way to righteousness, but rather hinders him."), Welker asserts that
Luther's "reasoning is that human beings, being fixated on their own works,
do not see the works of God, and, being satisfied with the mere appearance of righteousness, do not see God's actions."[42] Recognizing that God's
revelation in Jesus Christ is both *sans* "form or majesty" (Isa 53:2), and

---

40. Welker, *God the Revealed*, 145.

41. See Welker, *God the Revealed*, 144–45.

42. Welker, *God the Revealed*, 147.

demonstrated through the dramatic acts of "killing and bringing to life" (1 Sam 2–6), Welker notes that, for Luther, those who seek both divine and self-radiance not only misuse God's "good law," but "they misuse it insofar as they put all their stock in their own works, but do so with arrogance and without any fear of God."[43] Contrasting this dynamic, Welker cites thesis 11: "Arrogance cannot be avoided or true hope be present unless the judgment of condemnation is feared in every work . . . For it is impossible to trust in God unless one has despaired in all creatures and knows that nothing can profit one without God."[44] Such a reading of the *Heidelberg Disputation* leads Welker to ask, "What, however, can a person do in order genuinely to seek God and hope in God? How can a person avoid everywhere 'seeking himself in everything' (explication to thesis 16), thereby adding 'sin to sin' (thesis 16)?"[45] As well, "What can a person do to avoid sinking into despair or fatalism in this oppressive situation (cf. thesis 17)?"[46]

The answer, in Welker's reading of the *Heidelberg Disputation*, is exclusively informed by the "famous theses 19 to 21."[47] As Welker observes, a logic profoundly developed in theses 19–21, "a person must hold to God's revelation, or, more precisely, to the revelation of God's grace in Christ . . ."[48] Commenting on thesis 20, Welker remarks that "God turned his humanity and weakness toward the world. God wants to be known from suffering. God wants the 'wisdom of invisible things' to be rejected by the 'wisdom of visible and manifest things.'"[49] To be sure, such a distinction regarding wisdom issues in thesis 21 and its delineation of two specific, mutually exclusive categories of theology, "designating," in Welker's words, "as theology of glory the theology that would know God from his invisible nature, from his glory, wisdom, power, and divine nature, and the other theology as theology

43. Welker, *God the Revealed*, 147.

44. Welker, *God the Revealed*, 147.

45. Welker, *God the Revealed*, 147.

46. Welker, *God the Revealed*, 147.

47. Welker, *God the Revealed*, 147. Theses 19–21 are: (19) "That person does not deserve to be called a theologian who looks upon the invisible things of God as though they were clearly perceptible in in those things which have actually happened"; (20) "He deserves to be called a theologian, however, how comprehends the visible and manifest things of God seen through suffering and the cross"; (21) "A theologian of glory calls evil good and good evil. A theologian of the cross calls the thing what it actually is." See Welker, *God the Revealed*, 147–48; Luther, *Works* 31.52–53.

48. Welker, *God the Revealed*, 147.

49. Welker, *God the Revealed*, 148.

of the cross."[50] Welker cites thesis 21: "A theology of the cross calls the thing what it actually is . . . A theology of glory calls evil good and good evil."[51]

But why does Luther evaluate the theology of glory so severely? "He does so," in Welker's analysis, "because it abstracts from God's revelation in Christ; that theology knows neither Christ nor the God who is concealed in suffering." He adds,

> The result, Luther believes, is that it comes to prefer God's magnificent works to suffering, his glory to the cross, and his strength to weakness. Theologians of glory hate the cross and suffering, but love magnificent works, both God's and their own, which is also why they call the good of the cross evil and the evil of a deed good.[52]

On the other hand, the "theology of the cross," Welker observes, "enables one to acknowledge and bear one's own incapacity for good and to orient oneself, with the fear of God, toward the creative God, then allowing God's influence to come to bear in one's life precisely through the cross and suffering."[53]

Bringing his sketch of the *Heidelberg Disputation* to a conclusion, Welker—employing thesis 25 as his culmination's point of departure—observes that it is through this orientation, or one's recognition of one's incapacity for good and a corresponding fear of God, both oriented toward the creative God (thus "allowing God's influence to come to bear in one's life precisely through cross and suffering"),[54] that the righteousness of God, infused through faith, becomes the basis by which good works corresponding to the law are performed; by which faith attains what the law commands.[55] "Prior to faith," Welker perceives, a revaluation of values and their corresponding preferences—cross over glory, weakness over strength, suffering over magnificent works—issues from God's cruciform revelation.[56] For, ultimately,

> By focusing human beings wholly on Jesus Christ in his humanity and suffering, the theology of the cross counters all notions of self-righteous triumphalism, be they emphatic or moderate, and all open and concealed forms of self-trust by instead

---

50. Welker, *God the Revealed*, 148.
51. Welker, *God the Revealed*, 148.
52. Welker, *God the Revealed*, 148.
53. Welker, *God the Revealed*, 148.
54. Welker, *God the Revealed*, 148.
55. Welker, *God the Revealed*, 148–49.
56. Welker, *God the Revealed*, 149.

teaching radical trust in the power of the Spirit and in the God who even from within suffering and distress remains creative.[57]

Regardless of the revolutionary nature—both at its inception and certainly today—of the theology articulated by the *Heidelberg Disputation*, Welker notes, it must be continually reaffirmed in light of "powerful theologies of glory."[58]

To be sure, as he begins his explicit critique of Luther's theology of the cross as delineated by the *Heidelberg Disputation* Welker asserts that "Even Luther's own explications [in the *Heidelberg Disputation*] reveal two problematic sources of tension that for centuries have considerably burdened theology and Christology in particular."[59] The first source of tension, for Welker, in Luther's explication revolves around theses 20 and 21 and the implication of their seemingly restrictive location of God's recognition. The second source of tension, emanating from the *Heidelberg Disputation's* early theses on law and works (Welker specifically refers to theses 1, 2, and 5), a tension which Welker also sees evidenced in other writings of Luther, concerns "an imbalance" with regard to the law.[60]

Though Luther in thesis 21 emphasizes that "God can be found only in the cross and suffering. By contrast," Welker observes, "in his explication to thesis 20, [Luther] maintains that it is not sufficient for anyone, nor does it do anyone good, to recognize God in his glory and majesty unless he simultaneously recognizes him in the humility and shame of the cross."[61] Welker identifies the problem—and its implications—according to what he views as an unbalanced emphasis upon the crucifixion to the exclusion of talk of the resurrection: "A theology of the cross cannot and must not abstract from the resurrection lest it come to a sad end in a mysticism of suffering that is as bottomless as it is problematical, or in obstinate evocations of paradoxes as alleged 'revelations.'"[62]

The second source of tension Welker cites in Luther's explication is an "imbalance" with reference to a law, an imbalance which has, in Welker's view, burdened much theology in the trajectory of the Reformation in general, and Lutheranism in particular. On the one hand, citing theses 1 and 2, Welker notes that "Luther insists that God's law is 'the most salutary doctrine of life, holy and unstained, true, just, etc. . . . given man by God as an aid beyond his natural powers to enlighten him and move him to do the

57. Welker, *God the Revealed*, 149.
58. Welker, *God the Revealed*, 149.
59. Welker, *God the Revealed*, 150.
60. Welker, *God the Revealed*, 150.
61. Welker, *God the Revealed*, 150.
62. Welker, *God the Revealed*, 150.

good."[63] But, Welker observes, "On the other, Luther quite justifiably cites Paul's assertion that God's righteousness has been disclosed 'apart from the law' (Rom 3:21), and that the law not only makes sin recognizable as such, but indeed can also strengthen it ("the power of sin is the law," 1 Cor 15:56)."[64] Recognizing what seems to be a contradiction, an unresolved tension, in statements with regard to the law, its role and value, Welker asserts, "Rather than articulating these various points by differentiating between them and explicating their interrelationships, however, Luther's entire critique instead focuses on the polarizing opposition between God's works and human works."[65]

Thus, observing that "mortal sins"[66] in particular are most severely attacked by Luther as "human works," or, namely, those which appear good yet are "fruits of a bad root and a bad tree," Welker notes that Luther refers to these under the general category of "works of the law" "rather than analyzing more closely the peculiar problem of how some works, by seeming to correspond to the law, appear good and yet are nonetheless bad fruits of a bad tree."[67] Perceiving what he senses to be a lack of a set of distinctions with regard to the law, an absence which, for Welker, seems to compromise the unambiguous goodness of the law, Welker proposes that Luther should have made a distinction. It is a distinction, or set of distinctions, consisting on the one hand between the "good law," and "the law as misused by sin, on the other, and certainly also between the law that allows us to discern sin and the law that is too weak to disclose even its own misuse by sin. *This slide into impotence on the part of the good law is a central theme of every theology of the cross . . .*"[68] He quickly adds, "Unfortunately, the *Heidelberg Disputation* exhibits no signs of being capable of drawing these distinctions, nor do countless theologies of law and the gospel include such. And yet precisely the capacity for making these distinctions is indispensable for perceiving and understanding what actually happens on the cross of Christ."[69]

But Welker's fundamental criticism of Luther's theology of the cross as explicated by his *Heidelberg Disputation* revolves around the tenuousness of a theological epistemology oriented and funded by a God who is "to be

---

63. Welker, *God the Revealed*, 150.

64. Welker, *God the Revealed*, 150.

65. Welker, *God the Revealed*, 150–51.

66. According to medieval Scholastic philosophy, these are the kind of sins—in distinction from pardonable venial sins—which kill the soul.

67. Welker, *God the Revealed*, 151.

68. Welker, *God the Revealed*, 151.

69. Welker, *God the Revealed*, 151.

found only in the cross and in suffering."[70] If earlier he asked whether such a concentration on the cross rendered "knowledge of God impossible,"[71] ultimately Welker asks,

> For why does it not follow that his God is dead, or, indeed, that there *is* no God? Why does God not become utterly unrecognizable on the cross, though also utterly unrecognizable in Jesus Christ? For even had God yielded to death only temporarily, such would, after all, have called God' divinity into question. Even had God hovered above the entire occurrence, as it were, and then, after three days, remembered his divine power and resurrected Christ—would such not undermine our trust in God' beneficence and faithfulness? Indeed, would such not have called into question even Jesus' true communion and union with God?[72]

Though a crucified God—a God found in the depths of suffering and death, tribulation and guilt—for Welker *prima facie* appeared to be a revolutionary breakthrough, in the end this God "proves to be an unfathomable theological problem."[73]

But could it also be the case the Welker is responding to a construct of his own presuppositions? a caricature of his own perpetuating? Or could it be that his Reformed set of lenses are just too powerful? As we will see, it is often the case that misunderstanding can be more clearly detected through an analysis of omission than that of admission.

If, as was developed (chapter 4, above), Luther in his *Heidelberg Disputation* unravels through his first 17 theses layer after layer of illusion—law (thesis one), works derived from the law (theses two through 12), and free will (theses 13 through 17)—with regard to one's ability to actively attain righteousness and value before God (law, works, and free will all working in consort to fund an ability to *facere quod in se est!*); that such an attempt actually exacerbates sin's self-seeking nature, thereby farther and farther separating one from God, then thesis 18 becomes the pivot-point in the *Disputation* by which righteousness and value shift from "active" to "passive" categories. "It is certain that man must utterly despair of his own ability before he is prepared to receive the grace of Christ."[74] The following theses, especially the "famous" theses 19–21, only make sense in light of this

---

70. Welker, *God the Revealed*, 150.
71. Welker, *God the Revealed*, 150.
72. Welker, *God the Revealed*, 151.
73. Welker, *God the Revealed*, 151.
74. Luther, *Works* 31.51.

crucifixion of "active" righteousness and value (and its accompanying epis-temology, one no doubt grounded in some species of analogy).

To be sure, if the epistemic point of departure of Luther's theology of the cross as delineated in his *Heidelberg Disputation* is a crucified God, then such a point of departure is not simply the choice of one theological methodology (no matter how modish!) among others on the buffet table of theological methodologies. Instead, Luther's *Disputation* articulates the epistemic point of departure for the *theologian* who has suffered the agency of God's Word, or Promise. It is the point of departure for the one who has been crucified on the tree of active righteousness and value, its law, works and so-called free will; crucified of the pretense of seeing through creation and crucified corpses to a "meaning behind it all"; cast onto the crucified Christ in order to await with him the Promise of God's life-creating agency. Crucified of one's own ability (thesis 18), the *theologian* of the cross awaits—*vita passiva*—"The love of God [which] does not find, but creates, that which is pleasing to it" (thesis 28). The *Heidelberg Disputation* elaborates not the seeking of a crucified, hidden God, but describes the experience of the hidden God's life-giving agency. Specifically then, we might say, not only is thesis 18 the pivot-point by which righteousness and value (*coram Deo*) shift from "active" to "passive" categories with regard to personal agency, but thesis 18, together with thesis 28, provide the two, central *foci* by which the continuum of God's agency, its experience, through the Word is catego-rized: crucifying (theses 1 through 18) and resurrecting (theses 19 through 28). Far from theoretical, the *Heidelberg Disputation* elaborates an agency which will only be experienced, suffered. It is in the process of creating the perception of, and thus the ability to confess, that agency that a *theologian* of the cross is created.

When the "famous" theses—theses 19–21—are pulled from this continuum of agency (grounded in theses 18 and 28 and the trajectories that lead to them) the *Heidelberg Disputation* simply becomes another pro-posal—shifting from description to prescription, from experiential to theo-retical—for theology's epistemic point of departure. It becomes a point of departure which now, perhaps, is evaluated as to its "usefulness" according to the *insight* it garners for contemporary theology and the academy.

Reflecting this theoretical perspective in his elaboration of thesis 21—in which Luther distinguishes between "glory" and "cross"—Welker mis-takenly asserts that "Luther then defines these two theologies in thesis 21, designating as theology of glory the theology that would know God from his invisible nature, from his glory, wisdom, power, and divine nature, and the other theology as theology of the cross."[75] Whether Welker is simply introducing new vocabulary—"theology" as opposed to "theologian"—into Luther's formulation, perhaps an expression of unscrupulous theological *eis-egesis*, or an attempt to "pour new wine into old wineskins" is immaterial. Regardless, the result leaves the theologian the subject of a *Disputation* whose chief function is prescriptive. In Welker's words: "The theology of the cross enables one to acknowledge and bear one's own incapacity for good and to orient oneself, with the fear of God, toward the creative God, then allowing God's influence to come to bear in one's life precisely through cross and suffering."[76] Not only does Luther speak only of *theologians*, but the theologian of cross, for Luther, far from harnessing their faculties "toward the creative God," suffers the agency of God's crucifying and resurrecting Word. *Vita passiva*. The *Disputation* describes this agency of which the theologian is the passive object.

If, as was said above, omission is as telling as admission, then it must be noted that Welker's outline of the *Heidelberg Disputation* includes theses 1, 2, 11, 16, 17, 19, 20, 21, and 25, with a critical analysis that is centered both on the early theses regarding law and works, and theses 20 and 21, or those explicitly addressing the recognition—and its implications—of God hidden in suffering and cross. Theses 18 and 28 are conspicuously absent. *Sans* these theses the focus quickly becomes a *prescription* for doing theology.

In short, when the *Heidelberg Disputation* is understood as driving toward thesis 28, the revelation that the Word of God is a presence whose agency creates from nothing, then thesis 21 becomes not simply a prescribed epistemological starting point for theological method, but the point of departure for a theological method crucified of all active human faculties, their agency and value. Having become a theology crucified of prescriptive methodology, the theologian awaits the creating agency of the true subject of theology, or the *sub contraria specie* action of the Word of God. Thus, the theology of the cross does not simply delineate an epistemology which *de facto* becomes another instrument in the professional theologian's toolbox to examine God's presence, no matter how problematic or paradoxical that presence may be. Instead, it describes the manner by which that presence, the agency of Promise, creates the objects of God's love.

With this said, we can now address what Welker has deemed Luther's "two problematic sources of tension" and his fundamental criticism with regard to the *Heidelberg Disputation*. The first source of tension, for Welker, revolves around Luther's restrictive location of God's recognition, or the

75. Welker, *God the Revealed*, 148.
76. Welker, *God the Revealed*, 148.

emphasis that "God can be found only in the cross and suffering." Again, Welker: "A theology of the cross cannot and must not abstract from the resurrection lest it come to a sad end in a mysticism of suffering that is as bottomless as it is problematical, or in obstinate evocations of paradoxes as alleged 'revelations.'"[77] The second source of tension is what Welker perceives as "an imbalance" with regard to the law, an observation which ultimately permits him to speak of a "slide into impotence on the part of the good law [which] is a central theme of every theology of the cross."[78]

Responding to the first source of tension, let it again be noted that, far from abstracting from the resurrection, Luther's *Heidelberg Disputation* is informed, threaded, from beginning to end with the hidden God's life-giving agency through the Word, one experienced both as crucifying law and resurrecting Gospel. Responding to the second source of tension in the form of a question, let us ask: how can a law which crucifies one of its self-serving misuse so that one may be raised in faith to serve the world according to this "most salutary doctrine of life" be considered "impotent"? Its power to crucify is only outdone by its power to serve life. Perhaps, hearkening back to what Welker coined Bonhoeffer's "double legacy," could it be that Bonhoeffer was actually referencing within "one legacy"—in the piecemeal fashion of private correspondence—our crucifixion to a theoretical, abstract god in order to serve and heal where the "most salutary doctrine of life" drives us, namely, amid the concrete polyphony of creation which is a mask of God's creative agency?

Let us rehearse Welker's fundamental criticism: if God is "to be found only in the cross and suffering," does not such a concentration render "knowledge of God impossible?" Should it not follow that there is no God? Should it not follow that God is completely unrecognizable? Should it not follow that God's divinity is called into question? Should it not follow that our trust in God's "beneficence and faithfulness" is called into question?

Perhaps it is the case, at least from Welker's perspective, that each question must be answered in the affirmative. They have to be. To be sure, these are questions posed on the windward side of thesis 18, or the crucifixion of active righteousness and its corresponding epistemology. For who wants to anticipate the recognition—epistemology—expressive of solidarity with the crucified Christ and the suffering of a divine creativity which translates theology into *vita passiva* existence *coram Deo*, and not a profession?

77. Welker, *God the Revealed*, 150.

78. Welker, *God the Revealed*, 151.

Luther's *theologia crucis* is not a theology of God's absence, but one of God's hiddenness. Luther's *theologia crucis* permits us to confess not an unrecognizable God, but one who chooses to be recognized—by faith—in the crucified Christ. Luther's *theologia crucis* leaves not the door open for us to call God's divinity into question, but, instead, with the Word of God revealed *sub contraria specie*, permits us to call false valuations of God—and life before God—into question. Instead of calling into question our trust in God's "beneficence and faithfulness," Luther's *theologia crucis* permits us to confess that the Triune God is committed, without reserve through God's Word, to God's creatures.

Conclusion

Christological Existence

An Elusive Presence

"Israel," Samuel Terrien observed, "maintained her historical existence as a people only in so far as she remembered and expected the manifestation of divine presence."[1] The divine presence created her as a people. That same divine presence was ritually, cultically, anticipated in the final epiphany. Most importantly, as Terrien pointed out in his pathbreaking study of biblical theology entitled *The Elusive Presence*, the Hebrews/Israelites developed a unique theology of presence according to which "They worshipped a God whose disclosure or proximity always had a certain quality of elusiveness. Indeed, for most generations of the biblical age, Israel prayed to a *Deus Absconditus*."[2] Terrien added (and I quote him at length),

> In the celebration of her festivals, Israel commemorated the intervention of the Deity in her past, and she anticipated his manifestation in her future, at the end of history. Standing ceremonially between sacred protology and sacred eschatology, she summoned the beginning and the end of time into a liturgical present, but she could remember only a handful of ancestors, prophets, and poets who had actually perceived the immediacy of God. The rank and file of her people experienced divine closeness by cultic procuration. Nevertheless, Israel's cultus produced a mode of communion which appears to have been unparalleled in the religions of the ancient world, for it implied

1. Terrien, *Elusive Presence*, 42.
2. Terrien, *Elusive Presence*, 1.

172

a religious reality of a special character, which became semantically associated with the word "faith."[3]

As a result, knowledge of God could not be divorced from service of God, the former being predicated upon the latter. "*Theologia* could not be separated from *Theolatreia*."[4] But, it must be stressed, for a people situated ceremonially between past intervention and the anticipation of future manifestation, as cultus and faith are inextricably identified with one another, the Hebraic motif of God was that of "the elusiveness of presence in the midst of liturgical fidelity."[5] In other words, though integral to its mediation, liturgical fidelity was not synonymous with, did not equate to, or guarantee, divine presence. Let us unpack this dynamic further in order to develop the emergence of Christology within this framework of elusive presence and liturgical fidelity.

Though the religion of the Hebrews, of Israel, and of postexilic Judaism is permeated by the presence of God, that same divine nearness, being "historically limited to a few men,"[6] is perpetually informed by an experience of absence.[7] To be sure,

> The prophets, the psalmists, and the poet of Job often allude to their sense of isolation, not only from the community of men but also from the proximity of God. Theophanies of the heroic past are not repeated. Prophetic visions are few and far between. Even with the life span of special men of God, like Abraham, Moses, and the prophets, the immediacy of the Godhead is experienced only for a few fleeting instants. "The presence" as well as "the word" was rare in biblical days.[8]

But recognizing, as the record demonstrates, that instances of awareness of divine proximity were not only fleeting, but appeared historically to have been the "privilege of an extremely restricted elite,"[9] the question becomes: what manner of access did the "average Israelite or Judahite" have—one removed from the so-called "biblical days" of the patriarchs and prophets—to the divine presence? According to Terrien,

---

3. Terrien, *Elusive Presence*, 2–3.

4. Terrien, *Elusive Presence*, 4.

5. Terrien, *Elusive Presence*, 8.

6. Terrien, *Elusive Presence*, 28.

7. Terrien, *Elusive Presence*, 29.

8. Terrien, *Elusive Presence*, 29.

9. Terrien, *Elusive Presence*, 29.

As a member of the cultic community, he believed in the real presence of Yahweh at a shrine, he rehearsed the memorial of Yahweh's *magnalia* during the celebration of the seasonal feasts, and he expected—nay, he experienced liturgically and proleptically—the final epiphany of history, when Yahweh would at last bring creation to fulfillment, renew the earth, and unite mankind into a family of nations.[10]

Specifically, "A cultic form of presence was sacramentally available. A God who remained historically absent manifested his proximity to the average man through cultic communion."[11] Though that presence was sacramentally available, again, it was elusive, remaining in the category of expectation.

Framing this cultically instantiated, sacramental expectation of divine presence with reference to the patriarchal epiphanic visitations, Terrien observed that

Israel looked at these narratives in her festive ceremonies as models of her own religious stance from generation to generation. As the fathers knew their God, so also the sons could in some way duplicate, imitate, or stimulate in themselves a receptiveness to the renewal of divine entrance into their history. Moreover, the stories of the epiphanic visitations to the patriarchs carried with them promises and warnings for the future. The recital of the appearances of Yahweh to the ancestors of the special people had in effect already assumed the character of a dynamic canon: they were concrete parables of the standards of the faith, they contained the seed of a new life.[12]

Terrien elaborated,

The coming of God in the past meant more than a simple revelation (*Offenbarung*): its cultic recital promoted an expectation—the hope for fulfillment and the wait for the final manifestation (*Erscheinung*). He who came to the fathers is also *He That Cometh*. From the beginning, Israel's faith was eschatological.[13]

Cultic fidelity was situated between a protology of presence—elaborated in the narratives of the ancestors—and an expectation defined by divine, eschatological elusiveness. But how did this combination of cultic/

---

10. Terrien, *Elusive Presence*, 29.

11. Terrien, *Elusive Presence*, 29.

12. Terrien, *Elusive Presence*, 65–66.

13. Terrien, *Elusive Presence*, 66.

liturgical fidelity and divine elusiveness lend itself to the development, ultimately, of Christology?

With the emergence of Christianity from Judaism came a new theology of divine presence derived from its complex of cultic fidelity and faith.[14] To be sure, the divine presence, radically transformed by the experience of the resurrection and the person of the risen Lord by the Christians of the first generation, was no longer mediated through the Temple. Yet the stories of Jesus' appearances "were couched in a literary form reminiscent of that of the Hebraic theophany."[15] Noting the improbability that the first attempts to interpret the person of Jesus were shaped by the Messianic prophecies,[16] Terrien observed that "the Christians of the first generation sought to express their remembrance of Jesus in terms which they borrowed from the Hebraic theology of presence. The Messianic imagery, when applied to Jesus, was radically transformed and interpreted by the motif of cultic presence."[17]

Although this process of the interpretation of Jesus through the lens of the Hebraic theology of elusive presence manifested itself in various ways—from the structure of Mark's gospel, to the synoptic traditions on the Transfiguration, to the birth and infancy narratives in Luke's gospel, to the sermon of Stephen in Acts, to Paul's allusion to the New Temple, to the prologue of John's Gospel, to the epistle to the Hebrews—it is the manner by which the evangelists developed the annunciation from the perspective of this theology that will detain us here. Specifically, the gospel of John's Prologue, with its literary form derived from "The Tent of the Presence," most poignantly and profoundly captures our attention, which illustrates the Promise of *nihil*, the body of Promise, that has been developed throughout the course of this project.[18]

14. Terrien, *Elusive Presence*, 5.

15. Concretely, Terrien notes, "Stephen and Paul developed a theology of presence in which the temple ideology was applied to the spiritual body of the risen Jesus and thus, to the church. Like the prophets and psalmists of Israel, the early Christians waited for the final epiphany conceived as the *parousia*." Terrien, *Elusive Presence*, 5.

16. Terrien asserts, "The traditional figure of the Messiah may have proved to be embarrassing to the early church since it was suggestive of political, military, and racially exclusive manifestations of power." Terrien, *Elusive Presence*, 5.

17. Terrien, *Elusive Presence*, 5.

18. Terrien observes that "The words and the deeds of Jesus which were preserved in the oral tradition of the first Christians were eventually assembled and presented within a framework of three pivotal moments. At the beginning, a *preparatio evangelica* or 'annunciation' introduced the public ministry of Jesus through the preaching of John the Baptist (Mark), the stories of the nativity (Matthew and Luke), or the prologue on the *Logos* (John). The center of the synoptics was provided by the scene of the transfiguration. The four gospels ended climactically with the stories of the resurrection." He adds, "In these three pivotal moments—annunciation, transfiguration,

Taking John 1:14 as his point of departure ("And the Word became flesh, and lived among us, and we have seen his glory, the glory as of a father's only son, full of grace and truth."), Terrien focuses our attention to the phrase "*kai eskenosen en hemin*" which is more aptly translated as "and he pitched his tent among us," "he encamped among us," or even "he tabernacled among us." Contrary to the common rendering of this phrase, one depicting, it would seem, a stable, static presence—"and he dwelt among us," following the traditional Vulgate's "*et habitavit in nobis*," which "has received the connotation of an enduring quality which includes both the historical ministry of Jesus in the years 29–30 and the spiritual mode of divine presence which the church associated with the living Lord"[19]—according to Terrien "*kai eskensosen en hemin*" instead unmistakably suggests a "temporary stay." That is, "the nomadic tent of the wilderness was used as an image of the elusive presence, but it referred this time to the swift passage of the historical Jesus on earth."[20]

Having observed both that the emphasis of John 1:14 is upon the spatial and temporal reality of the elusive presence, and that this spatial and temporal presence had previously been mediated by "cultic space and time," Terrien has drawn our attention to the reality that this "elusive presence" had never previously been identified with a human, in this case, the man Jesus. According to Terrien,

> Here indeed lay the stumbling block of the gospel. Eternal divinity had become temporal humanity. The Prologue did not promote a theology of eternal presence. On the contrary, presence remained elusive, for it was contained in the frailty, the finitude, indeed, the mortality of human flesh. It was that very frailty which carried a virtue, hidden to most, discerned by a few, and which the Johannine poet expressed through the theologoumenon of the glory. The fullness of the divine reality was present in a peculiar hiddenness.[21]

That frailty, that finitude, that hiddenness, though, is no mere wrapping to be discarded, or stage of development to be superseded, in the perception, the apprehension of the divine presence. To be sure, "The glory was not

---

resurrection—the evangelists have presented an original interpretation of the Hebraic theology of presence. Interrelating the motifs of theophany, temple, and final epiphany, they interpreted the person of Jesus in the context of divine manifestation." Terrien, *Elusive Presence*, 411,

19. Terrien, *Elusive Presence*, 419.

20. Terrien, *Elusive Presence*, 418–19.

21. Terrien, *Elusive Presence*, 420–21.

superimposed upon the carnal finitude. The body of a historical man was not a window through which the glory could be glimpsed. It was the body itself which at once concealed and revealed the glory."[22] The "glory" of the divine presence, then, as Terrien observed, is communicated in terms of human finitude. Thus,

> Only those who receive him perceived with the sensorial apprehension of sight the quality in this man which set him apart from other men because it communicated the hidden reality of the divine. The verb "we saw" (*etheasametha*) did not mean a vision of spiritual ecstasy. It belonged to the realm of daily existence with the normal limitations of human finitude.[23]

The spatial/temporal reality of the elusive, divine presence, mediated within the framework of cultic/liturgical fidelity, is now—within the framework of that same Hebraic theology of the elusive presence, now translated christologically—mediated by the frailty, the finitude, the mortality of human flesh. Divine elusiveness, once situated in a cultic framework between protology and eschatology, and thus of memory and expectation, is now articulated by the evanescent finitude, the frailty and fragility, the body of Jesus Christ. The body, its mortality and fleeting finitude, is the structure of the divine, and, hence, the source of its "elusive presence."

Although—from the perspective of Luther's radical interpretation of the *communicatio idiomatum*—Terrien leaves us desiring a more robust understanding of the phrase "*kai eskensosen en hemin*" in John 1:14, or a conceptualization of the humanity of Jesus Christ which extends beyond the "historical Jesus on earth" (what Luther articulated as the first mode of Christ's presence), his work prompts a question. That question is this: if the earliest and most fundamental Hebrew/Israelite liturgies confessed an elusiveness of divine presence, one ultimately translated christologically by Christianity's first generations into a revelation in the concealment of a human body, its frailty and finitude, then why should we expect Christology to think and speak from, or even point to, a divine presence apart from such elusiveness, apart from such a revelation in finitude's concealment? apart, ultimately, from such crucified concealment? Why would we expect theology to elaborate the divine presence apart from an elusiveness which was, to be sure, translated, and thus inscribed, into the earliest christologies in the New Testament? Better, what would motivate theology to elaborate the divine presence apart from such finitude?

22. Terrien, *Elusive Presence*, 421.

23. Terrien, *Elusive Presence*, 421.

Though an outline of such motivations would require a project of its own, it can be safely asserted that the protection of divine impassibility was a powerful motivator amid the christological controversies of the early church. Indeed, as was observed from Heinrich Schmid's classic presentation of doctrinal Lutheran theology (see Introduction, above), the excision of the *genus tapeinoticum* by later confessional Lutheranism was done to protect divinity's impassibility within the Word of God.[24] Is it not universally accepted that what is divine is not permitted to attract flies and fill our nostrils with the stench of death? But if such an excision was conducted for the sake of honoring—within the Word of God—divinity's impassibility, it was also a testament to just how far classical Lutheran theology deviated from the theologian—his epistemic point of departure, its implications for theological method and christological formulation—whose name became synonymous with the tradition within which it was formulated, namely, Martin Luther.

The Communicatio and Christological Existence

To be sure, as Luther asserted, "[T]rue theology and recognition of God are in the crucified Christ."[25] Translated into the language of classical Lutheran Christology, such a point of departure is the *genus tapeinoticum*, or, according to Luther' radical interpretation of the *communicatio idiomatum*, the direct communication of the human attributes to the divine within the person of Jesus Christ, true God and true man. Indeed, the crucified Christ is both the epistemic point of departure for a theologian of the cross, and the locus by which the structure of Promise is perceived. As the divine attributes are communicated to the human within the person of Jesus Christ, so, also, that which is created, that which dissolves, rots, and—ultimately—attracts flies, is communicated to the divinity within the Word of God, Jesus Christ, true God and true man. Which means: Promise, the body of Promise, is not only concealed in, but bound to the created, the ephemeral, the evanescent, the ultimate *nihil* of what is created.

Ultimately, Luther's radical interpretation of the *communicatio idiomatum* has permitted us to translate its genera—the *genus tapeinoticum* and

24. Though the human nature partakes in the divine attributes through the personal union, Schmid adds, "*But there is no reciprocal effect produced*; for, while the human nature can become partaker of the idiomata of the divine, and thus acquire an addition to the idiomata essential to itself, the contrary cannot be maintained, because the divine nature in its essence is unchangeable and can suffer no increase." Schmid, *Doctrinal Theology*, 314.

25. Luther, *Works* 31.53.

the *genus majestaticum*—into categories of theological existence within the crucified body of Promise; to articulate, through the third mode of Christ's presence, humanity in its countless expressions of particularity as the *genus tapeinoticum* writ-large. In the crucified Christ is both the reflection of humanity's *nihil*, and the *sub contraria specie* revelation of God's *ex nihilo* life-giving agency. Christological existence is one which, as an expression of the body of Promise perceived through the third mode of Christ's presence, suffers the concealment, the *nihil*, of Promise's revelation, or its *ex nihilo* creating agency.

But there is caveat which looms over this project. One issued from an unlikely source.

Although most noted for the development of its thesis,[26] it is the concluding remarks of Karl Barth's lecture from October, 1922[27]—delivered to pastors and theologians in post-World War I Germany at Elgersburg and Emden—that instead captures our attention. If, for Barth, it is the task of—and, ultimately, the warning which hangs over—theology "to say that *God* becomes *human* and to say it as the Word of *God*, as God would say it,"[28] "that our goal is the speaking of *God himself*,"[29] that such a *Divine* Indicative is the fundamental-yet-impossible task for theology ("[Which] means the certain *defeat of all* theology and *of every* theologian."[30]), then it is Barth's concluding paragraph that frames, from the perspective of this project, the *real* christological caveat. Precisely, it is Barth's expressed reservation on two "Lutheran" points that will be also be employed, yet harnessed from the perspective of this project, for the sake of our own christological caveat. Thus:

> My lecture today is given in the vein of the Old Testament and Reformed theology. As a Reformed theologian (and in my opinion, of course, not only that), I must maintain a certain distance toward the Lutheran concept of the real presence—the Lutheran "is"—as well as toward the Lutheran certainty of salvation [*Heilsgewißheit*].[31]

26. "As theologians, we ought to speak of God. But we are humans and as such cannot speak of God. We ought to do both, to know the 'ought' and the 'not able to,' and precisely in this way give God the glory." Barth, "Word of God as the Task of Theology," 177.

27. Barth, "Word of God as the Task of Theology."

28. Barth, "Word of God as the Task of Theology," 185.

29. Barth, "Word of God as the Task of Theology," 196.

30. Barth, "Word of God as the Task of Theology," 196.

31. Barth, "Word of God as the Task of Theology," 197. Immediately following the selection quoted, Barth states, "The question now, is whether theology can and ought to get out beyond being a prolegomena to Christology. It could be also indeed be the case

With regard to the first point, for those wishing to formulate Christology within the trajectory of Luther's *theologia crucis*, a certain level of reservation, "a certain distance toward the Lutheran concept of the real presence—the Lutheran 'is'" is *also* advised. Precisely, that one evaluate whether it is *Luther's* "is"—expressed by his radical interpretation of the *communicatio idiomatum*—that is "on the table," so to speak. Is this the "is" expressive of God's complete commitment to humanity through the Word of God, Jesus Christ, true God and true man, the "is" in whom—the divine-human One—impassibility itself is crucified for the sake of that same commitment? Is this the "is" expressive of a Promise bound to body?

An affirmation on this point necessarily translates into the advising of a "certain distance" on the second point, or the "Lutheran certainty of salvation [*Heilsgewißheit*]." That is, unless the "is," the body of Promise, is one bound to, and thus concealed in the fate of what is created, its *nihil*, concealed—in all of its modes—*sub contraria specie*; revealed as God's *yes* concealed under God's *no*, it may be "certainty" about which we are talking, but not that of the evangelical variety.

If "our theology is certain" in that "it snatches us away from ourselves and places us outside ourselves, so that we do not depend on our own strength, conscience, experience, person, or works but depend on that which is outside ourselves [*extra nos*] . . . on the promise and truth of God, which cannot deceive,"[32] then such a "certainty" is concealed, and thus suffered, in the crucifixion of all anthropologically initiated avenues and capabilities—whether they be intellectually or affectually commandeered or funded by some combination of law, works, and free will—of taking what will only be unilaterally gifted by the Triune God.[33] The "certainty of salvation" for the theologian of the cross is concealed in the crucifixion of all

---

that with the prolegomena everything is already said." Barth, "Word of God as the Task of Theology," 197–98. Or, shall we say, that Christology/justification by faith is foundation from which everything that need be said can be said? Many will view this as a reductionist perspective. From the perspective of this project it is quite the opposite.

32. Luther, *Works* 26.387.

33. Articulating the reality that the "certainty of salvation" is not to be confused with any human faculty, that "faith" is not to be confused with either an intellectual or affectual capabilities, Karl Barth expresses this reality in a similar fashion in the second edition of his commentary on Romans: "Faith, unlike piety, is not a thing which can be vaunted and paraded before God and man, or played off against them. Faith is born in fear and trembling from the knowledge that God is God. All that is not thus born is not faith, but that unbelief which is the cause of rejection. 'Assurance of salvation'—the phrase is of doubtful legitimacy—is not a possession which can be claimed either against or on behalf of the Church. Only complete misunderstanding of the Reformers could lead to such an opinion. The decision is God's. His goodness and His severity are—because they are His—new every morning." Barth, *Epistle to the Romans*, 411.

capabilities for seizing what the Triune God will only categorically gift: life, righteousness, and, ultimately, a new creation. When one can confess one's self as both *nihil* and the mask of God's *ex nihilo*, life-giving agency, the "certainty of salvation" is experienced. To confess the "certainty of salvation" means that one has suffered God's life-giving presence and agency; that one is an expression of the crucified body of Promise.

I close with a quote (too good not to repeat) from Luther. Let us call it a confession. Or a prayer. Perhaps a prayer tinged with lament. Certainly the articulation of Promise's structure, the Promise of *nihil*:

> Therefore our life is simply contained in the bare Word; for we have Christ, we have eternal life, eternal righteousness, help and consolation. But where is it? We neither possess it in coffers nor hold it in our hands, but have it only in the bare Word. Thus has God clothed his object in nothingness.[34]

Is this not the same "object" which filled the gaze of Dostoyevsky's Ippolit? Could it be that it was in this "object" that Ippolit—the depressed nihilist quickly dying of tuberculosis—saw his own demise, his own *nihil* mirrored? Regardless, there is obviously no indication that Ippolit regarded this "object" as the body of Promise (though perhaps he did regard it as a "promising body," or one confirming his nihilist worldview).

It is Prince Myshkin who, earlier in the novel, standing before the same "object" with Rogozhin, gazing upon the same corpse sealed in the deafening silence of the burial vault, depleted of life-force and exsanguinated of all self-designation, de-aura-fied of all divine traces, suddenly cries out regarding the implications of such an "object" filling one's gaze, "A man could even lose his faith from that painting!"[35] Certainly.

Or, confessing that God can only be apprehended where there are "no signs of transcendence, no religious clues,"[36] that we "can only speak from the cross in sheer faith without evidence,"[37] may we not consider such a prospect, namely, "losing one's faith," to really be the crucifixion of one's agency—and all that one may have previously associated with "faith"—by which Promise is experienced? If one's existence can be

---

34. Luther, *Werke* 32.123, 25–29; cited in Hummel, *Clothed in Nothingness*, xii.

35. Dostoyevsky, *Idiot*, 218.

36. Williams, *Christian Spirituality*, 146.

37. Westhelle, *Scandalous God*, 114.

confessed as a veil for Promise's life-giving agency, may not "faith" itself be a crucified mask of God?

Perhaps all we have really done in these pages is attempted to outline the subject and task of theology. Or, more precisely, we have developed—funded by the terms of classical Lutheranism—the contours of an existence completely determined by its living, crucified Subject: a christological existence, one suspended from the cross with Jesus Christ.

"Let us hold fast to the confession of our hope without wavering, for he who has promised is faithful." (Heb 10:23) Or, in Luther's words, "If it weren't for the promise, I wouldn't pray."[38]

As Daily Bread that Promise will always be more than enough.

---

38. Luther, *Works* 54.42.

Bibliography

Althaus, Paul. *The Theology of Martin Luther*. Translated by Robert C. Schultz. Philadelphia: Fortress, 1966.

Angelus Silesius. *The Cherubinic Wanderer*. Classics of Western Spirituality. Translated by Maria Shrady. New York: Paulist, 1986.

Anthony, Neal J. *Cross Narratives: Martin Luther's Christology and the Location of Redemption*. Eugene, OR: Pickwick, 2010.

———. "Resurrectionism." In *Encylopedia of Martin Luther and the Reformation*, edited by Mark A. Lamport, 661–63. Lanham, MD: Rowman & Littlefield, 2017.

———. "Undecidability." In *Encyclopedia of Martin Luther and the Reformation*, edited by Mark A. Lamport, 783–85. Lanham, MD: Rowman & Littlefield, 2017.

Barth, Karl. *Church Dogmatics*. 4 vols. Edited by Geoffrey W. Bromiley and T. F. Torrance. Edinburgh: T. & T. Clark, 1936–77.

———. *The Epistle to the Romans*. Translated by Edwyn C. Hoskyns. Oxford: Oxford University Press, 1968.

———. *Evangelical Theology: An Introduction*. Translated by Grover Foley. Grand Rapids: Eerdmans, 1963.

———. "The Word of God as the Task of Theology." In *The Word of God and Theology*, translated by Amy Marga, 171–98. London: T. & T. Clark, 2011.

Bayer, Oswald. "Creation as History." In *The Gift of Grace: The Future of Lutheran Theology*, translated by Martin Abraham, edited by Niels Henrik Gregersen et al., 253–63. Minneapolis: Fortress, 2005.

———. *Creator est Creatura: Luthers Christologie als Lehre von der Idiomenkommunikation*. Herausgegeben von Oswald Bayer und Benjamin Gleede. Berlin: de Gruyter, 2007.

———. "Justification as Basis and Boundary of Theology." *Lutheran Quarterly* 15 (2001) 273–92.

———. "Luther as an Interpreter of Holy Scripture." In *The Cambridge Companion to Martin Luther*, edited by Donald H. McKim, 73–85. Cambridge: Cambridge University Press, 2003.

———. *Theology the Lutheran Way*. Edited and translated by Jeffrey G. Silcock and Mark C. Mattes. Lutheran Quarterly Books. Grand Rapids: Eerdmans, 2007.

————. "Toward a Theology of Lament." Translated by Matthias Gockel. In *Caritas et Reformatio: Essays on Church and Society in Honor of Carter Lindberg*, edited by David M. Whitford, 211–20. St. Louis: Concordia, 2002.

Beck, Richard. *The Authenticity of Faith: The Varieties and Illusions of Religious Experience*. Abilene, TX: Abilene Christian University Press, 2012.

Billman, Kathleen D., and Daniel L. Migliore. *Rachel's Cry: Prayer of Lament and Rebirth of Hope*. 1657. Reprint, Eugene, OR: Wipf & Stock, 1999.

Bonhoeffer, Dietrich. *Christ the Center*. New York: Harper & Row, 1966.

————. *Letters and Papers from Prison*. Enlarged ed. Edited by Eberhard Bethge. New York: MacMillan, 1971.

Braaten, Carl E. "The Person of Jesus Christ." In *Christian Dogmatics*, edited by Carl E. Braaten and Robert W. Jenson, 1:469–569. Philadelphia: Fortress, 1984.

Brueggemann, Walter. "Faith at the Nullpunkt." In *The End of the World and the Ends of God: Science and Theology on Eschatology*, edited by John Polkinghorne and Michael Welker, 143–54. Harrisburg, PA: Trinity, 2000.

————. "Reading from the Day 'In Between'." In *A Shadow of Glory: Reading the New Testament after the Holocaust*, edited by Tod Linafelt, 105–16. New York: Routledge, 2002.

Bustard, Ned. "God Is Good Like No Other?" In *It Was Good: Making Art to the Glory of God*, edited by Ned Bustard, 17–32. 2nd ed. Baltimore, MD: Square Halo, 2006.

Caputo, John D. "Hermeneutics and the Secret." In *More Radical Hermeneutics: On Not Knowing Who We Are*, 1–16. Bloomington, IN: Indiana University Press, 2000.

————. "Holy Hermeneutics Versus Devilish Hermeneutics: Textuality and the Word of God." In *More Radical Hermeneutics: On Not Knowing Who We Are*, 193–219. Bloomington, IN: Indiana University Press, 2000.

————. *The Insistence of God: A Theology of Perhaps*. Bloomington, IN: Indiana University Press, 2013.

————. "Only as Hauntology Is Religion without Religion Possible: A Response to Hart." In *Cross and Khôra: Deconstruction and Christianity in the Work of John D. Caputo*, edited by Marko Zlomislić and Neal DeRoo, 109–17. Eugene, OR: Pickwick, 2010.

————. "The Possibility of the Impossible: A Response to Kearney." In *Cross and Khôra: Deconstruction and Christianity in the Work of John D. Caputo*, edited by Marko Zlomislić and Neal DeRoo, 140–50. Eugene, OR: Pickwick, 2010.

————. "Undecidability and the Empty Tomb." In *More Radical Hermeneutics: On Not Knowing Who We Are*, 220–48. Bloomington, IN: Indiana University Press, 2000.

————. *The Weakness of God: A Theology of the Event*. Bloomington, IN: Indiana University Press, 2006.

————. "What Does the Cross Mean?: A Response to Sanders." In *Cross and Khôra: Deconstruction and Christianity in the Work of John D. Caputo*, edited by Marko Zlomislić and Neal DeRoo, 54–60. Eugene, OR: Pickwick, 2010.

Caputo, John D., and Gianni Vattimo. *After the Death of God*. Edited by Jeffrey W. Robbins. New York: Columbia University Press, 2007.

Chretien, Jean Louis. "The Wounded Word: Phenomenology of Prayer." In *Phenomenology and the "Theological Turn": The French Debate*, translated by Bernard G. Prusak, 147–75. New York: Fordham University Press, 2000.

Cone, James H. *The Cross and the Lynching Tree*. Maryknoll, NY: Orbis, 2011.

Derrida, Jacques. *Deconstruction in a Nutshell: A Conversation with Jacques Derrida.* Edited by John D. Caputo. New York: Fordham University Press, 1997.

Dostoyevsky, Fyodor. *The Idiot.* Translated by Richard Pevear and Larissa Volokhonsky. New York: Vintage, 2001.

Eiseley, Loren. *The Invisible Pyramid.* Lincoln, NE: University of Nebraska Press, 1998.

Forde, Gerhard O. "Law and Gospel in Luther's Hermeneutic." *Interpretation* 37 (1983) 240–52.

———. *On Being a Theologian of the Cross: Reflections on Luther's Heidelberg Disputation, 1518.* Grand Rapids: Eerdmans, 1997.

———. *Theology Is for Proclamation.* Minneapolis: Fortress, 1990.

Gorman, Michael J. *Inhabiting the Cruciform God: Kenosis, Justification, and Theosis in Paul's Narrative Soteriology.* Grand Rapids: Eerdmans, 2009.

Gregersen, Niels Henrik. "Deep Incarnation: Opportunities and Challenges." In *Incarnation: On the Scope and Depth of Christology*, edited by Niels Henrik Gregersen, 361–79. Minneapolis: Fortress, 2015.

———. "The Extended Body of Christ: Three Dimensions of Deep Incarnation." In *Incarnation: On the Scope and Depth of Christology*, edited by Niels Henrik Gregersen, 225–51. Minneapolis: Fortress, 2015.

Gudmundsdóttir, Arnfríður. *Meeting God on the Cross: Christ, the Cross, and the Feminist Critique.* Oxford: Oxford University Press, 2010.

Hagen, Kenneth, "The Testament of a Worm: Luther on Testament and Covenant to 1525." In *The Word Does Everything: Key Concepts of Luther on Testament, Scripture, Vocation, Cross, and Worm*, 99–110. Milwaukee, WI: Marquette University Press, 2016.

Hall, Douglas John. "Theology of the Cross: Challenge and Opportunity for the Post-Christendom Church." In *Cross Examinations: Readings on the Meaning of the Cross Today*, edited by Marit Trelstad, 52–58. Minneapolis: Fortress, 2006.

———. *Waiting for Gospel: An Appeal to the Dispirited Remnants of Protestant "Establishment."* Eugene, OR: Cascade, 2012.

———. *What Christianity Is Not: An Exercise in "Negative" Theology.* Eugene, OR: Cascade, 2013.

Harrisville, Roy A. "Encounter with Grünewald." *Currents in Theology and Mission* 31:1 (2004) 5–14.

———. *Fracture: The Cross as Irreconcilable in the Language and Thought of the Biblical Writers.* Grand Rapids: Eerdmans, 2006.

Hickson, Sally. "Grünewald, *Isenheim Altarpiece*." *Smarthistory*, August 23, 2015. smarthistory.org/Grunewald-isenheim-altarpiece/.

Hummel, Leonard M. *Clothed in Nothingness: Consolation for Suffering.* Minneapolis: Fortress, 2003.

Iwand, Hans Joachim. *The Righteousness of Faith according to Luther.* Edited by Virgil F. Thompson. Translated by Randi H. Lundell. Eugene, OR: Wipf & Stock, 2008.

———. "The Theology of the Cross." Translated by Aaron Moldenhauer. Prepared for the Beinroder Konvent in Herbst, 1959. Accessed May 15, 2020. https://www.doxology.us/wp-content/uploads/2015/03/33_cross-iwand.pdf.

James, William. *The Varieties of Religious Experience.* New York: Penguin, 1982.

Janz, Denis R. "To Hell (and Back) with Luther, The Dialectic of *Anfechtung* and Faith." In *Encounters with Luther, New Directions for Critical Studies*, edited by Kirsi I. Stjerna and Brooks Schramm, 17–29. Louiville, KY: Westminster John Knox, 2016.

Johnson, Elizabeth, A. "Jesus and the Cosmos: Soundings in Deep Christology." In *Incarnation: On the Scope and Depth of Christology*, edited by Niels Henrik Gregersen, 133–56. Minneapolis: Fortress, 2015.

Käsemann, Ernst. *Commentary on Romans*. Translated and edited by Geoffrey W. Bromiley. Grand Rapids: Eerdmans, 1980.

Kolb, Robert. "Luther on the Theology of the Cross." *Lutheran Quarterly* 16 (2002) 443–66.

Kristeva, Julia. "Holbein's Dead Christ." In *Black Sun: Depression and Melancholia*, 105–38. Translated by Leon S. Roudiez. New York: Columbia University Press, 1989.

Lienhard, Marc. Luther, *Witness to Jesus Christ: Stages and Themes of the Reformer's Christology*. Translated by Edwin H. Robertson. Minneapolis: Augsburg, 1982.

Livingston, James C. *Modern Christian Thought: From the Enlightenment to Vatican II*. New York: MacMillan, 1971.

Loewenich, Walter von. *Luther's Theology of the Cross*. Translated by Herbert J. A. Bouman. Minneapolis: Augsburg, 1976.

Löfgren, David. *Die Theologie der Schöpfung bei Luther*. Göttingen: Vandenhoek & Ruprecht, 1960.

Luther, Martin. *The Book of Concord: The Confessions of the Evangelical Lutheran Church*. Translated by Charles P. Arand. Minneapolis: Fortress, 2000.

———. *Letters of Spiritual Counsel*. Translated and edited by Theodore G. Tappert. Vancouver: Regent College Publishing, 2003.

———. *Werke: Kritische Gesamtausgabe*. Weimarer Ausgabe. 73 vols. Weimar: Bohlau, 1883.

———. *Works*. Edited by Jaroslav Pelikan et al. 75 vols. St. Louis: Concordia, 1955–76.

Marty, Martin E. *A Cry of Absence: Reflections for the Winter of the Heart*. New York: HarperCollins, 1983.

Murphy, George L. "The Theology of the Cross and God's Work in the World." *Zygon* 33 (1998) 221–31.

Musee Unterlinden. "The Isenheim Altarpiece." Accessed June 19, 2019. https://www.musee-unterlinden.com/en/oeuvres/the-isenheim-altarpiece/.

Nilsson, Kjell Ove. *Simul: Das Miteinander von Göttlichem und Menschlichem in Luthers Theologie*. Göttingen: Vandenhoeck & Ruprecht, 1966.

Oberman, Heiko A. "The Cutting Edge: The Reformation of the Refugees." In *The Two Reformations: The Journey from the Last Days to the New World*, edited by Donald Weinstein, 111–15. New Haven: Yale University Press, 2003.

Pascal, Blaise. *Pensées and Other Writings*. Translated by Honor Levi. Oxford World's Classics. Oxford: Oxford University Press, 1995.

Paulson, Steven D. "Lutheran Assertions Regarding Scripture." *Lutheran Quarterly* 17 (2003) 373–85.

Prenter, Regin. *Luther's Theology of the Cross*. Philadelphia: Fortress, 1971.

Rambo, Shelly. *Spirit and Trauma: A Theology of Remaining*. Louisville, KY: Westminster John Knox, 2010.

Rilke, Rainer Maria. *Rilke's Book of Hours: Love Poems to God*. Translated by Anita Barrows and Joanna Macy. New York: Riverhead, 1996.

Rollins, Peter. *The Idolatry of God: Breaking Our Addiction to Certainty and Satisfaction*. New York: Howard, 2012.

———. *Insurrection: To Believe Is Human, To Doubt, Divine*. New York: Howard, 2011.

Russell, William R. *Luther's Theological Testament: The Schmalkald Articles*. Minneapolis: Fortress, 1995.

Sanders, Theresa. *Body and Belief: Why the Body of Jesus Cannot Heal*. Aurora, CO: Davies Group, 2000.

———. "Festivals of Holy Pain." In *Cross and Khôra: Deconstruction and Christianity in the Work of John D. Caputo*, edited by Marko Zlomislić and Neal DeRoo, 37–53. Eugene, OR: Pickwick, 2010.

Scarry, Elaine. *The Body in Pain: The Making and Unmaking of the World*. Oxford: Oxford University Press, 1985.

Schmid, Heinrich. *The Doctrinal Theology of the Evangelical Lutheran Church*. 3rd ed. Translated by Charles A. Hay and Henry E. Jacobs. Minneapolis: Augsburg, 1889.

Schwanke, Johannes. "Luther on Creation." *Lutheran Quarterly* 16 (2002) 1–20.

Schweitzer, Albert. *The Quest of the Historical Jesus*. Translated by W. Montgomery Reprint, Mineola, NY: Dover, 2005.

Sellers, R. V. *The Council of Chalcedon*. London: SPCK, 1953.

Sittler, Joseph. "The View from Mount Nebo." In *The Care of the Earth*, 33–48. Minneapolis: Fortress, 1994.

Snider, Phil. *Preaching after God: Derrida, Caputo, and the Language of Postmodern Homiletics*. Eugene, OR: Cascade, 2012.

Southgate, Christopher. "Depth, Sign and Destiny: Thoughts on Incarnation." In *Incarnation: On the Scope and Depth of Christology*, edited by Niels Henrik Gregersen, 203–24. Minneapolis: Fortress, 2015.

Steiger, Johann Anselm. "The *Communicatio Idiomatum* as the Axle and Motor of Luther's Theology." *Lutheran Quarterly* 14 (2000) 125–58.

Steinmetz, David C. "Luther and the Hidden God." In *Luther in Context*, 23–31. 2nd ed. Grand Rapids: Baker Academic, 2002.

Stoeger, William R. "Scientific Accounts of Ultimate Catastrophes in Our Life-Bearing Universe." In *The End of the World and the Ends of God: Science and Theology on Eschatology*, edited by John Polkinghorne and Michael Welker, 19–28. Harrisburg, PA: Trinity, 2000.

Taylor, Barbara Brown. *Learning to Walk in the Dark*. New York: HarperCollins, 2014.

———. *When God Is Silent*. Lanham, MD: Rowman & Littlefield, 1998.

Taylor, Mark C. *Erring: A Postmodern A/theology*. Chicago: University of Chicago Press, 1984.

Terrien, Samuel. *The Elusive Presence: Toward a New Biblical Theology*. Reprinted, Eugene, OR: Wipf & Stock, 1978.

Thacker, Eugene. *In the Dust of This Planet*. Vol. 1, *Horror of Philosophy*. Alresford, Hants: Zero, 2011.

Thompson, Deanna A. *Crossing the Divide: Luther, Feminism, and the Cross*. Minneapolis: Fortress, 2004.

Tracy, David. "Form and Fragment: The Recovery of the Hidden and Incomprehensible God." In *The Concept of God in Global Dialogue*, edited by Werner Jeanrond and Aasulv Lande, 98–114. Maryknoll, NY: Orbis, 2005.

Vercruysse, Joseph E. "Luther's Theology of the Cross at the Time of the Heidelberg Disputation." *Gregorianum* 57 (1976) 523–46.

Weil, Simone. *Gravity and Grace*. Routledge Classics. Translated by Emma Crawford and Mario von der Ruhr. London: Routledge, 2002.

Welch, Claude. *God and Incarnation in Mid-Nineteenth Century German Theology.* Edited and translated by Claude Welch. New York: Oxford University Press, 1965.

Welker, Michael. *God the Revealed: Christology.* Translated by Douglas W. Stott. Grand Rapids: Eerdmans, 2013.

Wengert, Timothy J. *Reading the Bible with Martin Luther, An Introductory Guide.* Grand Rapids: Baker Academic, 2013.

Westhelle, Vítor. "Apocalypse: Yet-Time and Not-Yet." In *Transfiguring Luther, The Planetary Promise of Luther's Theology,* 155–63. Eugene, OR: Cascade, 2016.

———. "Beholding the Core: Reading Chalcedon." In *Transfiguring Luther, The Planetary Promise of Luther's Theology,* 95–110. Eugene, OR: Cascade, 2016.

———. "Enduring the Scandal: *theologia crucis.*" In *Transfiguring Luther, The Planetary Promise of Luther's Theology,* 111–23. Eugene, OR: Cascade, 2016.

———. "Foreword." In *Cross Narratives: Martin Luther's Christology and the Location of Redemption,* ix–xii. Eugene, OR: Pickwick, 2010.

———. "Luther on the Authority of Scripture." *Lutheran Quarterly* 19 (2005) 373–91.

———. "Luther's *Theologia Crucis.*" In *The Oxford Handbook of Martin Luther's Theology,* edited by Robert Kolb et al., 156–67. Oxford: Oxford University Press, 2014.

———. *The Scandalous God: The Use and Abuse of the Cross.* Minneapolis: Fortress, 2006.

Williams, Rowan. *Christian Spirituality: A Theological History from the New Testament to Luther and St. John of the Cross.* Atlanta: John Knox, 1979.

Wilson, H. S. "Luther on Preaching as God Speaking." In *The Pastoral Luther, Essays on Martin Luther's Practical Theology,* edited by Timothy J. Wengert, 100–114. Grand Rapids: Eerdmans, 2009.

Wolterstorff, Nicholas. *Lament for a Son.* Grand Rapids: Eerdmans, 1987.

Yalom, Irvin D. *Staring at the Sun: Overcoming the Terror of Death.* San Francisco: Jossey-Bass, 2009.

Zahrnt, Heinz. *What Kind of God? A Question of Faith.* Minneapolis: Augsburg, 1971.

Name Index

Subject Index

Scripture Index

Scripture Index